She Said What?

She Said What?

(A Life on the Air)

Turi Ryder

Tortoise Books
Chicago, IL

FIRST EDITION 2019

She Said What? © *2019 by Turi Ryder*

ISBN-10: 1-948954-04-4
ISBN-13: 978-1-948954-04-4

Disclaimer:

This book doesn't claim to be an actual memoir. My memory would have to be a whole lot better if it did. Nor is it entirely a work of fiction—since it's based on my all-too-real life. However, if you think you may have identified a real person, it's a coincidence. The names of people, places, cities, and radio stations have been significantly altered, or entirely fabricated, in order for me to tell either more of the truth, or bigger better lies.

Cover concept by Howard Hoffman
Cover Artwork by Brian Clarke

Contents

For Scott, Colman, and Simon

Part I

American Idiot

Sometimes the listeners are right, and you are an idiot. As a talk show host, I was prepared to admit this—on general principle. But this particular afternoon, I thought my audience didn't know what it was talking about. Even though the phone lines were completely lit up with callers who normally found me amusing or infuriating—but entertaining—this time, they all agreed: I was wrong, and in horrible taste.

The argument concerned that day's edition of one of my regular bits: a segment called "Nature Weeding out the Stupid." Nature Weeding out the Stupid stories were culled from the news. The nominees were the people who raced to the coastline to photograph thirty-foot tidal waves, or consumed record-breaking amounts of pizza on a bet after having gastric bypass surgery, or who drank cases of beer and then climbed atop the cabs of moving pickup trucks to wave at pedestrians. Nature, the weeder-outer, would variously take the form of a tsunami, a ruptured stomach, or a low freeway overpass. Alcohol was frequently nature's errand boy.

My audience was usually prepared to defend me from allegations of tastelessness in the aforementioned cases, but not this time. This time, I had gone too far. A girl wearing a Santa Claus light up plastic necklace had become entangled with a spring as she jumped on a backyard trampoline, with horrific results. I found the idea of losing your life to a Santa Claus necklace darkly ironic. Plus, I said, I didn't believe in giving kids plastic light up made-in-China landfill material in honor of religious holidays.

"You have no idea what you're saying. You're talking about a child," screamed one caller.

"Normally, I save these stories up for you, but not if this is the kind of thing you think is funny," added another.

"You're not a mother. If you had kids, you'd understand," explained a third. After the show, my boss, a wonderful woman who had already forgiven me a dozen times for listener blowback, tried to explain.

"Turi, I can tell you as a mother that these things go straight to your heart. This was a tragic story. A girl lost her life. Her family is grieving. Can't you understand how wrong it is to make fun of people in this situation? Do you really think it's funny?"

"Well," I replied, "I'm not really focusing on the kid. It's more the deadly Santa Claus necklace that got my attention. And while it's true that I don't have kids, I don't think I'll change much, if I ever do."

"I really, really, hope you do," my boss concluded. "I know you have a heart in there." I didn't realize the truth in the words of my audience or my station manager until about five years later. They were right, and I was an idiot. I don't particularly like telling this story. It's cringe-worthy. At the time, however, my existence outside radio was fairly thin, emotionally speaking. I dated. Occasionally, I'd considered getting married. Kids were something to avoid on airplanes.

Some years later, after I'd moved into a different market, I guest-hosted for a few days at my former Midwestern station. I was there for a week, but I had to pack light, because I was hauling around a breast pump while still wearing maternity clothes. (Actually, I will admit that I continue to occasionally wear maternity clothes. In truth, I keep three sizes of clothing in my closet at all times: optimistic, realistic, and don't-care-to-discuss-it. I tell friends that it is important to like your maternity wardrobe, since you may be using it longer than you'd thought.)

Married for six years, a mother of two, I began the show with an apology for all I'd said about how motherhood would not change me. I told my listeners that they had been completely right in their predictions that things that were funny then, are not funny now. I did not mention the Santa Claus necklace incident, but they knew. They knew, and I hope they forgave me. I imagined them shaking their heads gently as they waited for their bread to pop out of their toasters, or their coffee to percolate. "That Turi Ryder. I had a feeling she was a nicer person than she let on." Someone thoughtfully emailed me a few local "Nature Weeding out the Stupid" stories. We had a good week of shows.

Did having kids make me a better talk show host? Yes, in the sense that it made me aware of what most of my listeners live with, worry about, and feel. Yes, because kids are an endless source of broadcast material. And yes, because I don't think it's weird anymore to end up with a house full of plastic, light-up, made-in-China, religious holiday-themed necklaces—even if I don't buy them myself.

I do try to protect my children from what I say and do on the radio. They're not supposed to listen, for starters. (My eldest was recently astonished to hear, at a dinner party, that a woman seated across the table from him was a listener. "I didn't know anybody listened to my mom," he said.) Other hosts take different tacks. One made his son such a large part of his broadcast that the kid has his own gig now. Another hired his daughter to be his producer. I try to give the progeny some kind of anonymity, both because I exaggerate a lot of what they do, and because I like them to be free to act the way they want to act without worrying that their behavior will embarrass them on the radio.

The children of media personalities, even relatively small-scale personalities, should have a layer of privacy. It's safer. There are actually people who listen to the radio who are dangerous, like the guy who used to send me graphic Valentine's Day drawings with a return address at the federal prison in Joliet, Illinois. Every year, when the card showed up at the station, I took a moment to close my eyes and hope fervently that the envelope contained its usual handmade porn, and not an announcement of his imminent release from the maximum-security unit. Each card featured a detailed ink drawing of me in some variation of thigh-high, spike-heeled boots and a bustier, holding a carefully rendered assault weapon. Each card contained the convicted man's latest fantasy about me. The cards were all signed identically: "Love, the Men at the Max."

At the other extreme, a man who lived six states away accused me of being the mother of his "star child." The alleged father of this "star child" would ship me boxes of mildew-scented letters about the life we could have together, if I would only return his child to him. Once, the morning show host alerted me to a strange man waiting for me in the driver's seat of my open-top Jeep. It was the star child's dad. Our local police were happy to remove him, though the boxes of longing letters kept arriving at the station for months.

For a few weeks during my very brief stint as a morning talk show host, a white supremacist group, whose leader was being sued for conspiracy to murder, followed me around Portland, Oregon. They sent me drawings of the route I drove to work. I was so terrified that I sought the advice of a military friend on the safest way to get into a car that I thought might have been wired with explosives. After that, I always started my vehicle with the doors wide open. Evasive measures continued until Bryce, a highly placed acquaintance in the boxing and wrestling world, sent out a guy he called "Low Blow Samoa" to give the Aryan Fellowship what Bryce called, "counseling."

I am both relieved and amused to overhear my kids telling their friends, "My mom's on the radio, so I can't tell you her name." But mostly, except for the fact that there's a studio in the attic and it is difficult to broadcast on a Seattle station while an earthquake jolts your home in Oakland, California, it's a normal life. It's just the kind of life my listeners predicted I'd have someday. They were right. I was an idiot.

RIP Big Bird

The American Women in Advertising, Radio, and Television chapter in my Midwestern city invited me and several other women air talents, to be their guests at the unfortunately acronymed "AWART" monthly luncheon meeting. I would sit on a panel of women who worked on air. I'm not sure what they expected to hear from us. In general, the women who sell ads, and the men, too, haven't got a lot of interest in the product itself. They care about the research and the data and the numbers telling them about their listener demographics. They care about the listener's gender and age and how much money he has or whether she prefers bagels or yogurt for breakfast.

Sales people prefer not to get a hard time from their friends and golf buddies about who said what offensive thing on the air. As long as you don't interfere with their earnings, or their social life, you could be singing polka in the nude or chanting to Hawaiian ukulele music for three hours a day; or, as often happens in live talk radio, predicting the end of the world for any reason, from global warming to immigration, for all they would care or notice. Many sales people I've met never listen to their radio stations at all.

Do you remember the advertising slogan made famous by the president of the Hair Club for Men? In his commercials, the hirsute spokesman always ended with the tagline, "I'm not only the president, I'm also a client." Radio is, in lots of ways, the opposite. To make your living in radio, you do not have listen to radio, or even like it. You only have to be able to sell something that nobody can see: air time. If you can do that well enough, you might buy your own radio station, and demand that the sales people who work for you sell more air time, while you, the owner, get rid of pesky and expensive things like the real live people who play the music, or present spoken word programming on the air. That's why, in those instances when I have worked for someone who really loves radio—even if he or she isn't particularly a fan of talk radio—I feel like I've won the lottery.

The members of the Women in Advertising group may or may not have been actual fans of radio. I gave them points for trying, at least, to get to know—if not to like—the women who were on the air in their market. We were a mixed panel. One was the news personality for the album rock morning show. Another was the other half of the local "adult contemporary," or A/C (pop music for women) format. A rather bizarre inclusion was a lovely young woman who modeled for a shop-from-home TV station, and hosted a local children's radio program three hours a day

Each of the women made a brief speech about what her job involved and answered a question or two from the audience. If she worked with a male host, she talked about how well they got along, and how their show was just like a marriage. In my mind, I played a running commentary. "No. You are not in anything like a marriage. Because in your real-life marriage, you can tell your husband that he's just made a tasteless joke that's not funny. At work, you have to laugh and pretend everything that comes out of the male host's mouth is either hilarious, or childishly charming. And, most importantly, if the situation warrants it, you can ignore a real-life husband."

When it was my turn, with a mind-boggling lack of humility, I told the assembled sales professionals, "There's a reason I'm the only thirty-one-year-old woman up here with her own show. I don't have a husband. I don't have kids. I can move where I want and work where I need to work, like the men in our industry. In radio, if you are the male host at the top of the marquee, you get paid more. You get better gigs. When the ratings aren't there, you're the one who gets fired. Usually the woman, as the supporting player, stays put. It has been my goal to be at the top of the marquee. It's a tradeoff. It's a choice."

Part of me, remembering this panel, wishes I could reach back in time and scruff-shake myself for my arrogance. If you had told me that less than a decade later, I would decide to stay in a city where there was little work for me, in order to keep my kids in a school they liked; or work, under a pseudonym, as a news and traffic announcer where I had once been heard as a program host in order to stay home during the day and raise toddlers; if you had predicted I would join the legions of women who wrestle with the obligations of being a mommy, a worker, a home owner, and a spouse, just like those other women on those rock and A/C stations, I would have rolled my eyes at you and gone back to preparing that day's show.

And then it was the children's radio host's turn to answer this question: "What is the hardest thing you've ever had to do on the air?" In the seconds it took the pixie cut, lithe, blue-eyed host to form her answer, I speculated inwardly as to what she might say: Had there once been a power outage during story time, so that she'd had to recall the rest of "The Princess and the Pea" from memory? Did the owner of a toy store, in exchange for advertising, insist on a live broadcast from his business, and then make passes at her during the commercial breaks? Did she regularly have to give tours of the broadcast booth and explain how a radio station works to groups of girl and boy scouts while running her own soundboard?

Her answer, when she slowly, soberly, and with no trace of irony, spoke it aloud, nearly left my eyeballs permanently rolled ceilingward. "My toughest moment on the air," she confessed with a deep sigh, "was the day Big Bird died."

I grabbed for the glass of ice water that was thoughtfully placed before me on the dais and took a big swallow. A lot of my listeners think I'm quick with a comeback, but what do you say to a woman who has just virtually ripped the human stuffing out of their favorite television friend, then practically murdered him before their tiny eyes? I wanted to ask her whether she'd previously treated her young listeners to a behind-the-scenes look at Sesame Street, cheerfully slashing green fake fur and upending the trash can of Oscar the Grouch; or pointed out the nearly invisible sticks that control Bert's "hands" and revealed, in deeply sympathetic tones, that Cookie Monster wasn't able to eat so much as a Rice Krispy Treat, seeing as he lacked both an epiglottis and a digestive tract. I'm not sure the anatomy lesson would have atoned for the psychological damage.

Instead, I focused on not laughing. I would have taken deep breaths, but the mouthful of ice water was now threatening to shoot up and out of my nose. The effort to contain it kept me from doing anything other than forcing myself to look serious. The Donna Karan suit-clad saleswoman who posed the original question raised her hand for a follow-up. "So how did you handle that?" I looked around to see whether I was the only person in the entire church auditorium who thought death coming to children's radio in the form of Carol Spinney's sad demise was a dark, unnecessary, cruel joke. To force five-year-olds behind the feathered curtain was bad enough. To ask them to witness the death scene of a beloved character seemed either heartless or witless.

While the young pixie-haired woman may have been a lot of things, she didn't appear to have a mean bone in her model-esque body. She answered the question as though the event had just occurred, and she was sitting in her boss's office, explaining how she'd finished her show that day. "Well," she replied earnestly, "I told the children to go get their responsible adult. I told them I'd wait while they did that. And then...I believe I played some commercials...and then I told them Big Bird was dead."

Before I choked on my ice water, the woman from the rock station morning show came to my rescue. She wondered, with a bit of skepticism, whether it was perhaps even *more* confusing for the kids to hear that Big Bird had died, while Big Bird—now in the form of a replacement actor—could plainly be seen and heard every morning on Sesame Street: nasal accent, clacking beak, and all. The rest of the audience, and the panel, too, nodded approvingly. I kept myself, by extreme force of will, from quoting the Monty Python pet shop sketch joke, "He's not dead. He's resting." I looked around the room and back at the news-bearer of Big Bird's demise and thought to myself. "I am going to have to leave this place." By which I meant not only the AWART luncheon, but the Twin Cities altogether.

Tomato Soup and the Theory of Relativity

For some people, normal comes easy. Others have a tougher time coloring between the lines. One person related to me by marriage had to learn about normal by reading women's magazines. For this reason, she has decorated her house to look like an ad from *Better Homes and Gardens,* and makes sure a version of every item in her wardrobe was recently worn by a daytime TV personality. But *normal* is not nearly as good a qualifier for a career in broadcasting as *weird.* You could bemoan the fact that you came from a house where you were left to your own devices as soon as you could read; your mother walked down the street singing risqué Broadway show tunes (I learned Judy Holliday's "Bonjour Tristesse Brassiere Company" before I knew what a brassiere was), and a father who liked to teach you the pathology of plague at the dinner table. Or, you can figure out that a home where you are expected to entertain yourself means that you find out what interests you. What interested me was entertaining other people.

I wasn't aware that our family was not "normal" until later. It was normal, I thought, to have a scientist father who explained the theory of relativity using your bowl of hot, canned, Campbell's Tomato Soup ("Why is it, Turi, that when your hands are cold, you blow on them to warm them up, but when your soup is too hot, you blow on it to cool it off?" "Because my breath is cooler than my soup, but warmer than my hands?" "Aha! Relativity!") and who periodically confiscated everything in the medicine and kitchen cabinets containing the latest suspected cancer-causing ingredient. One day, I came home and all the antiseptic soap was gone. On another occasion, I returned from school to hear my mother demanding her right to use artificial sweetener in her coffee. I thought everyone in my first-grade class talked about carcinogenic ingredients at dinner. And, while it might seem implausible, I had no idea professional sports teams were considered topics of conversation.

My mother spent a lot of my childhood surreptitiously tossing pieces of her Orthodox Jewish upbringing overboard, while pretending to her still proudly Orthodox mother, my grandma Rose, that we were steering the prescribed religious course of observance. A lot of our family's activities, from eating cheese pizza in restaurants to driving on the Sabbath, began with the phrase, "Don't tell your grandmother." I thought that hiding your car keys in your bra so nobody knew how you'd gotten someplace was normal.

Both of my parents, but especially my dad, were grammar snobs who made bad puns. My mother talked to strangers and my dad barely spoke to anybody who wasn't a first-degree blood relative. Mostly, though, they were connoisseurs of a good story. Every evening, they ran through the latest goings-on of the people at their workplaces, whom they called, "the cast of characters." If one of my dad's fellow professors experienced a mental breakdown and was arrested by the police for directing traffic in his underwear, we heard about it. If my mother's adult "English as a Second Language" students made a particularly madcap malapropism ("All day people telling me my dress it is becoming. 'So becoming, your dress,' they say. Please to tell me, Mrs. Teacher, *what* is my dress becoming?"), we heard about it.

The lesson of my childhood: a day well spent was a day that ended up with a good story. It was excellent training for "show prep," which is a jargon-y word for collecting material that you will be able to use on the air—whether you're a music jock, a reporter, or a talk show host. As my friend, John, put it years later, "Turi, *everything* is material."

The Caller on Hold

In movies with a radio studio scene, you will usually see a control room. Somewhere near the microphone, there will be a bank of flashing telephone lights, signifying that there are callers on hold, waiting to make their song requests, talk to the DJ, or tell their stories over the air. And now, of course, I'm going to tell you that this image is, like so many movie images, a big fat lie.

In a real radio station, sometimes you have a full board of calls—but only sometimes. A lot of top 40 stations record song-request phone calls. Then they play the request on the air just before the song is originally scheduled. That way, it sounds like the station actually plays an "instant request;" something it almost never does, unless you are sleeping with the DJ.

In top 40 radio, or on any station that plays hits, nearly every song is in a fixed rotation. Boxes of index cards—one from the "A" box, two from the "B" box, one from the "C" file—once formed the databases for these schedules. By the time I worked in top 40, we had three-ring binders filled with computer printouts for each show's scheduled music. As I write this, the songs are often set up, and sometimes even played on a computer that's been programmed at a corporate office a thousand miles away.

I remember one jock, Hash Henderson (very popular with pre-teen girls), who used to answer the request line, then hang up quickly until he got a call from a girl whose voice he liked. He'd prompt her to request whatever song he was already going to play next. Hash was the fastest tape editor I've ever seen. He could screen, prompt, and record a "request call" conversation, edit the tape for brevity, and get it on the air in less than sixty seconds.

Talk radio phone calls are different than music radio calls. It doesn't necessarily mean your show is boring if you don't have a board of waiting callers. Sometimes, if you're a good storyteller, they're not calling because they are listening. Some radio shows, usually public radio shows, have a producer to call listeners who have previously submitted questions. If the producer thinks the person who has sent the question seems interesting, or the problem is funny and airworthy, they set up a recorded call with the host, edit it to make it sound fascinating or funny or clever, and present it to the public as though the lady with the chicken nesting in her car's air filter just happened to phone in. This is one reason why people assume all public radio listeners are so much more interesting than other listeners. We do not hear the fifteen calls the producer of the auto repair show makes to people who just want to know how often to change their oil.

Some air talent become nervous if nobody is calling. They forget that your phone lines blowing up doesn't necessarily mean you have a vast audience hanging on your every word.

Proof of this is what happens when hosts who don't know any better put an astrologer on the air. "It lights up the phone lines!" you'll hear them say. Yes, it does. And the only people listening are the people who are on those phone lines. Because if there is anything in the world more boring than listening to a complete stranger's horoscope reading, I cannot think of it.

It helped me enormously, in both music and talk radio, that I was comfortable talking to strangers on the phone. I get along with most people over the phone—even customer service people in the Philippines who are trying to sell me airline travel insurance I have no intention of buying. I learned phone techniques from two of the best: Grandma Rose and my mother.

I'd like to say that I have powerful memories of my mother talking to Rose in long, emotional conversations, laden with gossip, politics, and plans, but that came years later, when the price of calling state-to-state dropped. As children, my siblings and I were raised to believe that long-distance calls were fantastically expensive things. Long-distance time was precious. A genuine long-distance call, if not answered directly by the intended recipient, summoned that person to the black rotary dial phone in our shiny orange kitchen in the kind of excited state you'd expect from a team of rocket scientists who've just successfully guided an observation craft into orbit around Saturn.

What was considered fantastically expensive? I'm not sure. My grandmother was a frugal person, and my parents were struggling young academics, so to this day I have no idea whether the price of a long-distance call at that time was comparable to lunch at a five-star restaurant, or a drink at its bar. To keep family members from having to pay what was considered "unnecessary" money to AT&T—at the time, the universal American phone company, hated universally—my mother and Rose developed a strategy:

The phone would ring. "Get it, somebody!" my mother would call. I'd pick up the phone, giving my drilled "This-is-Turi-Ryder-speaking-who's-calling-please" greeting, and a stranger with a strong Bronx accent would say, "Loowang distance cawling fowah Aynnee Babowyit." I'd drop the phone on the kitchen counter like a burning marshmallow. "Annie Babayit, Mom! It's Annie Babayit long-distance!" Suddenly my mom, who seconds ago had seemed ready to chuck my swaddled infant brother onto any level-padded surface and race to the phone, was tranquil, as though the call had already ended with news that she had an extra two hours to fill before an appointment. "Tell the operator that Annie isn't here," she instructed me. Back to the phone I'd go. "Annie isn't here." "Thank you," said the operator, as she disconnected the line.

Eventually, I learned that the person-to-person call had communicated all my mother was meant to know: my grandmother was at home. Long distance calls in my family were placed using a complex series of signals featuring names originating in foreign languages. It helped that in Hebrew, the word for "I am" was pronounced *ah-nee*. *Ah-nee*, transposed into the first name "Annie," was matched with a series of last names; all designed, when employed in person-to-person phone calling, to make sure the phone company never saw an extra dime in charges. *Babayit* meant, "At home." Annie's last name was, depending on the message, variously translated into Americanized versions of the words for arrived, sick, coming in the morning, and sending a package.

Years later, working on a radio station whose signal could be heard from coast to coast, the toll-free number that allowed listeners to phone the station at no charge, whether from Maine or from Monterey, simply to request a song, seemed like a huge luxury and a bit of a miracle.

Up Your Nose

As an adult, it occurred to me that perhaps there was a reason my parents lived a long-distance call away from my grandmother. Specifically, Kansas, where my New Yorker father fled after getting a soft coal furnace cinder up his nose. My parents moved from the East Coast to the shores of Lake Michigan. The plan was for my microbiologist dad to continue his studies and research at a large university in Chicago. It seemed like a good fit for a young couple who wanted to settle in a city as far away from my grandmother as possible without crossing the Rockies. It all might have worked, too, except for the cinder.

At the time, the basements of Chicago apartment buildings housed giant coal or oil furnaces that generated cheap heat. Flying, partially burnt cinders, as well as a prodigious amount of grime, coated the lungs and windowsills of Chicago's South Side. The cinders seemed to possess intelligence when it came to their ability to stick you in the eye.

The story we were told as children was that my father had finished his post-doctoral work in Chicago. He was en route to interview for a faculty position at his university when the cinder-nose collision occurred. Although the cinder caused no lasting physical damage, it made an impression on my dad.

My father was known to be a quiet, thoughtful man, but in some ways, he lived his life like a covered pot set on "simmer." Periodically, something would irritate him to the point where he boiled over. At such moments, he would swear some sort of eternal oath such as "I will never take my daughter fishing again." (I believe that one was in response to countermanding his direct orders about standing up in a row boat.) In this case, the coal cinder caused my father to swear that he was going to move someplace with clean air. Other than that, he wasn't too particular, which is how our family ended up in Manhattan, Kansas; or, as my grandmother called it, "the wrong Manhattan."

If you've ever wondered how many Jewish ex-New Yorkers live in Manhattan, Kansas, the answer, at that time, was five. Over the years, my siblings and I have unsuccessfully tried to tease out some other, more reasonable explanation for our family's exit from Chicago—a city with an active theater scene, world class museums, symphony, opera, architecture, and the blues—to a town of thirty-five thousand, where the major cultural events were the open house at the veterinary medicine school (among the highlights was an actual window into a cow's stomach) and the K-State Wildcats Homecoming Purple Pride Day. If anyone should ever accuse you of being overly dramatic, you may take comfort in the fact that you never relocated your family over a sinus infection.

Not in Kansas Anymore

Even at the age of seven, it was clear to me that Kansas would require some adjustment. I'm not sure how many nights we spent on the road in our newly purchased dirt-colored Dodge Coronet, but it was daylight when we approached our new home: the newly constructed faculty housing development across from Kansas State University's bull barn. An eight-foot long metal sign outside the steel structure read, "Artificial Insemination Project."

I was a pretty good reader, but I had to sound that one out. "Ar—ti—fi—"

"Drive faster," I heard my mother say.

"Art-i-fi-cial...Mom, what's artificial in-se-mi..."

"*Drive faster,*" my mother pleaded.

"Artificial insemination. What is *artificial insemination*?" I wanted to know.

"Well," my mother took a deep breath, "it's a scientific method for raising cows."

Although faculty housing was directly opposite the bull barn, giving the apartments a distinctly rural ambience, the artificial insemination of cattle never occupied my attention again. The bulls, however, fascinated me. You could walk right up to the fence of the outdoor area, where the bulls were tethered by nose rings to a circular steel bar that rotated around a large pole. It looked like one of those old-fashioned clotheslines, or a Ferris wheel on its side. The bulls, one behind the other, would march in a circle; though if only one bull were in the mood to walk, I can't imagine he got very far without consensus from his fellow circuit-walkers. Other massive bulls grazed in a field that was over a double razor wire fence, so you couldn't get very close to them. But you could go right up to the gate of the pen holding the clothesline bulls and smell their animal breath. I spent hours observing them, but they didn't walk around in a circle very often. I was told they could move quite quickly, if they were allowed, but they looked so serene that I didn't really believe it.

Two years later, my mother took us to see the travelling rodeo. The rodeo occupied the K-State Field House for one week of every year, and held the attention of the entire town. On the afternoon that my family attended (minus my dad, who was at his lab) a bull broke free of the rodeo ring and catapulted itself into the stands. I have no idea if bulls are any good at climbing stairs. My inclination would have been to move higher in the stands, to get a better view of the action, but my mom was adamant about leaving immediately. I couldn't see exactly how fast the bull was moving, but I can tell you that my mother got out of there with a degree of speed she usually saves for times when she's running late to the theater.

Kansas came with different rules of living than the South Side of Chicago. My parents warned against picking up snakes, to come inside if I heard the tornado siren, and that it was not a good idea to mention, in a "dry" state, that your parents kept a liquor cabinet. They explained that the phrase "Dirty Democrat" was something the kids learned at home, but they probably didn't understand unless their mothers were in the League of Women Voters, in which case they would never say such a thing.

Also unlike the neighborhood where we'd lived in Chicago, I could ride my bike anywhere in town without worrying that somebody would steal it. They might, however, knock me off the seat for being a Jew. Not that my primary school classmates could have told you exactly what a Jew was. Explaining Jews to a class of second graders became my responsibility.

Multicultural education for me, and probably for the rest of the eight Jewish kids in the Manhattan, Kansas school system, consisted of being asked to stand and tell the class why we did not celebrate Christmas. Thinking back on it, this shouldn't have required much explaining, considering the nearly universally expressed belief that I had killed Jesus.

Shortly after my attempt to justify my inexperience with Santa Claus to my classmates, I got to live out a frequent talk show topic among political hosts: Separation of Church and State. My younger brother, a kindergartner, was sent home just before winter break with a gift from his teacher: a small, plastic, glitter snow-encrusted Nativity scene, with some non-species-specific farm animals gathered around a pink plastic baby Jesus in a peanut butter-colored plastic cradle. My mother hit the manger roof over it. She marched over to the school to speak with the principal, Mrs. Guthbertson. I was familiar with Mrs. Guthbertson because she kept a tank full of guppies outside her office. The guppies reproduced prodigiously. If you brought in a well-rinsed Nescafé instant coffee jar, you could take home some guppies and instructions on how to set up your own fish bowl, as well as a small piece of freshwater plant. I liked Mrs. Guthbertson.

Perhaps my mother wasn't happy about our own rapidly expanding guppy collection, or maybe she simply didn't realize that her children would bear the fallout of being branded not only Christ-killers, but also the enemies of Christmas, because she told Mrs. Guthbertson that while she—my mother—was sure my brother's teacher had meant well, it was not appropriate for public schools to give the children—her Jewish children—religious symbols.

Mrs. Guthbertson was genuinely shocked. Not because one of the members of her teaching staff was distributing worship icons to six-year-old public school students, but because she, the principal, didn't understand what my mom had against the baby Jesus. On the plus side, Mrs. Guthbertson didn't ask whether my mother's objections to the crèche stemmed from two-thousand-year-old guilt.

In fifth grade, Mrs. Post, one of the more enlightened teachers, told my schoolmates they should stop beating me up for killing Jesus, because I had been forgiven.

The World's Best Microwave

You may be wondering what kind of radio my family owned, and where I became aware of radios as physical devices. The answers are: *Consumer Reports* best-rated transistor, and the bathtub, respectively.

My parents owned a Dodge Coronet, which they considered a "practical car." I learned later in life that my parents, Harry and Eva, used the word *practical* to mean, *what we can afford*. *Impractical* or *luxurious* were pseudonyms for *what we cannot afford*. Harry and Eva's first automobile was a practical Morris Minor. The Morris Minor, a tiny English-made vehicle that looked like a hat, never really caught on in the United States. One reason for its lack of success was that the Morris Minor broke down about every two hundred miles. When it did, you had to order the repair parts from England. The parts were shipped by boat. So the car was usable only about ten days out of every month. Still, the Morris Minor was considered a practical car by my parents because, after they got married, they had just enough wedding-gift money to buy one.

From the experience of driving something that almost never worked, Harry and Eva flipped to the other extreme: they became worshippers at the altar of *Consumer Reports* magazine. My parents' devotion to *Consumer Reports* lasted decades. It was so complete, that once they made a decision to buy something for the house, they only purchased the top-rated product (assuming it was practical), regardless of whether it was suited to our family or not.

Take the case of the Ryder family's first microwave, bought while I was in high school. The number one, hands down, best microwave that year, according to *Consumer Reports*, was a model sold by a now-defunct department store called Montgomery Ward. This microwave could have easily served as a garage for their old Morris Minor, if they'd still owned it. *Consumer Reports* raved that the oven was powerful and sizeable enough to cook an entire Thanksgiving turkey. The fact that a turkey cooked in a microwave takes on the properties of a well-inflated basketball was of little importance to my parents.

I'll say this for *Consumer Reports*: that microwave was huge and indestructible. Almost the size of a conventional oven, it rested on its own cart next to our family dinner table. Long past the time when other families had acquired microwaves that tucked into cubbies or perched on corners of office coffee nooks, my parents microwave lived on. Their children, all moved away with kitchens of our own, were each offered the microwave. None were interested. Finally, my brother agreed to haul it to the Salvation Army donation station. I'm sure, wherever it is, the *Consumer Reports* top-rated microwave inspires observers to exclaim "Wow! Aren't microwaves supposed to be smaller than regular ovens?"

For years after I moved out of my parents' home, any major purchase would spark a version of this conversation:

"That's a new toaster?"

"Yes, Dad."

"Is it a good one?"

"It makes toast."

"How's it rated?"

"I don't know."

"Well, how did you decide to buy it?"

"I needed a toaster. I went to the hardware store and looked at the toasters, and chose this one."

"And it's good, you say?"

"Yes. It makes good toast."

"OK. I hope it holds up. Did you look it up in *Consumer Reports*? I can look it up for you."

"Thanks, Dad, but I already bought it."

"And you say it makes good toast?"

After the Morris Minor, my parents chose cars for being reliable and safe, according to *Consumer Reports*. They were not about to waste money on luxuries like power windows. They chose cars that were beige, because beige doesn't show dirt, and thus would not require frequent washings. The car wash was a waste of money, in Harry and Eva's opinions. So was carpeting, and so was FM Radio, both of which had become a standard package in new vehicles. Harry and Eva paid extra to have a fifth seatbelt for their third child added to the back of their soon-to-be-delivered new Dodge Coronet; and my mother, after having made a move from Fredrick, Maryland, to Chicago in the middle of August, insisted on air conditioning. She was willing to wait six weeks for Detroit to manufacture a stripped-down beige Coronet with AM radio, black plastic flooring, and A/C. Harry and Eva got what they ordered. This car looked like an anvil, instead of a hat.

So it was AM radio in the car, and a carefully researched AM/FM transistor radio on the counter in the kitchen of our small faculty-housing apartment. When we first moved in, my mom was thrilled to discover that our unit was located on the top floor of one of the highest structures around. If she had been a Kansan, rather than a New Yorker, my mother would have realized fairly quickly that being on the third floor of a building surrounded by prairie and barns in tornado country is like living at the starting gate of a race that can begin any minute. At the sound of the tornado siren, day or night, my brother and I were required to zoom down three flights of outdoor concrete stairs to the ground-level apartment of a sympathetic neighbor, where it was marginally safer to weather the storm. In the event that we were too late to leave the apartment, or that the neighbor was not at home, we huddled in the bathroom, our apartment's only interior room, with a flashlight and our trusted battery-powered radio. We listened as it spat out, in urgent lists, county by county, news of funnel touchdowns and, eventually, the all clear. Sometimes, we spent hours hunkered down inside the bathtub, with my infant sister wailing in my dad's arms, gusts of wind pelting the building with rain, and the whining sound of roof tiles losing their positions, giving us the feeling that we were living in a foreign, inhospitable territory.

The kitchen radio, which also ran—very practically—on house current, was not only the most reliable source of severe weather watches and warnings; it also broadcast local shows interviewing residents about upcoming events. (We might have missed the geology department's *Rock Show*, where you could scoop up a bag of polished stones for a nickel, had we not heard about them on KMAN.) The station also broadcast the legendary radio commentator, Paul Harvey.

Paul Harvey, a consummate storyteller, vied with *Ellery Queen's Minute Mysteries* for my rapt attention. Each created a short feature; in Harvey's case, *The Rest of the Story*, where the cliffhanger unspooled like cotton candy, with a crackerjack surprise at the end. You never would have guessed that the little boy who watched his twin brother drown and lost his eyesight as a result of the trauma, lived to become one of the most famous pianists of all time. Nor would you suspect that the kindly old lady showing the police around her garden grew her prizewinning peonies using human remains as fertilizer. Wherever I was and whatever I was doing when Ellery Queen or Paul Harvey came on the radio, I stopped and homed in like a missile on the broadcast, in order not to miss a word.

Mr. Harvey was also the first person I'd ever heard or heard of who supported the war in Vietnam. It was a raw moment of shock for me to hear Mr. Harvey, with more than a touch of disdain in his flexible voice, suggest that anyone who was not in favor of America's decision to fight the Communist Threat in Southeast Asia was a danger to the nation. So it was the radio that alerted me to the presence of others beyond my parent's fellow *The New Republic* subscribers. People, I soon learned, read *Readers Digest* at places other than the dentist's office. The war had abundant supporters, many of whom had sons and daughters serving overseas. I was at once titillated and horrified by Mr. Harvey's pro-war commentaries, but impressed by his style and sincerity. Later, when Paul Harvey reversed himself on Vietnam and opined, "Mr. President [Nixon], you're wrong," it produced an equally violent vibration in my universe. But by then, my obsession was less with Harvey or Ellery, and more with radio itself.

In the Air

If you ask radio hosts of my generation why we fell in love with being on the air, we tend to fall into one of two categories:

One group are those who do it, as songwriter Steve Goodman used to sing, for "The Loving of the Game." They're like my friend, Hank, who has worked in both the music and the talk radio aspects of broadcasting. Hank spent hours of his childhood sitting cross-legged in his closet, not because he had abusive parents, but because he was practicing announcing records, or calling ballgames, into a microphone he'd fabricated out of a paper towel tube. By junior high, Hank had advanced to building his own primitive radios, though he still worked on his sports calls among the sports coats.

Disappearing from this group are the folks who used to practice "segues," or transitions from record to record, as well as the people who dream of a career where they will have the opportunity to introduce listeners to new artists and music. Love of music was a major motivation behind my decision to work in radio. To my dismay, outside of college, community radio stations, and some increasingly endangered commercial exceptions, that's no longer something radio does very often.

(Even if I'd been one of those kids who'd run around the neighborhood with a pad of paper in hand and a pencil behind her ear, "interviewing" the neighbors, as some of my friends did, I wouldn't have been training for a growing job market. The excellent reporters and news-gatherers who used to be a part of all radio formats continue to vanish, year by year, as stations have changed from meeting a government-imposed mandate of "serving the public" to a deregulated focus on financially serving their owners.)

The second group of radio hosts, who came to the business older, figured out that radio is a great way to get people to like you *before* they meet you. Often, the goal, especially for male on-air talent, was to get these prescreened listeners to like you enough to have sex with you. This accounts for the disproportionate number of radio personalities who are better off being heard and not seen. One DJ from a Chicago radio station, described by a co-worker as "a smelly bowling ball with eyes," was known to fish for hot dates via the station's request line. This, by itself, was nothing unusual. But the Bowling Ball added a "fail safe" mechanism: once he'd decided on a likely sounding candidate, The Ball would offer to meet her on the lower floor of a large suburban shopping mall, just outside of Marshall Field's department store, an hour after his shift ended. The Ball would arrive about twenty minutes early, positioning himself on an upper floor balcony of the mall at a spot where he could easily view the woman arriving for their date. If the young woman was not deemed to be sufficiently good-looking, The Ball escaped by a different exit, never descending the escalator to their assignation.

I belong to both groups. I've loved radio before I even understood exactly what it was, starting from the time I was in kindergarten, listening underneath my parents' dining table to the Wednesday afternoon rebroadcast of classical station WFMT's *Midnight Special*. A pastiche of eclectic comedy, folk music, and miscellanea, the *Midnight Special*, which originated every Saturday night, opened the world of adult humor for me by playing Nichols and May, Bob Newhart, Second City routines, and Broadway musicals. While WFMT broadcast in stereo, at the Ryder house, the sound flowed from a single, silk covered speaker. Framed by a wooden cabinet four-feet tall, three-feet wide and as many feet deep, the giant speaker served my parents' monaural amplifier, glowing with tubes, and a tuner with a magical green indicator light.

By high school, I'd received my first AM/FM radio as a gift. It was about the size of a thoroughly researched hardback book about World War II, and made of black plastic with a silver metal grill. It also included the option of listening to the *Weather Band*—a frequency that repeated, every ninety seconds, the water temperature, wave height, and wind velocity over Lake Michigan. My dad had consulted *Consumer Reports* electronics reviews before buying my radio, but I believe he may have wavered from his path of strict review compliance in order to have this feature, which he thought was cool.

The new radio was good company during the day, but it was a true friend at night: my ticket to music and places I hadn't known existed. With my radio safely wrapped inside a disused half-slip and stashed between my pillow and the headboard of my bed, I forfeited hours of sleep in order to hear the new alternative rock station, WFFL; which was, at that time, only on for a few hours at night. WFFL played Traffic. They played Jefferson Starship. They played John Lennon. And their advertisers were fascinating—at least they were fascinating if you were a thirteen-year-old high school student exiled in suburbia. There were head shops, Army/Navy surplus stores, and concerts in stadiums and local bars. The whole world seemed to be wrapped in smoke, heavy bass, and black light. I wanted to be one of the people who could go out and hear all of that music live. But it never occurred to me to be *on* the radio...until I joined the second group of wannabees: the ones who found radio because of their sex drives.

My high school had a radio station, WNTT. WNTT broadcast at the power output of your average dresser lamp from a tiny tower at the top of one of the most privileged high schools on Chicago's North Shore. That high school radio station was a second home for kids who were into music, newsgathering, writing, and engineering. It was the latter group that caught my attention—specifically Jasper, a six-foot-five, technically brilliant, soft-spoken and shy engineer with long curly hair and a wide, seldom seen smile. A girl I knew brought me up to the radio station to meet him. She thought he was adorable. So did I. She flirted. I managed to get a one-hour weeknight air shift on WNTT during the hours Jasper was signed up to work as the station's engineer. A stranger to traditional feminine alluring techniques—my mother considered lipstick to be the limit of tolerable cosmetic enhancement—I made myself alternately obnoxious and what I hoped was attractive, until Jasper noticed me. Jasper had his own car, and a completely dysfunctional family. That left us pretty much to our own devices. Just like most of the kids at the radio station.

We did pretty well at WNTT. We had a board with elected officials. We took orders for and sold Texas Ruby Red Grapefruit and Oranges by the truckload to pay the United Press International Teletype service bill, and whatever other costs were involved in managing the station. The citrus fruit arrived in Chicago in the dead of winter. We delivered crates of it for three days straight, even though the weather had started to turn our oranges black from frostbite. None of the suburban parents who bought it complained.

A lot of the kids on the air at that radio station were hoping somebody was listening, but were not overly optimistic about it—which was about the same situation many of us experienced at home. My fellow students typically lived in extravagantly large, luxurious houses, frequently under minimal supervision. It was not unusual for sixteen-year-olds to be left on their own, for days at a time, with cash to spend, cars to drive, and a cleaning lady who was expected to call the parents if anything looked seriously, or dangerously, amiss. Others were escaping the fallout of their parents' divorces. A few had actually fallen in love with radio. No wonder we preferred the radio station to being at home. In my case, with two parents at work and several cross-country moves in my past, I wanted a place where I could feel in charge of something. The radio station—and my show, in its eight-by-ten, equipment-filled, tall-windowed, and hushed studio with my new boyfriend watching for cues through the soundproof glass—was that space.

My relationship with the charming Jasper did not last as long as my love affair with radio. Two of my best radio station friends, Tom and Michael, compared me favorably to the women on "WSDM, The Station with the Girls" (and to prove they were sincere, drove me to the Federal Building downtown to sit for the then-mandatory third-class broadcasting license), and I started imagining myself making a living in radio.

Arm Candy

The thing about lying is, if you do it long enough and with enough embroidery and detail, after a while you start to believe yourself. After navigating myself through three years of college (the degree came later, after I finished seven recalcitrant chapters of Italian), I remained, for a time, in Boston. I had just turned twenty. Having passed myself off to my classmates as an actual disc jockey at a real live radio station, instead of confessing the truth—which was that I had spent perhaps twelve hours total breathing into a microphone on my high school "light bulb" radio station—I felt I was qualified—no—*entitled* to a real radio job.

I started sending out résumés and a very bad demo tape, which I'd made by sneaking into the campus not-over-the-air radio station (you could listen by plugging something into the wall of your dorm—I'm not even sure now how it worked). By mailing out cassette tapes to every radio station within one-hundred miles of Boston, and by showing up in tight double-zipper jeans and three-inch-high Candie's heels to hand-deliver the accompanying fabricated résumés, I finagled myself the position of volunteer assistant to Ace Axton, program director at a suburban Boston alt-rock station.

This, I was certain, was the beginning of my real radio career. I would work around the station filing records, answering request lines, preparing contest rules, and advertising copy. The payment for all this would be running the control room on Sunday nights, before the religious programs. Then, I would get to play a few records in between the religious shows, and everyone would see that I was smart and talented. Then, I'd get the overnight shift and soon I would have my own daytime personality radio show.

Here is what actually happened: I showed up at the station, located about sixty miles outside the city, with the help of a car borrowed from a friend who was still in school. I asked for Ace, who was in a meeting. No one, from Ace himself to the receptionist to the unwashed music director, seemed willing to explain to me what my job at the station would be. After the first day, Ace was in meetings whenever I showed up. I hung around the office and studios doing nothing at all, received a station T-shirt and some free records, and got in the way of the disc jockeys preparing their shows. The jocks, having seen Ace's methods of "hiring" interns before, had in retrospect, completely understandably, no use for me whatsoever.

On the fourth day, Ace the Suburban Program Director called to say there was no need for me to come in, but that I was invited to a record company dinner at one of Boston's most hard-to-get-a-table restaurants, and that he, Ace, would be picking me up in his car on his way there. The guest of honor would be a woman named Janna Roman. Janna, whose given name was something like Gladys Rabinowitz, was a cult rock and roll icon returning from a druggy, boozy, hiatus. Considered an old lady in rock and roll years, she looked about twenty years older than she actually was (which, thanks to Wikipedia, I now know was thirty-four). As a teenager, Janna had been part of a girl group, Janna and the Jam. Later, after being discovered by a super-famous record producer, she'd fronted one of the more influential underground rock bands of the seventies. Janna had some very bad luck with her recording career—the most notable setback being when another group, headed by a beautiful, androgynous young man, recorded the single that had been a hit for her in Europe before she could record and release it in the United States.

Janna had a new record deal, and her A&R (Artist and Repertoire, also known as promotion) people wanted the suburban Boston station to play her album. What Ace wanted was to go to dinner on the record company's expense account, with me as his comely assistant, and order whatever the record company was willing to pay for, which was anything. It was the first time I'd gotten close to the excesses of late '70s/early '80s record promotion. (Not counting the time while I was still in high school that I'd crashed a music industry convention held at Chicago's Playboy Club Building and rode an elevator with the fully made-up gold-spandex-and-platform-boot-wearing members of the soon-to-be-world-renowned band, KISS. KISS had completely ignored me. Wise, on their part, since I was only fifteen at the time.)

The restaurant boasted large windows overlooking downtown Boston, white tablecloths, and a menu featuring foods that I'd only heard of people eating. The program director ordered the most expensive wine on the list. This seemed to be expected. The waiter poured for everyone. I spent a few minutes pressing my high school French into service to decipher the menu, then ordered quail. I knew approximately what quail looked like from the cartoon intro to the TV show, *The Partridge Family*. I figured quail were probably not too dissimilar from chicken, which I liked. In wild self-indulgence, or maybe fear of looking up from the menu at Ace, whose guest (or, more accurately, it was rapidly dawning on me, date) I was, I also ordered three appetizers.

When the quail arrived, they took me completely by surprise. Their tiny carcasses, golden brown, were nearly complete. The three miniature bird cadavers, arranged side-by-side, rested on a long, rectangular white china plate, next to what may have been carrot mousse, a sculpted mini-heap of teeny asparagus, and an artful graffiti of quince-flavored sauce. Each quail had its dainty legs bound together at whatever the quail version of ankles is. They didn't look like food. They looked cute, and heartbreakingly sad. I stared at them in horror, then tried to force myself to eat one. Fortunately, there's not a lot of flesh on a quail, so my exercise in willpower ended quickly. I passed two untouched specimens to Ace the Suburban Program Director, whose great appetite extended beyond comely assistants to gourmet food, and inwardly cheered when the waiter removed the remains of the one I'd attempted. Then I watched the tabletop theater as the A and R man—a pale complexioned, longhaired former hippie in a dark blue blazer, white shirt, and blue jeans who looked as though he'd been to a few too many expense account dinners—wooed the suburban Boston program director.

"You need to play Janna. She's gonna be *huge*. Bigger, maybe, than Blondie." Janna smiled vaguely, lit a cigarette, and gazed at the city of Boston below us, as though it were a game she were learning to play. "You're a smart guy," predicted the A and R man. "You'll get *all* the credit for being one of the very first to recognize this breakout record."

I recently donated my copy of Janna's album to the local Brown Elephant store. I dragged it around on my record shelf for years, as a memento of the day on which I realized I was viewed not, as the boys who were dying to be on the air were, as a poor, pitiable DJ wannabee, but as arm candy. I also mercenarily kept it because I hoped it might be worth something someday. (Today on eBay you can buy a sealed—as in never played, which was the whole problem in the first place—copy for fourteen dollars.)

I'd been poured another glass of wine. Expensive wine was dispensed as freely at these dinners as ketchup packets at fast food establishments. Wine pretty much was the ketchup of record company dinners. It got poured on everything. It was my second glass.

As a waitress, I had served a lot of drinks, but seldom actually consumed more than one at a sitting—so great was my fear of losing control. Although I couldn't say I was drunk at this point, I wasn't paying quite the level of attention to the conversation that I normally did.

Gradually, I became aware that I was being introduced as an employee of the radio station. For a moment, I hoped this was true. That I had somehow secured, between the vegetable terrine, stuffed squash flowers, fennel ravioli, and the alarming quail course, a real job at the radio station. But even on two glasses of wine, it was impossible for me to fool myself into truly believing that I had any function at the dinner beyond sitting at Ace's right hand, which was busily shoveling a rare steak and my quail into his mouth. Ace occasionally turned his blurred attention from the A and R man to leer at me in what, even then, I recognized as an unprofessional manner. I realized before dessert arrived that I was out of options for legitimate radio employment in the Boston area. I also realized I was going to have to get home by myself. Fortunately, since the meal was in Boston, and not the sixty miles away distant suburb, public transit was still running.

At the conclusion of dinner, as my "boss" was helping me with my coat, I thanked him profusely and explained how much easier it would be for him to get directly on the highway to get home, and how much simpler it would be for me to catch the T train. Once safely aboard the train, I slumped into my seat and fumed self-righteously: How dare Ace the Suburban Program Director not take me seriously? How dare he not see that I was a young-but-promising, raw, on-air talent? He dared because it was 1979, and I was a cute girl with a tiny adorable figure, tight jeans, and absolutely no real broadcasting experience. He dared because he had seen a dozen twenty-year-olds like me before. I didn't figure that out for a while, though. Even years later, with lots of air shifts under my 24-inch belt, it was still hard to get past the "cute girl" problem. I eventually solved it by getting old.

Steal This Book

This is how you get your first radio gig:

You listen obsessively to the radio. You are convinced (or your friends convince you) that you could do the same, or a better job, than the people on the air. You try, in various ways, to get your foot in the door at any radio station you can.

You try by offering to work for free as the assistant to a suburban program director, whose job description of an assistant turns out to be something between an escort service and rock and roll groupie.

You try by calling up a major market station and bluffing your way in: "I hear you have an opening." This often gets you in the door, but since you have no real radio experience, the door leads to a windowless little room where you end up spending eight hours a day in an enlarged closet; albeit one with a nationwide WATS line, enabling you to call other stations around the country and practice your "I hear you have an opening schtick" while writing down the record playlist in black and red sharpie pen. And you may *still* be asked to be a combination of an escort service and rock and roll groupie.

Finally, you decide to commit fraud, by fabricating your résumé. It's important that the résumé not be overly glamorous. You need to find stations in small—no, *tiny*—radio markets. Markets nobody in his or her right mind would make up working at, since they are completely without glory or reputation. Rantoul, Illinois, for instance.

If you live in a big city, you will need to find out about these stations, and where they are located. For this purpose, in 1980, there is nothing better than something called the *Standard Rate and Data Service Radio Spot Buying Guide*: a compendium of every radio station in the country, who owns it, who runs it, and what they do on the air, as well as what they charge for commercials. These books cost more than you make at your job as a swim instructor for senior citizens at the local YWCA, so you decide to check one out of your local library.

I show up at the huge, suburban, Skokie Public library, which I've already scoped out, so I know it has the book. It's late in the evening, because I am teaching a water exercise class for elderly ladies at the local YWCA during the day. After my morning shift as a lifeguard, a waste of my swim instructor talents, which rankles me, I cajole a group of about five octogenarians into sweeping gallon milk jugs filled with water back and forth through the pool in a sort of breast-stroking motion, and then run with them through waist high water across the width of the shallow end, while listening to their views about sex and matrimony. I'm not sure they get any more fit, but I learn a lot.

I arrive at the library prepared with my giant black leather bag, which I've bought at great expense from Off the Hoof in a nearby town, specifically to carry vinyl records around in my new career. I'm going to check out the book with my borrowed suburban library card, and use it to create a dummy résumé. The challenge will be to convince some station's program director that I am an experienced DJ. Naturally, I'll be making up that experience.

The idea makes perfect sense, if you assume that nobody at the sort of stations where I'll be applying has the inclination to make the calls it would take to actually verify someone's résumé.

The book, when I find it, is up on the highest of one of the library's towering black industrial metal shelves. I'll have to scale a wall of research volumes to snag it. From the top of the library stool, I notice the sign. "Research books are for library use only." If that means what it says, I'm screwed. I stop mid-reach. There is not enough time on any of my days off to copy all the call letters and addresses and phone numbers of all the teeny-tiny rural radio stations that I'm going to need. I need to be able to leaf through and start calling. I need to be able to copy down pages and pages of data and stick them into my phony résumé. I need the book to come home with me.

For a career in broadcasting, I am going to have to lie *and* steal. I spend all of an extra ten seconds balanced on that library stepladder, making up my mind to begin my life of crime. I snatch the heavy paperback book—roughly the size and weight of an old Sears catalog—clamber down, seek out a dark corner of the research shelving area, and stash the SRDS into my expensive black bag. I'm out the door ten minutes before closing.

I flee the Skokie Public Library, never to visit it again—though I do stealthily return the *Spot Buying Guide* via the afterhours book drop when I am done with it two months later.

Faking It

I **wasn't making** up that station in Rantoul, Illinois. Rantoul has (or had) a radio station. I've never seen it, heard it, or been in its town of license. I also chose a couple of call letters for stations in towns so small and obscure that their equipment was powered by automobile engines, and put them on my résumé, too. That is not an exaggeration. There really were stations powered by car engines. I know because, years later, I dated a guy who had actually started out at the very station in Rantoul that I had chosen for my fictitious résumé. He told me that the electricity for the transmitter was produced by a V-8 manufactured by Chrysler.

At WVPD, the very small suburban Chicago radio station where, thanks to my faked résumé, I was fortunate enough to land my first real radio job, there was a real general manager. Mr. Dean Smart was grateful to locate someone who could read, write, and speak English clearly. As far as his employees could tell, Mr. Smart did not possess any marketable skills, except one: He was an expert at trading out enough advertising time each year to secure for himself, his wife, and three daughters, a free, all-expenses paid trip to Walt Disney World.

WVPD, under previous ownership, had been a progressive rock outlet. By the time I started working there, the album collection had been shipped to the transmitter site—a mouse-infested shed in the middle of a field—to molder and crack in floods and freezing temperatures.

The new owner made money by "brokering," or renting, airtime. People who wanted to host or air a recorded radio program purchased a show. In the case of the preachers hosting religious shows, who sent us their programs on reel-to-reel tape, they solicited donations (some ministers charmingly called them "love offerings") to cover their costs. The foreign language shows usually brought their own sponsors, typically businesses seeking to market their services to those in their own communities. Sometimes, foreign language programs were the brainchildren of foreign residents who had money and a whopping big case of homesickness, like the show hosted by the wealthy German-born socialite wife of a prominent pharmaceutical titan. She hosted a show featuring German covers of American hits by artists like Pat Benatar, and her collection of 45s of vintage European pop stars years past their popular prime.

Mr. Smart's job was supposedly to make sure that all the live program announcers showed up for their purchased time slots, and didn't cause the station to lose its broadcasting license by uttering profanity (not that we, or the FCC, would likely have recognized profanity in Polish or German). Perhaps most importantly, Mr. Smart—or sometimes his designated employee—was to keep the hosts of the brokered shows *out* of the studios if they had neglected to pay their fees. Once or twice that task was passed to me. On these occasions, I had to face down a room full of angry, late-paying Spanish speakers from Mexico who were hell-bent on gaining access to the studio, turning up the reverb on their microphones as high as it could go, and talking over accordion music for two hours.

Mr. Smart did not broker out the morning show, probably in order to have advertising time to trade for his trip to Disney World. Instead, he gave it to me as the perk for turning on the station's transmitter at sunrise and running the tape of the various Gospel, Spanish, and Armenian shows that paid the station to use its signal beginning at nine each morning.

From sunrise to 9:00 a.m., I was on the air. Hired in late summer, by winter, when the sun rose late, my air shift was down to about fifteen minutes; but it was my first genuine, part-time radio gig. The pay was minimum wage, with an extra hour thrown in as the price of me emptying all the wastebaskets in the four-hundred-square feet of below-street-level office building that housed our studios. The audience would likely have been more entertained by watching me empty the trash. I was a terrible disc jockey. The situation was made far worse by the fact that I really didn't have any discs to jockey.

The morning show was a comically simple program. At one time in its distant past, the format for the entire station had been oldies. The staff and the records for that era were long gone, yet six scratchy "Best Of" vinyl albums had survived, tucked in a corner somewhere. These six records were the whole of our morning show repertoire. I was to mix the approximately seventy-five songs, along with a few banged up 45s, in various combinations for three hours every weekday. In between, I read the weather and tried to sound cheery as I announced whichever four of the cuts I had just played. The selection was further limited because some of the cuts were too damaged to use. The titles of these unplayable songs (though not all of them, as I soon discovered) had been lined out with an indelible marker on the cover. I found myself actually buying old vinyl records at yard sales with my meager wages, in order to keep from going entirely insane. Not that anyone would have noticed.

My job at the station was similar to the character of the king in the children's classic book, *The Little Prince*. The king is the only visible occupant of a small asteroid. He believes himself to be a legitimate ruler, because he has one subject: a small furry animal, perhaps a rat, which he sometimes hears at night.

At WVPD, I was able to verify that I had two listeners. One was a Holocaust denier. He sent me large, scuffed envelopes containing "evidence" debunking the existence of concentration camps. The other was a slightly depressed junior high school student who called each morning to request Herman's Hermits' "I'm Into Something Good," and to talk.

I was able to hoist myself out of WVPD, VapidRadio, within a year, thanks to my loyal high school engineering friends, Tom and Michael, who came into the station with me after hours, and put together a tape for WFFL—the station I most longed to work for in the entire world. I had listened to this station as a kid. I worshipped its disc jockeys, who were the essence of FM cool. They could put records together in such a way that you heard the actual songs differently. WFFL's jocks knew the music, hung out with the artists, and each one got every single new album that came out delivered to a cubby with his or her name on it. I was going to be one of them. It was everything I'd hoped for, and my second on-air job.

Unfortunately, my tape was far better than my actual abilities at that point, having been well edited in an all-night pizza-fueled orgy of splicing (an obsolete method of editing audio involving a metal block, a sticky-backed, extremely thin and flimsy tape, and a razor blade). My new job didn't last long. The competing progressive rock station, located in a remote exurb, changed format two weekends after I started my Sunday morning air shift. My new boss, Laughlin, understandably decided it was smarter to hire all the known jocks who'd just been fired from his competition, and skip the time-consuming process it would have required to make a great—or even a good—jock out of me.

Laughlin was perfectly correct, of course. I was in need of serious training. For example, I hadn't yet learned that when one's new boss said, "feel free to call me at home if you have any problems or questions this weekend," what he meant was "don't call me unless someone throws a hand grenade into the studio. And even if that happens, don't call me unless the backup production studio also explodes." So when I had some typical, beginners-level problem—like not being able to find a transmitter log, for example—and I called him, I was astonished to find he was angry to have been woken up on his day off. That's how stupid and ignorant I was. And now I had been sacked. I was devastated. My fantasy job had come and gone in three weeks. Still, my moment at WFFL left me with something memorable. It generated the nightmare that has kept me awake before the start of every new job since.

In my nightmare, I am in the WFFL studio. Just as it was in real life, in my nightmare the WFFL studio is lined, nearly floor to ceiling, with vinyl LPs, organized alphabetically, by artist. Some are commercial albums; others are special "promo" copies with songs recorded just for radio stations—often live, in-concert versions. In my dream, my record is ending, and I have to choose a song that will fit in well, or "segue," to play after it. I turn to the wall of records. Nothing looks recognizable. I cannot identify a single LP. But I have to choose something. The song on the turntable is drawing to a close. I head for the "B" section of the alphabet, knowing the Beach Boys, who recorded about a thousand albums, will be there. The Beach Boys will save me. Ah. There they are. I pull out an album, turn to the console, and remove the LP. To my horror, the album jacket contains, not a vinyl album, but a circular, ringed, one-inch-thick slab of cement, with a hole in the middle for the record player's spindle. Desperate, I yank out a handful of albums at random. They are, each and every one of them, cement. I have no choice. I must place the cement slab on the turntable and play it. I wake up.

There is a part two to this nightmare, if I am able to go back to sleep. It is also set in the WFFL studio:

I am playing an album. The door to the studio opens. It is one of my fellow DJs. One of the WFFL DJs that I admire so much. He sits down. I am nervous. I don't want to make any mistakes, or miss my announcing break, but I do not want to be rude. We chat. The door opens. It's another of the WFFL DJs. She looks for a place to sit down, but there's not a lot of room, so she perches near the turntable. I wonder how I will get to my record when it ends, but I do not want to be rude. The door opens. Another DJ. This one sits next to the other turntable. This happens over and over until the entire studio is stuffed with DJs, and I know my record will end, and I will not be able to reach either the turntable, or the microphone, but I am afraid to ask anyone to leave. My song is ending. I wake up.

Recently, someone I only know slightly, who is no longer in radio at all (he's now a minister), tagged me in a Facebook post. He asked me, along with a few other radio personalities, whether he is alone in his recurring dream about playing a record that is skipping, but the turntable cannot be turned off. He got forty-six responses. First, I was surprised at how many former DJs have become ministers. Then, I was surprised to read forty-six different varieties of radio station anxiety nightmares. Nobody else, however, reported the cement record problem.

Thank You for Your Couch

Some of the people I've met or worked for in broadcasting are lovely souls: kind, expansive, and generous. You work in this business long enough, and you learn that any radio station—or, at the very least, someone on the staff of any radio station—in any American town, will probably take you in during an emergency.

Other folks are more problematic. Probably, they would be just as hideous in a different occupation, but they seem to be drawn in and encouraged by radio's reputation (now rather compromised by a wave of corporate acquisitions) for creativity and quirky personalities; to create a corporate miasma of bad manners that embeds itself in office carrel walls like scum from a backed-up drain. You work with these people for a few years, and after a while, you realize how easy it would be to become...just like them.

Difficult broadcasters tend to come in three basic flavors: substance abusers, malevolent saboteurs, and the frighteningly spineless. I'm leaving out the merely self-serving and the sex-obsessed creeps—they are everywhere.

After losing my dream job at WFFL, I pasted together a combination of jobs that required the kind of commuting and stamina only a twenty-year-old can manage. For my day job, I bluffed my way into a position in the music department at a large country station by calling management and chirping into the phone, "I hear you're looking to fill a position in your programming department." The phone happened to be answered by the music director. She was just about to quit for a better gig at another station in our market, but had not yet announced it.

"How did you know that?" she demanded in a harshly whispered mixture of irritation and paranoia.

Thinking quickly, I answered in my most conspiratorial tone, "You know, there's not much that stays secret in the radio business." Convinced that I was a well-connected insider, she immediately brought me in as her assistant. I never told her that the "I hear you have an opening" approach was my standard strategy for getting past the "send us a tape we're not hiring" response that a more general query would have gotten.

The assistant music director position was rendered completely unnecessary about a year later by the introduction of song-scheduling software. But for a few months, I was the human music computer. (Later, computers generated these lists in under two minutes.) My job consisted of filling out the playlist: a schedule containing every song the station would play that day, in a pattern determined by research experts to be exactly enough to satisfy fans with short attention spans, but stopping just shy of causing madness in folks who listened for longer than twenty minutes at a time. Tools of the trade were red and blue fat-point indelible markers and boxes of three-by-five index cards.

Now, at some radio stations, the jocks don't even get a playlist; they just announce whatever the computer has been programmed to play. That's if they need to show up at a studio at all. Many DJs "voice track" for radio stations from microphones arranged in foam-mattress-pad-surrounded corners of our bedrooms.

But at my third radio job, writing out the music logs by hand took all day. Actually, it didn't take all day. Part of my day was spent wandering the halls of the iconic Materials Mart building where the company's radio and television operations were based. I met the TV station's promotion director, who was frequently on the radio floor of the building; hiding, I supposed, from the impossibly difficult actors she regularly shepherded around: the station's grouchy engineers and an amazingly talented newswoman who, as a former ballerina, found the oversized hallways of the Materials Mart perfect for keeping up her grand jeté. There was also a company store, where you could purchase, at a discount, products made by the company's other divisions. I got a great deal on a blender. At some point, the station's program director must have noticed me sticking my head into various studios and offices, trying to figure out what the people who weren't scheduling Kenny Rogers songs were doing all day.

You may now wish to take a moment to roll your eyes at my naiveté when I was confused as to why the program director of this radio station, Ernie Boyle, offered to bring me as his guest to a radio broadcasting convention in Florida. For the life of me, I couldn't figure out why someone in high management, over fifteen years my senior, would want me to join him in attending a professional meeting at a fancy resort. So I asked him. His answer: "I think you might learn a few things."

The main thing I started to learn, though not from Ernie Boyle, was to listen to the little voice in my head that said, "This makes no sense." I had moved a short pace—not far— from my days as "arm candy:" just stupid enough not to understand what exactly was being proposed to me, and just smart enough—and a teensy bit humble enough—to figure out that there were probably a lot of other people at the station who had better reasons to attend the convention than I did.

(I never gave Ernie much thought after declining his offer of professional advancement. He didn't pursue me or bother me back in my little closet of an office. It seems the out of sight, out of mind channel only ran one way though, because decades later, just days after I created a Facebook account, who should message me but good old Ernie. On one hand, Ernie was aware that I actually had a radio career. On the other hand, he let me know he was single—"My third ex-wife got the big house," was how he put it—and he called me "babe.")

In addition to spending my weekdays on a hamster wheel of markers and cards, on weekends I travelled two hundred miles, round trip, to work overnights at a Rockford, Illinois, album rock station. Blaze, an alcoholic program director who was impressed by the fact that I had worked for WFFL for less than a month, hired me. He sent the staff a long memo about it. Our relationship headed downhill the second that memo hit the breakroom bulletin board.

Every weekend, I'd drive for two hours, spend five hours on the air, and then be back behind the wheel cradling a thermos of overcooked breakroom coffee. Frequently, I'd wake up as my tires hit the gravel shoulder of I-90, correcting course and turning the air conditioner up high in order to remain conscious. My constant fear was falling asleep on the Fox River Bridge, where there was no warning track: only the railing and the gorge below.

Blaze, it turned out, was an abusive drunk. And who better to abuse than somebody who works for you in the middle of the night—someone who absolutely *must* answer the hotline phone when you call? It might've been possible to ignore the hotline if Blaze had been the only one with the number, but station hotlines are not just for program directors. They exist so that chief engineers can reach you with the news that a lightning bolt has hit your transmitter site and knocked you off the air, or so that the general manager can tell you to pull all the airline ads from the schedule because there has been a crash. I'm not sure whether anybody could have ignored the flashing red strobe lights of Rockford's hotline phone, even if she ran her mixing board while wearing sleep shades. In a clever example of upcycling, before that was even a word, the guys who had designed the studio had repurposed the Mars Lights of a state police car, so that when the hotline phone rang in Rockford, you could see it from three counties away.

Blaze loved calling that phone. "You're ruining my radio station," he would scream into my ear. "Blaze," I would explain, "I drive ninety-five miles each way in a borrowed car that barely runs just to *be* on your radio station. Why would I want to ruin it?" For the first few weeks, I imagined Blaze was actually preparing to fire me. I eventually figured out that he forgot the calls as soon as he'd made them.

The playlist in Rockford was heavy on heavy metal. Bob Seger was easy listening to the Saturday night audience. I honored listener requests for Black Sabbath and Uriah Heap and tried to sound like I thought an all-night DJ on an album rock station should sound. Surprisingly, a few listeners seemed to really like the show. The local concert promoter threw a few MC gigs my way. I was elated. You got paid more money to show up for an hour and announce the lineup of a local band's concert than you could make in an entire air shift. I tried to work around Blaze's now predictable routine.

Blaze would call, rage for twenty minutes, hang up, and then repeat the process about an hour later. So when I'd show up for work, I'd set out a little pile of the albums with the longest tracks, right near the turntables. We had plenty of four-to-seven-minute guitar solo anthems to choose from. The moment Blaze called, I'd hit the speakerphone button and cue up one of what were known to all DJs as "bathroom tracks."

"Stairway to Heaven" may be a classic anthem to you, but to a jock, it's a bathroom track. Often, I kept Blaze on the speaker while I left the on-air booth for the ladies' room; a project that, in addition to speed, required blocking open a large sound-proof door. The heavy portal, which also served as a fire barrier, automatically locked from the inside at night. It could, if not propped properly, swing shut, preventing you from re-entering the part of the building where the studios were located. If that happened, you had to de-program the burglar alarm, leave through the front office door, race around to the back of the building, and re-enter the studio wing from the parking lot. And that only worked if you remembered to bring your key with you to the ladies' room. This set up had caused problems for the station's other nighttime DJs. I know because the only training I got in Rockford, prior to going on the air for the first time, was how not to get locked out of the studio when you used the bathroom. I never did grow to be a fan of heavy metal, but I did develop an appreciation for Nazareth's "Please Don't Judas Me"—playing time nine minutes and forty-seven seconds.

Every radio job, no matter how demoralizing, comes with at least one lifetime benefit. At the Rockford station, I learned how kind relative strangers in radio could be to one another. I cannot tell you how many times I have tried to recall the name of the good-hearted salesperson who noticed me leaving the studio one Sunday morning, nearly intoxicated from exhaustion, and asked, "Do you need a place to sleep?" Surprised, and fearing unprofessional motives, I stared in confusion. "You can have the couch in my living room, if you'd like," continued my angel of mercy. "I won't even be there. I go to work. Here's a key. You can stop in any morning before you drive home, and rest, if you feel tired." That salesperson, whose name I pray I remember someday, but whose act of charity will remain in my heart forever, is probably the reason I survived.

That wasn't the only time the broadcast tribe has come to my rescue. One news director in the small town of Bakersfield, California woke up in the middle of his sleep cycle and met me at the Bakersfield freeway exit where my car had broken down. He waited with me by the side of I-5 for a tow truck, made sure my car was looked after by his mechanic, and gave both me and my dog sleep, supper, and an escort to my freeway entrance the next day. A kind program director in Sacramento filled my tank with gas when I lost my wallet, and presented me with some folding money "for the road," too. We are a roving people, and I never tire of the stories of bosses who throw coats over their pajamas and drive miles in the dark of night to bail their reporters out of jail, or fly around the world to sit at the bedsides of correspondents who've been injured in war zones. I work for crazy people, but I also work for and with some of the most generous, thoughtful, deeply caring human beings you could hope to meet in any profession.

Miss Indiana

WFLX, the exurb station that had dropped its progressive rock format just as I was starting with WFFL, was returning to progressive rock. Dale Tinker, a savvy salesperson with a love of new wave and the blues, had convinced the station's owner to give eclectic album rock another shot. I would be hired for nights, on one condition: I would have to spend my workdays selling airtime. Of course I said I could do it. And it *was* doable—just not by me.

First, there was the matter of the car. I was seeing a boyfriend imported from the UK—a defrocked Jehovah's Witness minister who had left his wife and signed on to a sailing ship in the Caribbean as crew. I also happened to be on this ship, as the guest of a wonderful gentleman with whom I was well-matched as a friend, but who was not nearly damaged enough to be appropriate as a boyfriend. At the time, I was only interested in men who were prone to compulsive lying, drinking, drugging, sexual identity issues, or any combination of these qualities, with an underlying layer of complete irresponsibility.

The one area in which the British boyfriend was reliable was as an auto mechanic. In fact, he was on his way to legal employment in the States, thanks to his abilities as a healer of Britain's more delicate and expensive engines. He also pronounced Jaguar, *Jag-you-are,* which I found endearing. I was fairly confident that whatever car I purchased, Mark would keep it running. For $500, which was just about everything I had in the bank, I bought an ancient Datsun sedan with a reliable engine, and an unpredictable everything else. There was no floor; just a mat over a rust hole. The windshield washers didn't work, making it necessary to pull over every few minutes during winter weather, when the roads are salted and slushy, and massage handfuls of snow onto the wiper blades. The radio antenna was bent and the doors were corroded, though touched up with primer paint. The car looked so poverty-stricken that I used to hide it from any business I called on as a salesperson. Mark told me not to bring it near his European car salon either.

Then there was my wardrobe. Broadcasting salespeople look extra good, perhaps because what they're selling can't actually be seen. As stand-ins for the product, they have to look successful, like walking money. There's a reason I like working where nobody can see me: I hate office attire, uniforms, and fancy dress of any description. Even more than wearing it, I hate shopping for it, and spending money on it.

I did my best to approximate normal on a budget, but no one was fooled. My one suit looked as though it was made out of burlap feed bags that had been died a not-quite-trendy dusty rose color. I added to it a couple of pencil skirts, boots, and a few blouses with heavily padded shoulders. These came in shades of polyester that were intended to match the suit and pencil skirts. I looked like I was wrapped in a shag rug ripped from the inside of a hippie van, and I felt awful.

I did enjoy spending time in the station's sales area. There was a gruff but competent sales manager, Mr. Reverso who, to his credit, figured out nearly immediately that I would never make him any money as a salesperson. As soon as he was resigned to this, he became an energetic raconteur of radio sales war stories, for which I was a willing audience.

The station's fresh and most ambitious sales hire lounged at the desk next to mine—a former Miss Indiana. I soon knew everything about Miss Indiana's pageant wardrobe, because she described it to me in great detail. She also described it on the phone to prospective clients, and she described it to every other station employee, including the guy who delivered the packets of Swiss Miss and coffee to the administrative staff's office coffee machine.

Miss Indiana was not going to be one of those former beauty queens who let herself go, post-pageant. She kept in shape by doing leg stretches and splits while seated at her desk, chatting into her phone, and narrating the details of her pageant wardrobe to whomever was on the other end of the line. She was also able to set her hair in hot rollers and polish her nails while filling out log sheets of prospective clients she'd called on. I found her fascinating.

After a few weeks, I started avoiding going out on sales calls. Instead, I hung around the station drinking coffee mixed with Swiss Miss hot chocolate packages in the station's administrative office area, while chatting with the bookkeeper, who had a horrible marriage, and liked to talk about it. I wasn't supposed to be there at lunchtime, or almost any other time before my show. I was supposed to be out, promoting the opportunities our station offered to advertisers. Businesses like bars, vitamin and health food stores, record shops, and other establishments appreciated the chance to have clever commercials produced for them by our creative production director, who was also our morning show host. Unfortunately, many of these clients did not appreciate being asked to pay their bills.

Sometimes, I stayed at home instead of coming in to make sales calls. Then I'd have to hustle to make it to the station for my show. Since my show started at seven, I had to be there at six, which meant I was commuting sixty miles to the station in rush hour traffic. Dale Tinker can still quote some of the excuses I gave for being late. His favorite is the one where I got stuck behind the Pope's motorcade.

I did manage to sell a few paying ads, mostly to listeners who had small businesses and were fans of the show. I think, to be honest, that many of them were actually put up to buying from me by Dale. He had talked the station's owner into trying rock again, and I always believed he threw some of his business my way so that the venture could succeed.

WFLX generated nearly zero in sales revenue for me, but it gave me a priceless appreciation for the hard work and creativity that goes into selling radio time. To this day, if there's anything I can do for a station's sales force, I'll do it. Just don't make me bring in the business.

I also met my friend Jane at WFLX. Jane scheduled the commercials for the radio station—a job title known as "traffic director." Jane didn't especially care for the music we played, but she did like me, and I liked her. She'd hang around the studio, and we'd talk while the records played. Jane was always planning something: a trip to China, a new crochet design, or a science fiction story she wanted to write. The difference between Jane and most other people who plan things is that Jane actually did nearly everything she said she wanted to do. This turned out to be a particularly good thing, since Jane died of cancer before she turned fifty-five. Jane taught me, among many other things, how to look at quilts: from the plain side. That, she explained, is the best way to see the quality of the piece—by looking at the stitch work from the side nobody usually sees—the side that's not fancy. It was good life advice, too.

Skip Columbus

Certain pieces of advice that people give you about starting your career in radio are a bunch of hooey. While I was commuting one hundred miles every day to work at WFLX, I applied to Edgar James, the program director of one of Chicago's two country music stations, for a job playing Eddie Rabbit and Crystal Gayle records. I am, in fact, a country music fan, just not *that* kind of country music fan. I am an Emmylou Harris, Gram Parsons, Johnny Cash, Kacey Musgraves country fan, but the station played some Willie Nelson along with its mainline countrified pop, so I figured I could stand it.

This was before I got used to the idea that you didn't necessarily have to like the music you played. All the DJs I'd met told me it didn't matter whether you liked the music on your station. "Because," they all explained, "even if you start out loving the songs on your playlist, if your station plays the hits, by the time you play a record 2,362 times, you hate it. So you might as well just play music you can't stand to begin with. Then you don't F-up something you like."

Edgar James told me that in order to move from my suburban Chicago station to any station within the borders of the actual city itself, I would first have to leave Chicago and

work in a smaller market. When I called him to see whether
he'd listened to my tape, he had a smaller market all picked
out for me. "You have the potential to be a great little DJ,
Trudy. You just need some more experience. Nobody is going
to hire you for a full-time air shift in the top radio market in
America, unless you have some medium market experience.
Columbus, Ohio. That would be the place for you to go."

There was no job for me at Edgar's station; but Edgar
James, programmer of the top country station in Chicago, had
graciously taken the time to listen to my tape—a tape that
was likely one of fifty or so he received every week. And
Edgar James, a bona fide industry pro with years, if not
decades of experience, had rendered his opinion: If I were to
succeed at this radio thing, I must move to Columbus, Ohio,
and work my way back. Edgar James even offered to put in a
good word for me at the country station there in Columbus.

"Thank you, Mr. James I'll send them my tape, and, if
they're interested, I would be grateful for any
recommendation you care to give." I hung up and thought
about what Edgar James had suggested. I said the words,
"Columbus, Ohio" out loud a few times, just to see how it felt.
"No," I decided, "there are a couple of other things you are
going to try before you head to Columbus, Ohio."

It's not that I was opposed to the idea of a medium radio
market. Madison, Wisconsin; Nashville, Tennessee;
Providence, Rhode Island, and at least a dozen other markets
I could name off the top of my head might have tempted me
with their hip college populations (I had forgotten about Ohio

State), music scenes, and history. But Columbus, Ohio? For all I knew, Columbus, Ohio, was, and is now, the great overlooked diamond-in-the-rough metropolis of the USA. But in my head, it was a depressed, scrappier version of Chicago—minus the music, sweeping lakefront, architecture, theater, and museums, with possibly worse weather. I could not imagine myself in Columbus, Ohio, unless I were on the run from the FBI and trying to think of the last place anyone would expect to find me.

I realize I may have just cut myself off from the public in a city in the heartland of America. Columbus, Ohio, is probably every bit as exciting as other mid-size American cities, but that's not what I thought at the time. So I thanked Edgar James for his advice, and carried my tape across town, to deliver in person to the competing country station, which had only recently signed on the air. I told the general manager, who was in his office when I arrived, that I would take literally any and all shifts that might be available.

That is when I learned one of the great truths of radio: you may not be the most talented, or experienced, or able person who has approached the program director of a station for work in the last month—but if you show up at just the right time (by which I mean the day their overnight guy has just been arrested on child pornography charges, or their weekend talent has been felled by a stomach virus, or the evening host has been given an escort out the door after a number of contest winners turned out to be his high school drinking buddies), you may just get the job anyhow.

Not two weeks later, without leaving my tiny Chicago studio apartment, and for reasons that probably had less to do with my ability and more with my willingness to allow myself to be moved from shift to shift like a human roulette ball, I was hired by the competing country station in Chicago to host two overnight shifts every weekend. It wasn't a full-time job, but it was still Chicago. I had not had to move to Columbus, or anyplace else. I was inside the station, inside the John Hancock Building, drinking the same horrible coffee as the full-time, big-money DJs. I told my new boss that if he could guarantee me three shifts a week—any three shifts—I would quit my suburban station and be available to him whenever he needed a shift covered. He carved out three shifts a weekend for me; three shifts that paid far more than I'd been earning on my grueling daily round-trip to WFLX and supposedly selling airtime. And this shift offered insurance: something I'd lived, fearfully, without for two years.

I resigned from the sweet little alternative rock station that I loved. I kept two good friends, and my notebooks of the sets of music that I'd played, knowing even then that it would be the last time I was likely to have any kind of creative freedom in choosing records. Those notebooks are still here, in my desk, to remind me of what was once possible in radio. My boss in the suburbs was not pleased, but he understood. A few months after I left, the station's owner pulled out of the alt-rock format for the second time in three years, leaving one commercial rock station, and a handful of college signals, to carry on some remnant of the "music the DJs like" format.

Edgar James, who didn't hire me, still taught me something important: you do not need to take every piece of advice you get, especially if you have another plan you think might work. If you're wrong, or if you fail, Columbus, Ohio, will still be there.

Free Beer

Drivin' 99 would have caused a huge improvement in my life, had it not been for Lon and Rickie: perhaps the most abusive and sadistic couple ever to call themselves radio professionals. Lon, a tall, doughy man of about thirty-five who favored tweed sport jackets and always looked as though he needed both a haircut and a good dandruff shampoo, was widely believed by the airstaff to be a dedicated cocaine user. Prone to verbal explosions and venomous public critiques of his airstaff, Lon's management technique included ordering you to get up in the middle of your sleep cycle. Lon would demand, often on very short notice, attendance at meetings where all the air personalities were expected to listen to tapes of each other, then savage one another's work.

Unlike healthy air check meetings, where a show's hosts and a trusted manager, coach, or consultant go over a piece of audio the hosts have selected, offering helpful observations and setting goals, these meetings resembled summer camp "bull sessions," where a group of kids picks out one suffering victim to deliver the "truth about why nobody really likes you" speech. "Hear that?" Lon would roar. "Hear how many times he said the word *fun*? Didn't know we hired Dick and

Jane, did you?" Unlike summer camp, you couldn't write a letter home to your mom about it, and you were going to have to endure the treatment for a lot longer than six weeks.

Rickie seemed pleasant enough, except that she had a strangely unrealistic idea of what a music disc jockey does. Among the tasks that Rickie seemed to think could reasonably be expected of me included tracking down her putatively drug-addled boyfriend—my boss—and getting him to show up to work. If this was not possible, I was to stay and cover his air shift until a better alternative could be found. I, and all the other members of the station's airstaff, were also required to read whatever the latest management philosophy book of the moment was, and adhere to its more stringent tenets. One of Lon's assigned readings suggested the airstaff do our entire day's work on a planned schedule, broken into three-minute increments. None of this was pleasant; but the real reason several of us lost our ability to even pretend we liked hosting our shifts every day was the forced pet-sitting.

I confess that I had not yet properly absorbed the industry standard practice of being at the station an hour before you're supposed to go on the air. Karl, who held the shift before mine, referred to me as "Turi who makes us worry." One day, when I popped into the studio about fifteen minutes before my shift, I found Rickie waiting for me. "You will never guess who I have in my office!" Rickie warbled. "His name is Dallas." She then added—as if I could not see the small gray fluffball shivering on its perch for myself— "He's a cockatiel."

Normally, the life expectancy of a cockatiel can reach twenty years, but that's assuming you don't have your tropical bird locked in a small, highly air conditioned, cubicle-sized room. Rickie's office was on the same air conditioning sub-system as the on-air studios. The thermostat regulating the temperature in both rooms was in a spot where stacks of electronic equipment heated things up considerably. Dallas' new room, with almost no heat-exuding equipment, was about twenty degrees chillier than the studio. Naturally, Dallas caught a cold.

We didn't have Ikea or The Container Store to provide cheap, stackable, plastic mini-cubicles yet. Even if you worked in one of the tallest, fanciest buildings in the entire world (which we did), state-of-the-art staff-management communication meant stacking stolen plastic milk crates from the closest 7-11 against the wall and cramming a bunch of instant coffee cans on their sides inside of them to create personal mailboxes for the "jock lounge." This, along with the coffee-stained couches discarded from the offices of long-forgotten former managers, piles of newspapers and sliced-up magazines used for show prep, plus the overflowing ash trays, and the rock and roll or country promotional posters on the walls, gave the performers' side of the radio station a distinctly dorm room ambience.

Inside the coffee can labeled "Ryder" a few days later, I found this memo, copied to each DJ, from Lon: "Dallas has a cold. In addition to your air shift and production duties, you will each be expected to check in on Dallas twice per hour. The thermostat in your studio must be set for 84 degrees, in order to keep the temperature in Rickie's office comfortable for Dallas. If Dallas' condition worsens, call Rickie at the condo. This is not optional." In other words, if the bird kicked the bucket on any of our shifts, our jobs would go into the ground with it. Rickie worked morning drive, and stayed on as a manager until about noon, so it was not a long shot to hope the bird—if its number were truly up—would oblige us by keeling over during one of Rickie's shifts. I believe that before our game of cockatiel roulette reached its conclusion, Rickie and Lon retrieved Dallas and brought him to their condo, where a tropical climate could be assured.

Aside from my unhappiness at running an exotic bird nursing facility, Rickie and Lon were often disappointed with me for a myriad of other reasons. One was my support of our union, AFTRA (now known as "SAG-AFTRA"). AFTRA was the proverbial thorn in Lon and Rickie's side. When Lon didn't show up for an air shift because he was pursuing what some believed were his interests in inhalable narcotics, the union would do something outrageous, like demand that the person who had covered Lon's hours be paid, even though

Lon had clearly said, "Fuck no," and thrown that person out of his office.

Drivin' 99, my first full-time major market radio job, nearly killed *me* as well as the bird. This is not an exaggeration. Requests for time-off for illness invariably elicited a repetition of the last line of every memo Lon sent: "If you can't do it, we'll find somebody else who will." One night, during my air shift, after fainting in the bathroom from an episode of influenza, hitting the floor face-first and knocking loose one of my front teeth, I stayed up till 9:00 a.m. to call Lon and tell him I was too sick to come to work that night, and would he please schedule one of the weekend talents to fill in. Lon gave me his "If you can't do it, we'll find somebody else who will" line, and hung up on me. I could barely drive, stand, or speak, but I made it through that next night. Then, I had to face the fact that while I was unwilling to abandon my air shift until I could find a replacement job, it would also be difficult to send out résumés if I were already dead. I started looking.

Snakes in Your Bed

Kyla, barely twenty, perky, clever, and blonde, arrived during my second winter at Drivin' 99, hired to host the evening shift. I'd become the full-time overnight jock several months earlier, and I'd hoped to be promoted to the evening shift myself. But Kyla, while younger, had been on the air far longer. A self-described army brat, Kyla had grown up on the military bases of the acknowledged epicenter of outlaw country music: Texas.

Kyla landed in Chicago mid-January with nothing in her wardrobe warmer than a station-logo-branded windbreaker. So I took her shopping for a down coat—and I honestly did *not* purposely help her choose one that made her look more like the Michelin Man than a Rangerette. That just happened. I gave her a vintage green rhinestone and faux pearl owl pin to make the taupe sleeping-bag-with-arms ensemble look a little fancier.

When Kyla's hotel allowance ran out and she still hadn't found a rental, in an effort to overcome my jealousy and emulate the good person I hoped I could actually become, I offered her the fold-out couch in my studio apartment. We each had a little privacy, thanks to the dining alcove I'd made into my bedroom by means of a curtain.

It didn't take long before I reconsidered my decision to play hostess. In the middle of her first night in my home, I was shocked into semi-consciousness by a loud stage whisper bearing a hardcore El Paso twang. "Turi! Get up! There's a rattlesnake in here!"

My eyes flew open as I tried to force my slumbering mind to consider how a rattlesnake could possibly have climbed three flights of stairs and snuck into my apartment. I stalled for time (as those suddenly awakened tend to do) by taking on the persona of a complete idiot. "What?" I asked her. "There's a what?"

"A snake!" came the voice, more urgently this time. "There is a rattlesnake here. In your apartment." I was, by now, awake enough to determine that whether or not the snake was real, a 3:00 a.m. conversation about it was definitely taking place in my apartment. Then I heard it: a hisssssss, followed by a clunk-clunk-clunk. "There!" the whisper ratcheted up in pitch and volume to a Texas-inflected shriek. "A rattlesnake!"

In the interest of kindness, before I collapsed backward onto my pillow to resume my previous dream, I said, "Kyla. That's the steam heat from the radiator. We don't have rattlesnakes in Chicago."

"Well," huffed Kyla in a haughty drawl, "we don't have steam heat in El Paso."

PINWWA

Jimmy Breslin, a famous New York City newspaperman, once wrote a book in which he mentioned keeping a list of "People I'm Not Talking to This Year." It is to Mr. Breslin that I owe the inspiration for creating my own list: "People I'm Never Working with Again." Periodically, I revise this list by adding names. Once you are on my "PINWWA" list, you stay there, so it never gets shorter (unless somebody dies). One of my life's small, secret pleasures is to occasionally review the list to see how the people on it are doing, professionally speaking. It's a point of honor that I am not allowed to celebrate physical misfortunes, though it can be tempting. Thanks to the internet, it's easy to find out whether somebody's rotten karma has come back to haunt them.

The top slot on my list of PINWWAs is still held by a DJ from Drivin' 99 we'll call "Stan the Scam." Stan was one of those people who embraced nasty behavior as his personal true north. With the personality of a children's book villain, The Scam was the kind of guy who'd have dug up your dead kitten in order to bring it in a box to school and taunt you with it. Having to masquerade as an adult with manners, The Scam amused himself in slightly less obviously sadistic ways by making your life around the radio station a constant emotional agility test. You had to jump over whatever unpleasant hurdle he set up for you, then smile and act as though nothing had happened.

I should mention that stations playing hits of any genre used to play them on a form of media called "carts." These were usually blue plastic rectangular boxes with see-through tops, about six inches long, four inches wide, and an inch thick. Each contained a looped audio tape recording of a single song. If you've ever seen the briefly popular 8-track tape, carts looked a lot like them. Placing the cart in a machine called a deck and pressing a start button "fired" the cart, which played that song and then stopped when the cart recycled to its beginning point.

Carts could stack, if you were tall enough, extremely high. One of Stan's entertainments was to stack all the carts he'd played in a four hour show on the counter in towers about eight feet tall, instead of re-filing them in the storage racks where they were organized for easy access. That's how you'd find them when you came in to do your show. If you were short and needed to take a song from the middle of the pile, even if you tried very, very, gently to move the top of the pile first, you'd knock the whole thing over. The sound of the tower of tape crashing to the ground was cacophonous, particularly if somebody's microphone was on.

Stan the Scam also liked to paste photos of the faces of the female airstaff (except, of course, for Rickie) onto *Playboy* centerfolds' bodies, and post them around the studio. This kind of stuff ranks way down the list of offensive behaviors from what some [usually] women still endure in the entertainment (and likely every other) industry. Still, it was disconcerting to come into work and see your face plastered atop the image of a nearly nude women wearing a G-string while crawling, with her ass in the air, across a cheesily-made-up bed.

As useless as he was, I still learned two very important things from The Scam. The first is not to ask a married man riding the radio station elevator with his arms around a Chicago Bulls cheerleader "Is this your wife?" even if you happen to know that the man's wife is a Chicago Bulls cheerleader. Cheerleaders are not, actually, interchangeable. The one in the elevator may not be, and in this case, was definitely not, the one who was expecting The Scam home for dinner.

The second thing Scam taught me was that being avaricious, nasty, and devoid of scruples can result in excellent career progress, but only for a while. Revenge came for Stan the Scam not long after he quit our country station, confident of becoming a famous actor. You may be wondering which famous actor Stan turned out to be, but it wouldn't help if I told you his real name unless you are a connoisseur of insurance company training films and late-night ads for heating and air conditioning services.

Before quitting, The Scam had improved his regular on-air source of income by sneakily finagling away the job of our afternoon host, a personable fellow I'll call The Governor. The Governor was a much more interesting air personality than

Stan. But Stan had an important off-air skill. In addition to his prowess at decorating the Drivin' 99 studio, he had, it was alleged, excellent sources of cocaine; something, you will remember, that was rumored to be very important to Lon, our boss. Stan dealt his way into the coveted afternoon drive position, which gave him a little less time to stack up carts and pin up doctored photos, but it put The Governor out of a gig. Fortunately, The Governor, after just a few days of unemployment, landed at a much calmer and healthier rock station across town.

A few months after he'd quit, Stan the Scam, whose acting career already wasn't going as well as he'd hoped, decided that a paycheck as a lowly disc jockey was useful for things like rent and buying drinks for Chicago Bulls cheerleaders. So he went looking for radio work at The Governor's new station. Knowing that he had worked with Scam, that station's program director asked The Governor for a reference on his old colleague. The Governor paused, considered for a moment, and responded.

"You're thinking of hiring Stan? Let me give you one or two other names." Which is how I found out that revenge does not have to look like the ending scene of an action picture, with cars on fire and a hero walking into the sunset. It can be very, very subtle.

No Job Is Worth This

There were now three women on the air at Drivin' 99. Kyla worked evenings; I held down overnights; and the third female on staff was Lon's girlfriend, Rickie, who read news during the morning drive show. Doing morning drive means you go to bed at about seven in the evening. Even if she'd been awake, Rickie was understandably reluctant to spend evenings inside the sort of bars that advertised on Drivin' 99. With Kyla on the air, I was, by default, the available DJ to be the station's emissary to our listeners in the places where they spent their free hours: those bars you hear about in Country Western songs. This fit right in with Lon's second-favorite pastime: devising horrific "personal appearances" for his airstaff.

"This weekend," he would bark at me on the phone at ten in the morning, which is the middle of the night for someone whose shift ends at 6:00 a.m., "you are going to a bar. Men like looking at women in bars. That's why you're going." I was also going because Lon had offered to provide Drivin' 99's country-music-bar-owning advertisers free beer for the evening. Every Saturday night, and usually Sunday nights, too, Lon would order me to travel to far distant suburbs (often sixty miles from my apartment) to hand out concert tickets and radio station T-shirts while the patrons drank free beer.

It's not unusual for radio stations to do "prize truck" promotions. They dispatch a "prize crew," consisting of a couple of attractive broadcasting students, a bouncer, and a station-branded van that dispenses station swag. But even if the students are unpaid interns, a prize crew still costs money. Lon's third most important goal in life, beyond the speculative goal of obtaining as much cocaine as possible and torturing the airstaff, was to avoid spending the broadcasting company's money. The formula that so far had well-served Lon's career with Drivin' 99's owner—a hotelier who thought radio would be a good business to "branch out" into—was this: the fewer dollars Lon spent, the greater the speed at which he would be promoted. So Lon would send me, unpaid and living in fear of immanent unemployment, on four-hour sojourns to the hinterlands of our city, to walk my then-115-pound, five-foot-four self into a smoky, loud bar full of third-shift drunks and country music. There, I was to attempt to give away concert tickets and T-shirts, while remaining fully clad and dry.

That's not strictly accurate. *I* wanted to remain dry. Lon would not have cared if I had offered to strip down to a bikini and dance on the jukebox while being bathed in pitchers of whatever draft beer we were giving away. I only survived because of the kindness of Karl, who happened to be a former major-league-baseball-draftee-turned-country-DJ, and was huge. Though Karl had a prodigious appetite for young blonde women, he nevertheless paid special attention to my safety, and would often arrive like a knight in shining armor to interpose his six-foot-three, 220-pound self between me and the drunken masses and escort me to the safety of my rusted-out Datsun 510. I cooperated by doing my best to speed my ancient sedan in pinball fashion between the salt-and-mud-encrusted pickup trucks and out of the parking lot. Once, Karl arrived to find me being carried aloft like a sack of onions by a particularly hearty group of Drivin' 99 fans, and only by throwing free station T-shirts and bottle openers as a diversion was he able to distract the men, enabling me to escape.

After nearly three years of misery at Drivin' 99, our union contract came up for renewal. The station's airstaff was invited by the union's negotiating team to attend a meeting. We would discuss what we hoped to achieve in our next negotiation. As a performing union, AFTRA contracts basically made sure on-air workers were paid at a certain rate, and the union provided health care coverage for working broadcast and commercial talent, providing they earned a relatively small amount of salary in an AFTRA-covered position. The health care option has historically been one of the great features of performers' union memberships, since members often make a living out of part-time work for a couple of stations or producers and wouldn't qualify for it otherwise. Unlike many other labor unions, SAG-AFTRA negotiates with the understanding that job security and seniority are not really something you can achieve in a ratings-driven industry where a station can be playing country music one minute, then fire the entire airstaff and switch to techno dance mixes the next.

We all took our seats, along with AFTRA's representative, around the station's oval, faux-walnut conference table, in the gray fabric-padded room where the sales people usually held their daily motivation sessions and marked their white boards with goals and ratings data. Mostly, the rank and file were hoping for a small raise, and some control over how far and how often we could be ordered to travel for personal appearances. Rickie, in addition to being the morning newsreader, was also the station's music director. She had finagled her way into the airstaff meeting by insisting she was not management.

According to the union contract, managers were defined as having the power to hire and fire people, and Rickie technically didn't have anyone reporting to her (unless you counted Dallas, the cockatiel). The fact that Rickie had a management job title, and was Lon's girlfriend, and that Lon was happy to fire or hire anyone at Rickie's request, was not something we could prove, so Rickie got to stay. She gave a speech about how we didn't need AFTRA, because the station's owners were just this side of sainthood.

"Trust me. Lon and I have worked for this company for nine years. They've been nothing but wonderful to us. If you decertify the union, the company will contribute just as much as it pays the union now, only directly into your personal retirement accounts. With the money they save not having to pay the union's staff and expenses, you can have raises." She spoke for about five minutes, which can feel like a very long time to listen to somebody who you happen to know is reciting to you the company's official handbook of complete horsewash. I waited. Nobody was going to say a word to Rickie, either because they believed her, or, more likely, because they were afraid of her. Perhaps my guard was down due to sleep deprivation, after yet another "bull session/ group critique." I raised my hand.

"Rickie, I'm not saying you're wrong. In fact, I'd like you to be right. I'd like the owners to be the very best broadcasting company in the whole world. If they are, why would it bother them to put all these promises in writing? Nobody is going to ask them so to sign anything they can't live with. So if this is the way they want to treat us, then let's put all the things you just told us they want to do for us in a contract, and they can sign it, and then we'll all be happy."

It took about a week for my job to disappear. Since, for the preceding three years, I'd always expected to be fired whenever I talked with Lon, the actual dismissal came as a relief. Like every other meeting we'd ever had, he scheduled this one via a memo left for me to read before my shift, requesting my presence at an hour that was normally the middle of my night.

"We've decided to make some changes, and you're one of them," Lon told me. I thought about this for a moment.

"Does this mean I am losing my job?"

"That's one of the changes."

"Ok. Would you be willing to tell me why?"

"We are tired of your bullshit. Every woman I've ever hired has been a great employee, because she was willing to work twice as hard as the men, to prove herself. You, Ryder, don't want to work any harder than anybody else."

That was my very best firing moment ever. The only thing I regret about it is that I didn't smuggle a tape recorder into the room, so that future generations of women would believe me.

Every now and then, the universe is kind. Shortly after Lon and Rickie showed me the door and got rid of the union and its irksome contract, I landed a dream job at a legendary and successful radio station: The Big Rock. Lon found out about it from Frank, the local newspaper columnist who covered radio for our town.

Frank, our town's media expert, is so well connected that it is an open secret that timid bosses use him to avoid sacking their jocks in face-to-face meetings. Managers can just leak the fact that they are firing so-and-so to Frank, and the hard part is over before they ever have that final clean-out-your-cubbyhole meeting. Once, when I was kept on at a station after the rest of the staff had been fired, I had to prove I was still employed to one of the trade magazines that followed

Frank's column by playing my show jingles to them over the telephone from the on-air studio.

A few hours after Frank ran a mention of my new air shift on The Big Rock in his column, my phone rang at home. I heard the whispered, muffled voice of a former co-worker. The co-worker was hiding in a remote sales office. It was still difficult to hear her, not only because she had her hand wrapped around her mouth and the phone receiver, but also because there was some sort of loud banging and swearing going on in the background. "I can't hear you, Lauren. Speak up please," I said. Since this was a 9:00 a.m. call, I was also half asleep.

"Do you hear that noise?" Lauren asked. "That's Lon. He's punching a hole in his office wall."

"Why should I care what he does?" I replied, annoyed at having been woken for the latest Lon complaint. "I don't work for him anymore."

"That is *why* he is punching the hole. He walked out of his office, waving Frank's column, shouting 'There are three stations in the country that any DJ would give his left nut to work for, and fucking Ryder just got a job at one of them.' And then he locked himself in his office and started punching the wall."

I figured Lauren's update was the end of my Drivin' 99 experience, but some months later, I was astonished when the receptionist at The Big Rock left one of those "while you were out" pink messages in my mailbox: Rickie wanted me to call her.

"Turi, things are not going well here," Rickie complained. "They've hired a bunch of broadcasting school graduates for eight bucks an hour, and the new insurance coverage is crap." I practiced deep, slow breaths and listened. Rickie was hoping I could help her out. "I've just sent my new demo tape over to The Big Rock. Would you put in a word for me?" It was shocking to realize that Rickie seemed genuinely unaware of my revulsion at the way she and Lon had managed the airstaff at Drivin' 99. Not to mention the fact that the current employment situation there was directly attributable to her. Perhaps she really had no idea how Lon treated any of the "regular" employees, or that the other disc jockeys might have resented her cherry-picking the best air shifts and overpaying herself to host them, or that she was allowed to trade commercial endorsements for anything she wanted: from a new pair of expensive headphones to—it was widely opined—a nose job and breast enhancement surgery. Perhaps she felt she had built a bridge between management and the humble DJs, creating a station of high hopes and esprit de corps. Perhaps she'd heard a rumor that I had undergone recent shock therapy resulting in short-term memory loss.

"Sure," I told Rickie, "I would be happy to let my program director know you are applying." I hung up, walked twenty feet to my boss's office, and stuck my head in the door. "Beau? Do you remember how I showed up for work for two days when I had pneumonia before you saw me and said I looked awful and sent me home? Do you remember that you asked me why I'd been coming in to work in that condition, and I told you it was because I was afraid that if I called in sick, you'd fire me? And you asked me if management at my old station would really fire someone for having to call in sick and I said 'yes?' Well, one of my former managers is sending you a tape. I told her I'd let you know her tape is coming. So. Her tape is coming."

"Got it," Beau nodded.

Sex (and Diplomacy) on The Rock

On my third night at The Big Rock, I met Lola, the ample, curvaceous wife of Brad, the station's hunky blond DJ. Brad resembled the lifeguards in 1960s beach movies. At first, I assumed Lola was there to meet her husband after work. Then I realized her husband's shift on our sister station had ended an hour ago. Perhaps Brad was in one of the studios, producing a bit for his show? No. Interviewing a music star? No. Giving a tour to a group of students? No. Lola was there to see me! I could not have been more flattered. This, I told myself, must be what legendary radio stations are all about. Not only do the men make you welcome, but their wives come down to the studios late in the evening, just to say "hello." I briefly wondered whether she'd brought cookies.

But something didn't track. Our conversation was starting to feel more like an interview, and all Lola's questions were about her husband.

"Turi, what do you think of Brad?"

"He's great on the air. I'm a fan."

"What do you think of Brad *off* the air?"

"Well, I've only just met him, but he seems extremely nice. Just like all the guys at the station. They've all been really welcoming. Friendly."

"And what do you think of Brad *personally*?"

"His person? What do I..."

Three days into the job, and a layer of naïveté shriveled like a salted slug. Of course! I'm the new girl-DJ. I must be after everybody's husband. It took me a few minutes, but now I understood. This smart, savvy, worldly woman—all icy blue eyes, high heels, and magazine-lovely blow-dried hair, was there to scope out whether I had any thought of dating her Beach Boy-handsome husband. Worse, if I said "I am not the slightest bit interested in your husband. I never even had a crush on any of the Beach Boys, and they can sing," she would be mightily insulted. If, on the other hand, I told her that her husband was the stuff of teenage fantasy, and that his image should be on posters over the beds of college dorms across America, she would be in my studio every night, or down the hall, substituting rat poison for the Sweet'n Low in the station's kitchenette. In one of my rare moments of diplomacy and insight, I sensed the answer that would save me:

"Lola," I said, "I'm sorry, but I can't answer your question. It's funny, but I never really look at the guys I work with that way. They're just 'guys-I-work-with'—it's kind of another category."

Lola released me from her wide, blue gaze. I felt the way I imagine I'd feel if I were a just-caught salmon, tossed back into the lake after being judged too small to eat: blessed relief, and the chance to swim away. Some other hook would get me, but for the moment, I was safe.

Ironically, Lola had married one of the men in broadcasting who seemed completely delighted with his wife. In fact, most of the married men at The Big Rock gave every indication of being devoted husbands. The most famous of them, Lincoln Lawrence, legendary for his acerbic personality on the air, and taciturn nature in the halls, transformed into an animated, cheerful, boyishly devoted suitor the minute he called his wife. He chatted. He smiled. He was utterly smitten. Ratings didn't scare this man. He'd been number one for years. Money was no problem for him, either. He was one of the first morning drive personalities in America to make six figures; and when he retired, he was, reportedly, well beyond that. Link was generous, quietly so, with his charitable work, but lived modestly. In the years I worked with him, the only thing I ever saw Link worry about was the safety of his wife. He warned me the day I started: "Ryder, you're going to call me three times. Every morning, starting at 3:00 a.m. You call me every fifteen minutes, until you hear me say, 'I'm up.' And never mention on the air what time I wake up, or when I leave for work. Jill is home. I don't want anyone to know she's alone in the house."

Maybe I'd arrived in rock radio too late to see the Mad Men era of free love and radio groupies, or maybe it's the fact that several of the jocks, on their second or third marriages, had gotten their wild yearnings out of their systems, but nothing risqué ever seemed to be going on in the darkened, disused production booths of The Big Rock late at night. Even the DJs who were single and dating behaved like pros. They cared about their shows, the station, and their listeners. They worked impressively hard. I would see them at 2:00 a.m., through the soundproof glass, in the station's other studios, using their off-hours to produce humor pieces or parody songs they'd be playing at ten the next morning.

They were at their desks, before and after their shows, hunting through the trades and press for material, learning details about the songs and artists we played. Link stacked a pile of newspapers around his desk that, after fulfilling their function as show preparation material, was high enough to serve as a privacy wall. The Big Rock's air personalities were entertainers, and they took their craft seriously.

The single DJs who were interested in dating mostly trolled the request lines for willing listeners. Dating listeners has always struck me as utterly creepy. Maybe it's a gender thing, because I don't know any other women who worked on the air while dating any of their listeners, either. I did everything in my power—from using a PO box for mail to changing the spelling of my last name—to keep my private life private.

Ironically, it was a woman who worked for The Big Rock's sister station, Andie Belmont, who accused me of turning the contest line into a dating service.

I discovered Andie believed I was traipsing off with any interested fan the day she called me on the station hotline.

"Turi, you need to get Clyde to return my money."

"Andie, are you sure you've called the right person? Who is Clyde? What money?"

"Don't tell me you don't know what I'm talking about. You've been dating Clyde for months. He even named one of his horses after you."

Now I was completely stumped. "I'm not sure if I should be flattered or offended that there's a horse with my name on it somewhere in the Midwest, but I still don't know what you're talking about. You know my boyfriend, and his name is not Clyde."

It turned out that Clyde had made his way into the lives of Andie and her partner, Genevieve, by claiming to be dating me. Andie, I intuited, operated under the assumption that if I dated any men, I would date any man. "He came up to the studios," Andie continued. "I let him in. He was here to see you." This creepy revelation prompted me to remember that Clyde had been Andie's guest one night while we were both on the air, though that was the only time I'd ever met him. I hadn't been able to get him out of my station's end of the hallway fast enough. The fact that Andie and I were essentially alone in a warren of soundproof booths in the middle of the night was one good reason that I did not welcome strangers to tour our studios. Clyde, I now recalled, had also mailed me a picture of a colt labeled "Turi's Toy." I'd thought it obsessively weird, and had tossed it into the trash. Andie, however, was an easier sell. "Clyde borrowed money from us to invest in breeding horses, and now we can't get it back," Andie whined. "I know you're dating him. He knows your whole schedule. He told us you were taking a night off, and you took the night off." The audacity of a coworker telling me that a stranger was my boyfriend made it fun to disappoint her.

"Andie, every single listener within the fifty thousand-watt, thirty-eight state listening area of this radio station knew I was taking the night off. It was Passover. I told the listeners I was celebrating the holiday with my family, and that I'd be off for two days." One of the loveliest sounds I've ever heard over the phone was the silence of Andie absorbing her $500 lesson.

Not that there were never any radio station romances. I became the legitimate topic of gossip a few months later, when I took up with our single, but not especially eligible, production director and part-time air talent, Blaine.

Harley to Nashville

There's not much sexier than somebody who is the very best at whatever he or she does. Being new at a radio station where brilliant—in some cases, legendary—talent is working can feel a bit like walking among the exotic flowers of a conservatory hothouse. It's very tempting to reach out and pick something. But in the decades I've spent in broadcasting, I've had only two serious romances with men who were in the business. That doesn't count the rumor of the hot lesbian liaison with a news reporter that I was alleged to have had, complete with accusations of being discovered with her in flagrante underneath a studio console. Hearing about that one, a year after the alleged "fact," made me skeptical of rumored office romances forevermore.

Blaine, on the other hand, was a real, if not particularly healthy, relationship. Six-foot-one, sporting a leather jacket and cowboy boots; gangly, befreckled, curly haired and lightly tattooed, he was a picture of rock and roll dissolution. Blaine made a point of telling everyone, on and off the air, that he was a Vietnam veteran. It's still not entirely clear to me to what extent this was true. One of the horrors Blaine claimed to have endured sounded somehow familiar to me. Later, I realized it was lifted straight from the pages of *Catch-*

22. Blaine's ex-wife told me, years afterward, that he never saw combat. However, Blaine's boozy mother, during the first and last Thanksgiving dinner I ever spent with his family (a dinner at which I was surprised to learn that there really were people who considered Jell-O infused with cream cheese and shredded carrots a salad) confessed that if she'd known what he would suffer at the hands of the Viet Cong, she'd have driven him to Canada herself. Whichever was the case, Blaine charmed me with his prodigious broadcasting talents, and alarmed me with his bourbon-and-coke-fueled binges. During these, anything and anyone who tried to prevent destruction by standing between TV sets and guitars and the walls they were aimed at, was in danger of breakage. Ours was a highly dramatic, if entirely cliché, radio romance. It is also how I ended up riding three hundred and seventy-five miles from Chicago to Nashville on the back of a Harley Davidson.

By the time I strapped myself to the "Queen" seat of Blaine's Harley, heading south on Highway 41, my extremely talented, seriously alcoholic and much older boyfriend had been a dramatic part of my life for about two years. Not only had he taught me about storytelling, humor, and on-air technique, but I also learned—by heart—the direct phone numbers of every emergency room in the city; acquired a shelf full of "self-help" material for "wives" of alcoholics; and became constantly alert to the variety of places—cowboy boots, toilet tanks—a man could hide a full-sized bottle of Seagram's.

Lest you think me a pushover, I wasn't the only one willing to put up with bad treatment in exchange for living close to the fire of an enormously creative and equally self-destructive talent. The top-rated station for which we both worked had sent him through rehab three times in an effort not only to do right by him, but also to keep him on the air. In the four years we were together, he blew more career opportunities than most people get in an entire performing lifetime: TV shows, production gigs, morning drive offers, and the chance to succeed the host of the most famous countdown show in the country.

I, on the other hand, had volunteered for a far less glamorous job. I signed on for the role of "therapeutic martyr/girlfriend." I now refer to this type of behavior as Lion Tamer Syndrome. You want to prove that you're the only one who can safely walk into the cage with the dangerous, beautiful lion, and make him do things for you. You climb in, provisioned only with your simple chair, a useless whip, and a skimpy, alluring costume, and show the lion who's in charge, over and over again, show after show, until one day, the lion eats you. So when Blaine decided to drive to Nashville on his pride and joy, a customized Harley Davidson motorcycle, I knew that since he was likely to drink his way down and back, it was my duty to take my vacation simultaneously, and ride with him.

On the list of stupid things I've done, this one hit the trifecta. Standing between an alcoholic and his intended binge is a little like walking in front of a fast-moving train, foolishly confident that it will stop in time. Inserting yourself into somebody's "dream vacation," when you were not part of the dream to begin with, is not likely to produce anything like the joyful cavorting pleasure breaks you see in Carnival Cruise line advertisements. And riding on the back of a road-absorbing Harley Davidson for three hundred and seventy-five miles makes your annual mammogram seem like a spa treatment. Harley Davidson back seats are not for feminists. The boyfriend had a tiny—some might have said bony—denim-clad backside that rested on a padded saddle nearly as wide as the Harley's handlebars. I, at the time an aerobicized, petite woman, most of whose non-bone, non-muscle flesh was concentrated in her backside, got to perch on a leather-wrapped fencepost. I'm sure I looked a little strange up there, wearing a helmet when the driver did not, and sporting a fashionable black leather short jacket with red snakeskin inserts and poufy 1980s padded shoulders like something from a Duran Duran music video.

By the time we arrived in Nashville, Blaine had been forced to miss visiting a world-famous bourbon company tasting event and a distillery tour. Instead, he suffered the bat- and stalactite-filled cave trail of Cumberland Caverns, and was force-fed samples of spontaneously purchased, locally made praline fudge. Blaine could not have been less interested in bats or stalactites, although I could sense for a fleeting moment, at the sound of water dripping, a momentary hope that early settlers had used stalactites as a primitive bourbon filtration technique.

On disrobing for the night, I discovered that the harsh ride had turned the insides of my thighs, from knee to hip, a deeply bruised purple. I looked like I had suffered an assault. Had I walked into the Nashville police station and demanded they arrest the local football team for criminally abusing me, I would have certainly been believed. So in the morning, I requested a detour, to the Nashville, Tennessee, Harley Davidson dealership.

There are rules about being the girlfriend-passenger on the back of a Harley Davidson—rules with which I was, up until that very moment, unfamiliar. Rule one is: if you're the passenger, you do not speak to the salesman. The man speaks to the salesman.

"I'm thinking about changing out the seat on the bike," said Blaine.

"Now why," drawled the salesman in an accent I thought existed only on the TV show *Hee Haw*, "would y'all want to do that? You got yer king'n'queen seat there. That's ah nice, expensive, custom seat."

My boyfriend looked pained. "I know. But my girlfriend's not comfortable," he explained.

"Wahl," continued the salesman, "that's ah king'n' queen seat. That's ah haigh end, top of the lahn seat. That's custom, the king'n'queen seat."

Blaine started to look a little panicked. The salesman was talking to him as though he, Blaine, had just asked to have his privates removed with a fish-filleting knife. That's when I found out about the rule—by breaking it.

"Well," I said sweetly to the salesman, "that may be a king and queen seat, but this princess is not getting back on that bike until you change it."

Blaine looked like maybe I was the one heading toward him with the fish-filleting knife. He turned several shades of white, which made the not-completely-soaped-away road dirt from the three hundred seventy-five-mile ride stand out like coarse sandpaper against the drink-exploded pink capillaries on his face. I remembered that this was supposed to be his vacation, on his dream bike, and that I commandeered my spot on the Harley entirely to keep him from enjoying it in the way he had wished, and that he was willing to let me do it. In such relationships, that is what passes for an expression of love.

"Never mind," I said, turning on my leather-booted high heel to leave the store. "I have an idea."

I can count on two fingers the number of times I've stolen anything from a hotel room. I'm sure it looked a little unusual to our fellow bikers, truckers, and vacationers as I rode past, perched on the pillow from the Knight's Inn Motel that I had bungee-corded to the queen seat—all the way back from Nashville to Chicago.

Ghostbusters on Secretaries' Day

Being one of the few, if not the only, women on a rock station with a 50,000-watt signal heard in thirty-seven states in the early 1980s had definite advantages. Since you were a novelty, you got a lot more press than you probably deserved. When someone wanted a photo of the airstaff, you got to sit in the middle. Station management, however, was not completely comfortable with a female air talent as "one of the boys." Women were just beginning to make their way in sales. Several of our best board-operators were female—the direct result, one of them told me, of a company training and internal hiring program designed to increase the presence of women of color in traditionally white male jobs. And, of course, there were female receptionists and secretaries.

I'm not sure whether anyone celebrates Secretaries Day anymore. One of the byproducts of the TV show *Mad Men* has been the nostalgic, yet frightening, portrayal of what it meant to be a secretary in the 1960s. By the time I showed up a few decades later at The Big Rock, the lot of the secretary had improved somewhat, but she was still typically the least-appreciated employee in any company. My boss' superior, a

kindly man, wanted to change that. He was determined that
the secretaries at The Big Rock would know, at least on
Secretaries Day, how much the company valued their
contributions.

About a year after I started at The Big Rock, I arrived an
hour before my show. There, in the on-air studio, in a tall
glass vase set next to the music logs, I discovered a dozen
long-stemmed red roses.

"Nice going," I said to Jed, the jock who held the late-
night shift before mine. "What did you do to impress the
young lady? No. I've changed my mind. Please don't tell me."

"These aren't mine," Jed explained, with a slightly
worried laugh. "They're here for you."

"For me?" I replied, dumbstruck, wondering what Blaine
had done that he felt required a blooming apology, and then
speculating some more about when and how and whether I'd
find out.

"They're from the boss. For Secretaries Day. He didn't
want you to feel neglected."

On the one hand, I felt touched, and a little surprised,
that my boss' boss (our legendary-in-the-business general
manager, Gary) even knew I existed. On the other hand,
imagining that one of your airstaff will feel left out if she is
not treated like one of your secretaries is the type of scenario
I'd have expected to see on *The Mary Tyler Moore Show*, which
by then had been off the air for nearly ten years. I decided to
appreciate the thoughtfulness of the gesture.

Gary was a man of an earlier era, and for some men of his generation, it was difficult to imagine any woman at the station who was not a secretary. I got proof that my assessment was correct the day I was asked to be the Ghostbusters' receptionist.

Do you recall those short films or animation pieces you sometimes see at movie theaters before the main attraction starts? I don't mean the coming attractions, I mean the "buy some refreshments" videos featuring animated raccoons cavorting with talking popcorn bags and singing soft drinks, or depicting a helpless looking couple becoming apoplectic when their fellow moviegoer's ringing cell phone interrupts the dramatic love scene? The Big Rock had been creating its own movie trailers for several years, mostly starring Link Lawrence and his sometimes-on-air partner and fellow air personality, Sparky. These employed Link and Sparky's legendarily dry humor to discourage smoking, talking, and otherwise bothering fellow movie patrons. They often featured sarcasm and deadpan humor and were wildly popular, especially with high school kids. It was also kind of fun to hear Link, a devoted smoker, whose press photographs often showed him with a cigarette in his hand, tell people they were not allowed to light up.

This year, however, things were going to change. The Big Rock had a new idea for a movie promotional reel to communicate its "Don't Smoke or Talk During the Movie" message. The smash hit movie of the previous year was *Ghostbusters*, and we would parody it. The guys from our station would all be cast as Ghostbusters. The guys. Not me. The guys were fitted for jumpsuits, just like the movie's. They practiced their scripts. Then they shuttled around the block and down the street to the historic landmark theater where the rehearsal and filming would take place. I did not get a jumpsuit or a script. I had been at the station for three years, but I was not going to be a Ghostbuster.

I'm still not sure how it happened, but sometime during rehearsals, somebody figured out that they needed someone to play a secretary to dispatch the Ghostbusters to the scene of the smoking, talking, littering couple in the theater. Could I zoom back downtown and play a "cheesy secretary"? Of course I could.

Ransacking my wardrobe for "cheesy secretary" attire, I located fishnet pantyhose and the high-heeled black leather boots Blaine had bought for me to wear on the Harley. A lavender sweater showed cheese potential, if I added sufficiently gigantic shoulder pads. A quick swing through Marshall Field's department store en route to the theater produced a teensy black leather miniskirt, and I was done— except for hair and makeup. Mindful of the Texas maxim, "The higher the hair, the closer to G-d," I instructed the makeup artist to make me look as heavenly as possible. Actually, I told her to make me look "slutty." We set my hair and teased it till I looked like a member of Mötley Crüe after a night on the town, caked my face with pancake makeup till it looked like tent canvas, and applied blush to my cheeks in a pattern similar to the racing stripes on a 1967 Camaro. My eyeshadow was the same lavender shade as my sweater, only sparkly, with a lighter sparkly shade up to the eyebrows, which left my eyelids looking like the tail of a My Little Pony doll.

Transformation complete. Mini-skirted, made-up, and moving like a prostitute, I ventured a grand entrance into the filming area. Slack-jawed, my stunned male colleagues alternated between awkward praise and silent horror. Until then, I had dressed just like them: jeans, boots, and button-down shirts. Underdressing for my job (which, after all, took place at an hour when most people were either working as cops or firefighters or else safely home in bed) was almost a matter of self-preservation.

My job in the video would be to answer a ringing hotline and send the jumpsuited boys out to the theater to vaporize smoking, littering, noisemaking audience movie-goers. "So," I queried the director, "where does the secretary sit?" He pointed to a desk. The idea of hiding my once-in-a-lifetime fishnet-stocking and stiletto boot covered lower half seemed like a cheat. I propped my feet up on my typewriter, struggling to keep the miniskirt covering enough of me that our little trailer wouldn't require an "R" rating, and ran through my two lines. The shoot went off perfectly.

Afterward, Link offered to walk me back to the studio. It was clear he feared I might be mistaken for somebody working as "conventioneer entertainment" if I traversed the two blocks to the station by myself. His unspoken desire to grab a paper towel to scrub my face and get me back to "normal" was almost palpable. At the station's lobby, I turned to Link.

"Thanks for the company. I'm going to run up to the station now to change and wash this gunk off my face."

"How long do you think your hair's gonna stay like that?" he mused.

"Don't worry," I reassured him. "I brought a hat."

Cheaper Than an MBA

I had been on the all-night shift at The Big Rock for three years. I was starting to think not only about work, but money. When it came to money, the people who held the overnight shifts were at a real disadvantage. You might entertain hundreds of farmers, waking up to combine peas; or be a conversation starter for thousands of people on their breaks from third-shift factory work. But ads on overnights were practically given away free as a bonus for buying time on the shows that aired during the day. There were a couple of exceptions.

Phil Sawyer worked overnights at a clear-channel country music station in a major radio market. A clear-channel signal meant that at night, there was nobody else on that frequency, or dial position, so they could be heard, on a night when the atmosphere cooperated, from coast to coast and by ships in distant oceans. As I heard the story, Phil proposed to management that he would sell ads for his show himself, but he'd give the station a cut. Management took the deal. Phil visited truck stops. He read twenty-minute weather forecasts listing the road conditions on every interstate from North Dakota to Miami. He created a radio "bulletin board" where truckers could post their availability for different kinds of cargo. The show became its own network, heard on as many as eighty radio stations overnight. Sawyer anticipated an industry-wide trend: targeting your programming to a relatively small but specialized audience. Before the internet was in every home, before smart phones, Sawyer made radio at its most useful.

I tried to follow Sawyer's lead by creating marketing materials for my overnight shift—producing a tape featuring callers describing their overnight working lives—with hope that I could encourage the sales people to sell the airtime. The salespeople continued to ignore overnights. So, for that matter, did management—a mixed blessing.

My only hope of making a better living at The Big Rock was to be moved to a better shift, and the chances of that happening were slim. I worked for union scale and had been glad to get it. It was a pretty good salary, but it was not the sought-after "personal service" contract you could land as a host of a successful, Arbitron-rated day part. It wasn't what the guys had. The guys, I noticed, also had agents.

I didn't know much about talent agents when I started in the radio business. Now, at least, I know this: do not hire someone who is telling you something you'd like to believe, but which makes no logical sense.

Once there was a talent agent. This agent—we'll call him "Bud"—was a parody of the genre. Loud, tall, sporting a substantial gut and a lot of gold jewelry, Bud's face was the color of the nearly-raw steaks he consumed regularly at a local institution known for the caricatures of local media celebrities festooning its walls. Bud was fond of the notorious Mel Brooks movie phrase, "It's good to be the king." Bud eventually went to prison for having fleeced several of his clients out of large sums of their retirement savings in a Ponzi scheme.

Before becoming a convicted felon, Bud was renowned in Chicago for negotiating amazingly lucrative deals for several of the city's biggest-name program hosts. Several of them were on the air where I worked. Agents could be handy things. You could use them to be the "bad cop" to your "good cop" during negotiations. One on-air talent I know, who happens to be a lawyer himself, still hires a different lawyer to negotiate his employment agreements. That way he—the talent—can always be the nice guy. As he puts it, "Let my boss think the cappuccino machine in my studio was my lawyer's idea." Maybe it was greed, or optimism, or maybe it was working with a lot of people who were making ten times my salary. Even though I had never thought I needed an agent, I hired one.

I can't remember whether I phoned his practice, or they phoned me; but Bud, the celebrity attorney, invited me to meet him at his office in a famous art-deco era downtown skyscraper with an elaborately decorated black marble and brass lobby. From there, I was escorted to the famous steakhouse. In this noisy setting, where everyone seemed to know his name, Bud offered to represent me for a sum equivalent to about four weeks of my pay. He promised me that if he couldn't find me a better gig, at the very least he could ratchet up my present salary.

Now, a little voice in my head said these words to me: "If your present station can pay you what they're paying you, and he can't find you someplace else to go, then why should your boss—nice guy though he may be—decide to give you a raise? Out of the kindness of his heart? Because the lawyer asks him to? That makes no sense."

And that is the voice I should have heeded—the voice asking: "Does this make any sense?" However, because I fall into the rather large group that likes to believe we will get our heart's desires, even if those heart's desires sound too good to be true, I shook Bud's hand and wrote out what for me was a big check, which he cashed. Then, I waited.

I can't say absolutely nothing happened. Bud's partner, a dynamic, savvy young woman who's a powerhouse agent in the business to this day, came to my house and ordered me to cut my hair and throw away every single piece of clothing in my closet—so that I could get a job in television, which was as likely as Harvey Weinstein being hired as a resident assistant in a college women's dormitory. After *that*, nothing happened.

A few weeks after the "steak and shake," I met Bud at his office and took a closer look around the place. About five giant cardboard boxes of demo tapes were on the floor. Five boxes! I wondered exactly how much of this guy's time I was going to get, when he had literally hundreds of people paying him thousands of dollars to "represent" them to management, having personally assured every one of them of great things to come. As time passed, with only one "meet and greet" non-interview at a local TV station to show for my new wardrobe and grooming regime, it dawned on me that there would be no new job, and no raise, coming.

Now my question was: since this guy had guaranteed me something, was he prepared to give me back my money when he couldn't produce? I decided to take a swing at retrieving some of my cash. The trick would be to do it in a way that let Bud off the hook for failing to live up to his promise. How would I get "The King" to give back my money? By making him feel like The King.

I can still remember, almost word for word, my carefully crafted speech to Bud:

"It's clear you've done everything you possibly could for me, Bud, and you've worked very hard. With your extensive contacts, and all the people you know, it's obvious that I'm just not cut out to be a TV personality. It looks like my current situation is the best I can hope for. You're not going to be making the kind of big percentage representing me that you'll get from your more successful clients. I'm sorry about that. Seeing as I'm going to have to manage on what I make now, how much of my retainer do you think you might be able to return?" I got lucky. Bud sent a check for about two-thirds of it. The experience ended up costing about as much as the fancy steak dinners Bud bought for us, plus a few rounds of drinks.

About a week after my refund check cleared, our station's big-money morning guy, Link Lawrence, represented by Bud, asked me how I liked dealing with him. "Well," I told Link, "it was cheaper than getting an MBA." That was the only time I can remember making the famously hard to crack Lawrence laugh out loud.

"Cheaper than an MBA" is actually my mom's philosophy, which I've adopted. When I make a crummy financial deal, I mentally tally the money I've lost against the cost of earning an MBA, and sometimes I feel like I got a bargain. "Well, it was cheaper than getting an MBA" is an extremely soothing phrase, assuming I don't have to use it too often. Also, by having made the occasional error in financial judgment, I've added to my portfolio of self-humiliating stories, many of which can be traded for lunch.

I was lucky to run into Bud early in my career. If I'd met him later, I might have lost the thousands, or tens of thousands, that many of my colleagues who'd invested with him lost. Because I didn't have it, I couldn't lose it. And, I went right back to working for a fairly good salary, under a reasonable union contract, in the middle of the night.

There are some attorneys who really are good at representing writers, artists, and performers. My favorite story about one of them involves the attorney for the iconic Chicago newspaper columnist and author, Mike Royko. Media Goliath Rupert Murdoch had recently devoured the *Chicago Sun-Times*, where Mr. Royko worked. Mr. Royko, in his typical way, was clear about his objections to his new publisher: "No self-respecting fish would be wrapped in a Murdoch publication," he was famously reported to have said. So Mike Royko accepted an offer from his employer's competition, the *Chicago Tribune*. The legendary columnist had a contract, however. The contract said he was prohibited from working for any newspaper distributed within one hundred miles of Chicago.

Mr. Royko had a very smart lawyer, E. Leonard Rubin. E. Leonard Rubin dispatched an intern to the local newsstand with instructions to buy one of every newspaper they carried. The intern fetched his boss enough publications to fill a grocery cart. He brought in papers serving cities and countries around the globe, from Mexico to Milwaukee, Iran to Iowa; none of which, according to Mr. Royko's contract, would have been able to hire him. Mr. Rubin presented the judge with the substantial stack of newspapers, all of them distributed within one hundred miles of Chicago. Since

America is not a land where you can legally sell yourself into slavery, the contract was, E. Leonard Rubin argued—and the judge agreed—unenforceable, if not illegal. Lawyers for the *Sun-Times* argued that this was not what the contract meant. The judge liberated Mr. Royko with these words: "I care what a contract says, not what you meant." Royko wrote for the *Chicago Tribune* till shortly before he died. My post-Bud wish was that one day I would be fortunate enough to have a real agent, or at least successful enough to need one.

Corsets and Qualifications

It was as obvious to me as the antenna on the Sears Tower: I would never get off the overnight shift. Overnight shifts were the unofficial "girl shift" of nearly every radio station. Since overnights were not officially rated, you were not going to get credit for the size of your audience, no matter how vast it might be. That meant no rating bonuses, and no chance to use your large listenership to leverage yourself into a better sleep cycle on a more visible shift. You didn't get to run the big station giveaway contests—the ones where listeners can win the sports car or the $5,000. Your job was to promote the fact that a listener could win on anybody else's show but yours. It was a bit of a Cinderella-cleans-the-fireplace-while-the-other-jocks-dance-at-the-prince's-ball kind of a shift.

The main advantage of the overnight shift was that station management was usually asleep, so you could get away with doing pretty much whatever you wanted between the records. Jealous that I had been passed over for the station's new evening "Sex Therapy" show, I created a parody talk show, "The Unqualified Sex Therapist," at three in the morning without anybody finding out about it until listeners started mentioning it in the station's research. My manager told me to cut it out. I gave up the bit, and felt miserable. A fellow staffer instructed me to just ignore management—a valuable piece of advice. In a week, the bit was back. By the time the next research project came out, the mini-talk show had become a hit with our morning man, who intervened on my behalf. The bit stayed.

Callers to "The Unqualified Sex Therapist" got exactly what was promised: advice and abuse from someone who was not professionally certified at either. That never stopped people from phoning in with questions they seemed to seriously expect to have answered. Like Rod, the guy who wanted guidance on how to retrieve a specialized costume he had bought for his former girlfriend.

"Hi Rod from Kankakee. Thanks for calling."

"Hi Turi. I have a question. It's about my ex-girlfriend. I bought her some leather and stuff."

"What kind of leather? What kind of stuff?"

"Oh…um…a corset—a really nice corset—and some handcuffs and a whip and some boots."

"Okay."

"So now that I'm not seeing her anymore, what I want to know is, can I get my stuff back?"

"Why do you want it back?"

"It was really expensive."

"Like, how expensive *is* a corset and handcuffs and— what else was there?"

"The whip and the boots."

"Yeah. The whip and the boots. What does that come to?"

"Well, I had the corset custom-made, by a guy in Chicago—"

"Rod, I don't care whether it was sewn by elves and brought to her by trained pigeons. What did this outfit cost?"

"Around twelve hundred bucks."

"And you want it all back."

"Yes."

"What for?"

"So I can give it to somebody else."

Here, I took a moment to form a few thoughts I shared with the audience. "Rod not only thinks he'll have no trouble finding someone else in Kankakee who will wear bondage gear; he's also pretty sure he'll be able to find someone who is willing to wear *used* bondage gear. That's optimistic.

"Rod, have you found somebody else to wear this corset and the boots? Already? Because you're talking like you already have someone in mind for it. I'm guessing the cuffs and the whip are one-size-fits-all."

Here's the part that scares me about callers: almost without exception, they answer every question. Even the ones you're not seriously expecting them to answer. "That's right. The cuffs and the whip are one-size, but I haven't found anybody yet."

"Okay Rod, let me clearly understand this. You give your girlfriend the leather gear, and she breaks up with you—"

"No. I broke up with her."

"Really? You find a woman who's willing to put on all this stuff because you want her to wear it, and then you break up with her? Why?"

"She wasn't really that into it."

"Shocking. She wasn't *really* that into it. So you broke up with her, and now you want your stuff back, because it's expensive."

"Yeah."

"Well, the way I see it, Rod, you have a few problems here. One is that it's not your stuff anymore; it's her stuff. Because you *gave* it to her. You didn't *lend* it to her. So it's not yours; it's hers. And the second thing is that if you want it back, you don't really deserve to have a woman who will use it on you, because you're not obedient enough. You should, pardon the expression, be willing to take your lumps. And *finally*, your main problem, as I see it, Rod, isn't that you like women who will put on uncomfortable footwear and handcuff you and beat you; it's that you're cheap."

"I kinda thought you might say that."

"It also occurs to me that you may have called me so I would tell you these things. Is that right?"

"No."

"That's a relief. For a minute there, I thought you might have called just so I could give you a hard time, seeing as you haven't found anyone to give you one in person, yet."

"No."

"Well, that's reassuring. So Rod, it's time for you to look for a woman who already has all that stuff. You'll be happier."

"Yeah. Probably."

"Good luck, Rod."

The other "girl shifts" at any radio station were middays, where you played ninety-five million songs in a row while saying as little as possible, aside from the time and outdoor temperature; and the morning drive sidekick. The sidekick position was sometimes camouflaged as newswoman, but there were ways to tell which you really were. The first test was if you were expected to laugh whether or not you actually found something funny. A friend of mine was once paired with a morning team so desperate for her to giggle at their every remark, that they secretly recorded a rare spontaneous *guffaw* and played it, without her knowledge, as a laugh track while she was back in the newsroom writing copy. That way, they could make her laugh at anything. The second test was if you were going to lose your job if the ratings stank. If you were, you were actually a part of the show. If you answered yes to the first test and no to the second one, you were absolutely the sidekick.

When you are a woman with a big on-air personality, you will eventually be offered a job as part of somebody's morning team. The program director will usually make a pitch about how you will be an equal player on the team, and not a sidekick. You will be, he will tell you, just as valuable as the men on the show. When this happens to other women, and they ask me whether they should give up their own shows and join a team as an equal member, I suggest they ask station management to show them a copy of the male hosts' contracts. Equality, I believe, lurks in the fine print.

Female sidekicks, whose job is to appreciate and admire the morning men, are often funnier and smarter than the starring show hosts, but they are invariably paid less, treated worse, and benefit very little from the ratings successes they help to create. Their advantage is that they often outlast the men on whose shows they serve, and so are frequently able to keep their marriages and families intact.

The all-night shift had once been the launching pad for morning drive shows. You could experiment, get your feet wet at a new station, and try working with different support people. But by the '80s, landing the overnight shift was no longer a sign that great things were in store for you. It was exile in Siberia. Unfortunately—with morning drive the last official place for personality radio on most music stations—for women who wanted to do personality radio, creating entertainment under managements' sleeping noses on the overnight shift was all there was.

To their credit, my station's managers had figured out that AM radio was becoming a better place for talk than for music. But the fact that I was already on their station, and could talk, wasn't helping. Meanwhile, entire weeks would pass without me conversing in-person with any human beings besides the jock ahead of me, the morning show and news anchors after me, and the guy at the mini-mart who took my credit card for gasoline and boxes of Entenmanns chocolate chip cookies; which, in my depressed state, I often ate for breakfast. For these reasons, I was overjoyed to get a phone call inviting me to move to a new, beautiful, city. It was an ocean-side tourist destination with one of the most expensive housing markets in the world. But none of that mattered. I would be hosting the evening show, from seven to midnight. I would be home by one, in bed by three, and sleep till ten. If I couldn't have late dinners, at least I'd be able to meet people for lunch without noticing that the salad might make a comfortable pillow. I was going to be a regular person, with a normal life.

Link Lawrence gave me these prophetic words of advice: "Ryder, never go anywhere for less than a two-year deal." Unfortunately, even with the help of Earl Rosen, my newly acquired entertainment lawyer, all I could muscle out of my new contract was a solid twelve months. I took it. My boss at The Big Rock asked whether I could extend my two weeks notice to a month, in order to allow him time to find and hire a suitable replacement. I agreed; in retrospect, a big mistake. A delay of three months might have averted the debacle to come.

Four weeks later, I gave away most of the furnishings of my first "own" studio apartment, and the movers arrived to pack my remaining possessions, including my nearly new car, onto a moving van.

Evenings with Hypatia Bedpan

Your deepest fears are not a secret. If you work in the entertainment industry, your contract, and the things you absolutely must have in it, reveal every professional indignity you've ever experienced. Did you work for a boss who demanded you show up for live remote broadcasts at car dealerships at what, for you, was the equivalent of three in the morning? That clause saying you must not be required to attend staff and sales events except between 2:00 and 6:00 p.m. guarantees you can get some rest. Were you required to read embarrassing commercials for erectile dysfunction products; commercials that implied you *used* these products? Now that you have approval over live copy, you can stop blushing. My deals, after the first contract I signed, specified that I could not be moved to an overnight shift, unless I agreed to do it. (One way radio stations can get rid of, for example, an unwanted afternoon host is to move him to the 2:00 a.m. to 5:00 a.m. air shift until he drops dead or quits.) After all, it had taken me over four years to earn the privilege of sleeping in the dark.

My first show for the new station—another aging, but far from defunct, AM top 40 signal—was something of an event in the industry. It was broadcast live, from a United Airlines commercial plane carrying our station's chief engineer, me, and my pet guinea pig, Velcro. We used what was then the new technology of the in-flight telephone, something that never quite caught on. As it turns out, a lot of things about that move were ideas that never quite caught on.

This was my first personal services contract. I had been courted, flown in to see the town, meet the managers, and ogle the station's brand new, state-of-the-art studios. The station was recovering from a temporary bout of insanity, during which it had jettisoned its slowly declining but still highly successful music format for something called, "game show radio." The four listeners who cornered the market on the station's prizes probably retired to Aruba on their winnings. But now there was new management. They believed the future of radio lay in providing unique entertainment between the hits. I was to be that entertainment. And, I would work human hours—evening hours.

The whole project was over in twelve weeks. It took six of those weeks for me to buy my first house; another two to see it out of probate court; and, on the last day of the third month, the moving company delivered my boxes while my new rock and roll radio station played its first day of "Music of your Life." I had unwittingly swapped all-nights of Madonna and Journey for "How Much is That Doggie in the

Window?" Perched on a pile of moving cartons in the middle of the kitchen of my just-bought fixer upper, I looked over the contract that said I would have to be paid for playing the Andrews Sisters for another nine months, and wondered whether I'd find another job before I jumped into the world-famous tourist destination's world-famous frigid bay.

My new program director and general manager were deeply apologetic. One of them left the station within days for a music trade magazine. The other took up a defensive position trying to stay out of the way of the same consultant who had brought the city "Game Show Radio." The corporate execs were giving him another run at the place. As a gift to me, my program director carved out an hour in the middle of my shift every evening so I could play Broadway show tunes.

I love Broadway musicals. But my tastes were a bit too diverse for the creator of "Music of Your Life." *Oklahoma*, OK. But they weren't too pleased about the hippy-ness of *Hair* or the sexy and soulful "And I'm Telling You I'm Not Going" from *Dreamgirls*. The Broadway show tunes were soon reduced to a playlist of about thirty old standards, to be mixed with the Perry Como we were already playing. I decided to change my name to Hypatia Bedpan, in order to avoid the humiliation of introducing Wayne Newton's "Danke Shoën" with a straight face. My general manager took pity on me and allowed me to come in twice a week and voice track—record the introductions and announcements—for the all-night shift. For this purpose, I got to use the smaller state-of-the-art studio that had been the exclusive province of the public service director. She wasn't happy about it. Neither was I. With seven months to go on my contract, I figured it wouldn't be all that hard to find something else. After all, I'd worked for the biggest rock stations in two of the four largest radio markets in America. It was logical. Logical, but wrong.

Some memorable quotes from program directors who got my then-current tape included "I *love* what you do. I'm just not sure Philadelphia is ready to hear a girl saying the things you say;" and "Have you thought about applying in Birmingham, or Syracuse?" (I had.) I continued reading the trades, working my contacts, and sending tapes. To vent frustration, and because it cost nothing, I'd go out and weed my yard. The yard was looking pretty good.

I also made a habit of crashing any kind of industry seminar or broadcasting convention within driving or bargain flight distance. I continued this practice of worming my way into industry conferences for years, even after I could afford to pay my way. It started out as financial necessity (conferences often cost several hundreds of dollars to attend, not counting travel and lodging), but became a sort of subversive sport—my version of what I imagine goes on in the pleasure centers of the minds of confidence game runners or Three-card Monte dealers.

It used to be fairly easy to dummy up a set of credentials for any of the big conventions. But the tickets and badges grew more and more elaborate, so that other kinds of sneakiness were required. I suspected that the reason the convention holders kept increasing conference badge security was that my friends and I (there was a small group of occasionally unemployed broadcasters who combined forces to forge credentials, spy out cheap housing opportunities, and locate the best options for dining on someone's company's expense account) were not the only ones cheating the various broadcasting organizations out of their $600 convention passes.

I confirmed my suspicions when, at one of the bigger conventions, I approached my former boss, Beau, and asked him to claim he'd lost his badge and buy a replacement for twenty bucks. Beau was working for a nascent research outfit, and its employees not only all had passes; they had a big hospitality suite with great food and an open bar. The plan was for my friend and partner-in-crime, Howie, to put the easily computer-faked passes Howie had made into Beau's harder-to-mimic plastic branded holder. My former superior refused. I was surprised, and disappointed. Beau was a friend. He typically helped me whenever he could. "What's wrong with you?" I whined. "Have you gone over to the dark side? Are you one of those guys now who toes the corporate line? It's just twenty bucks to get a new badge holder. We'll pay for it. What's the problem?" I continued my harangue, escalating it as I followed him down the hall to the cocktail party his company was hosting.

Finally, he turned to me in exasperation. "I can't help you," he hissed under his breath. "My badge is fake, too."

At one music industry trade conference, to which I had legitimately been invited, I met a young, adorably frothy woman who claimed to be my biggest fan. "Turi Ryder," Heather gushed, "you are my inspiration. I want your career." I was equal parts flattered and embarrassed, having only recently managed to maneuver myself off of voice tracking the "Music of Your Life" shift. I thanked Heather, wished her luck, and then watched as she literally ran, in four-inch heels, across the highly polished floor of the convention ballroom, to buttonhole a major market program director. "Brad! I'm Heather, from KRAS. Do you have any openings for female DJs?"

I managed to flag Heather down. "Heather," I stage-whispered as forcefully as I could, "if you don't tell Brad, or any of these other program directors that you are looking for work as a 'female DJ,' you might get a shift that a guy is doing." I wish I could say she took my advice. Alas, from here and there in the hotel's grand ballroom, I heard, throughout the evening, Heather's machine gunfire heels as she sped from PD to PD in her quest for a gender-specific air shift.

Heather isn't the only person I know who has sabotaged her own best chances at landing the next big gig. I have also been known to eliminate myself from consideration for some really great shifts. The one that springs to mind was a job hosting mornings at a Seattle rock station. I would have loved that job. The interview turned out to be, without a doubt, one of my all-time horrible job-seeking experiences; and it was, at least in part, my own fault.

The problem was that the Seattle program director didn't want to hire me. He had someone else in mind. I was the general manager's idea. You could best describe the tone of the meeting as: "You can make me fly her in, but you can't make me talk to her." I knew something was wrong the moment I stepped off the plane and was met by...nobody. If you've ever heard the phrase, "I don't want to jam this down your throat," I promise you that the experiences of the "jam-er" and the "jam-ee" are still far and away better than of being the "jam."

Having made my way to the station by a very expensive taxi ride, I was given a perfunctory tour of the place, then sent back to languish on the flocked gold polyester bedspread in my hotel room, unwanted for the evening. Fortunately, a former coworker from an old station had relocated to the city, and he picked me up and toted me along with him to a record company dinner that was being held, literally, in an underground music club. The performers were a band shortly to become extremely famous; the food, fresh and excellent; and, as used to be standard at record industry events, the wine was worth tasting. I forgot about the job for a few hours.

By morning, the two bosses had reached a compromise of sorts. I could have afternoon drive, if I wanted it. But for some inexplicably stupid reason, I stood firm on my desire for mornings. Was it ego? Probably. Ego, and a bit of anger.

Stations from Manchester, New Hampshire to Madison, Wisconsin wouldn't consider a woman for morning drive. Sometimes they said so to my face. This only made me more determined to have "the boy shift." So I told the Seattle managers sitting across the table from me that I wanted mornings. What a stupid thing to have done. I was sent back, like a misaddressed letter, with a station key chain as a souvenir, to spend the next year unemployed. If I'd been a little smarter, and a little less ego-driven, I could have lived in Seattle on a better sleep cycle, gained an audience, and would have been perfectly positioned for taking over mornings when the guy the program director had picked partied himself out of the shift eight months later. I kept that key chain for years as a reminder that to be offered a job in your chosen profession, especially when you are unemployed, is an honor, and, if at all possible, should be gratefully accepted.

You Sound Sweet

To keep busy while I looked for work, I acquired a boyfriend. Ari was age-appropriate and Israeli. Stereotypically dark, curly-haired, and wiry, Ari possessed a casual slouch and rare smile. He owned a small business and played the saxophone well enough to have come to the United States as a student at one of the preeminent jazz music academies.

Despite Ari's devotion to music, he had absolutely no interest in radio, which I decided was a good thing. I checked to be sure that in addition to his solar installation company, Ari also owned a legitimate green card, permitting him to live and work in the States. He was requested to bring the card on our first date, so that I would never have to wonder if it was me, or my passport, that he'd found alluring.

After we moved in together, our next-door neighbors complimented me on the beautiful music they could hear coming from our house when I was at work. Since Ari never played for me, I had to take their word for it. I didn't think this was odd; just mysterious. Since Ari was the first person I'd dated after spending several years with an alcoholic drug-addicted air personality, I guess I must have figured that not hearing my significant other play his instrument even once was still an easier life than looking inside trash bags and vacuum cleaners for hidden bottles of scotch.

What I did get to hear was Ari learning English, which was my version of homegrown improvisational theater. I watched from the sidelines as he called in orders for "tuning fish boats" (tuna fish subs). I particularly liked hearing him mispronounce the brand name of his car, a "Link-o-lin" Continental, of which he was very proud, but which I thought resembled a navy-blue bar of soap, with pin striping.

Enjoying being madly in love didn't change the fact that I was getting a bit desperate for work. The "Music of Your Life" format required absolutely nothing in the way of show preparation, since I wasn't allowed to do anything but announce song titles, the time, and the weather.

This left a lot of my day free for wandering semi-aimlessly through the Rainbow Food Coop, where the best produce in San Francisco was displayed in humble (but expensive) barrels and bins, then heading to the back of the store to buy whatever slightly bruised but organic fresh produce was on its last root-y legs. At home, I would combine these edible finds into elaborate meals of sautéed cauliflower and herbed tomato pasta for us. Between perusing the industry trades and calling stations from Birmingham, Alabama, to Yreka, California, to apply for any radio job I'd heard was open, I compulsively cleaned house and dug in the garden. Our bathtub could have doubled as an operating table.

All of this gave Ari the mistaken impression that I preferred housework to work-work, and that my career involved appearing at a radio station for a couple of hours a week; collecting a large-ish check for very little effort. He also developed the misapprehension, based on hearing my voice—naturally pitched low enough to be comfortably sandwiched between Petula Clark and Frank Sinatra's romantic ballads—that I was "sweet."

One Shot

Sometimes people come into your life for one reason, like those cicadas that wake up every seventeen years for the purposes of reproduction. They perform the function for which nature intended them, and then leave their desiccated carcasses all over your front porch.

After about six months of trying and failing to find full-time, on-air work, I was still having no luck. The list of stations that had either ignored me or turned me down was rapidly approaching the auctioneer-style roll call of towns in Johnny Cash's "I've Been Everywhere." I phoned Sims.

Sims had escaped the "Music of Your Life" format change and landed at Crazy103, the top-rated FM station in Los Angeles, with two job titles: music director and executive producer of the station's hit morning show. The host of the show, Zeke Sada, who was very famous and rich, was also a world-class jerk.

What is my definition of a world-class jerk? When visitors came to tour the station, they wanted most of all to see the city's number one morning man at work. This was usually impossible, because business hours started shortly after Zeke wrapped his show for the day. That, after all, is the definition of morning drive—you are on the air as your listeners are driving *to* work. But if prospective clients or other guests arrived shortly after 9:00 a.m., Zeke and his morning staff were still in the building.

At this time of day, a guest would be ushered to the morning show conference room, where Zeke Sada would typically be getting ready to bolt out the door to tape whatever TV pilot his agent had found for him. Zeke, despite his radio success, lived in hopes of achieving greater media stardom. Zeke's forty-three-year-old newswoman, Laura Geary—an industry veteran with excellent newswriting skills and the slightly burned-out look of a three-years-sober recovering alcoholic—also stayed in the conference room. Her solid-but-not-especially athletic body comfortably clad in a gray, pajama-esque sweat suit bearing the name of her state university, Laura worked till 10:00 a.m., compiling stories that might still be current news the next day. She'd head to an AA meeting when her shift was over. Her earlier drinking years had taken a visible toll on Laura's looks, but not on her sharp wit. Both before and after starting her recovery, Laura had maintained her spot as the much-loved newsperson and sidekick to Zeke. Along with her dependable presence, and husky tobacco-tinged voice, Laura also had a talent for reading the newswires while putting on makeup; something she didn't have time to do at 3:00 a.m., when she left her distant mountain house at the farthest northern end of the LA metro area in order to be ready with her first day's Crazy103 newscast at 5:30 a.m.

The guest might also see Zeke's producer, Sims, at a table in the show-prep area for the post-show meeting. He'd be writing comedy, looking through the joke-writing services' daily submissions, and scanning the papers for "kickers"—bizarre news items that might appeal to Zeke and his audience. Sims had a UCLA sophomore, a lithe suntanned intern seeking a career in marketing and public relations, to help him peruse the trades and papers, as well as bring coffee and make sure all the music and contest material was current.

If the prospective client arrived in time, Zeke would introduce him to "our morning crew." Turning to the winsome twenty-something-year-old music department intern, Zeke would gaze warmly at her and say, "This is our talented newswoman, Laura Geary." The guest would be overwhelmed. "Laura looks so much younger than she sounds," the visitor would likely exclaim. Or the visitor might tell "Laura" how beautiful she was, or that he loved her work, or he might just stand there gaping. Meanwhile, the actual Laura, two chairs away, would pretend not to notice that someone else—someone else twenty years younger, three inches taller, and thirty pounds skinnier, wearing a full face of makeup and a shiny '80s blowout hairstyle unmarred by headphones—was being introduced as her. That is what I mean when I say that Zeke defined the term "world-class jerk."

In response to my desperate phone call, Sims arranged for the station's program director, Scorch Brooks, to put me on the schedule for holiday fill-in work. Scorch seemed to like

my work. Perhaps more importantly, he liked the fact that by
hiring me part-time, he could say he had a woman on his
airstaff. After the Thanksgiving and winter holidays, Scorch
assigned me three regular shifts a week: a Friday overnight, a
Saturday night, and a Sunday night.

In one of the most generous gifts anyone has ever given
me, in addition to the job, Sims also invited me to move into
the second bedroom of his beige-walled, brown-carpeted Van
Nuys courtyard apartment. He would not accept rent.
Suddenly, I had a career again. Between my three regular
weekend shifts, plus all the fill-in work the station had—
which was a lot, since many of their jocks were legends, with
weeks of accrued vacation time—I could earn enough to
make ends meet. It was not so much money that I could
afford to commute and live in my house, but I figured Ari
and I could rent my house to somebody else and move into
an apartment until I located something closer to the Bay Area.

I worked so much fill-in, I was often mistaken as the full-
time overnight person on the number one rock and top 40
station in Los Angeles. Sims had effectively saved my career,
providing work, shelter, and even the occasional sushi
dinner. I will forever be grateful.

LA holds a lot of history, charm, and style—but Sims'
apartment had none of it. The U-shaped building surrounded
a tiny, irregularly shaped pool that one woman, who swam
like she was on Quaaludes, used for five minutes every day. It
was in a working-class part of the Valley—or maybe a little
lower than working class. One time, I locked myself out of my

car, and within five minutes, a guy with a slim jim showed up to help me open it. If you are unfamiliar with the slim jim, it is the tool one uses for breaking into cars. In the hands of an experienced car thief, tow truck driver, or cop, a slim jim will leverage the window against the gasket just enough to allow you to shove the slim jim down inside the door and release the locking mechanism. That car, which I still drive to this day, makes a whistling sound where the slim jim cracked the window gasket slightly. The whistling sound, and the sound of any loud and distorted phone message playback, always reminds me of the Valley, and Sims' apartment.

Distorted answering machines were the white noise of the typical Van Nuys apartment building. You could hear them night and day, through the walls, through the windows, dutifully taking messages—mostly the residents' agents, telling the struggling actors and actresses who comprised the majority of our fellow tenants where and when they had auditions. You could also hear breakup messages, demands for late child support, and the occasional drug deal. Privacy did not exist in the 1960s apartments of the San Fernando Valley. You heard everything your neighbors said, and smelled not only when they were cooking dinner, but when they were taking off their shoes. Yes, feet smell came through the walls. That is how thin those walls were. I have had window shades that provided more privacy. But I was more than glad to be there.

Sims let me stay in his second bedroom for free every weekend, and during the weeks as well if I was filling in for

someone. In exchange, I cooked, cleaned, and did laundry—
not that he asked me to. I gave up the laundry chore pretty
quickly. You can never predict who will be particular about
how you fold his socks.

The arrangement worked splendidly, until Sims met his
future bride who, quite understandably, decided the situation
was less than ideal for their privacy needs. She couldn't do
anything about the answering machine next door, but I had to
go. I relocated to an unused bedroom in the home of
Scientologist friends of Ari's. They were accommodating,
until it became clear that I wasn't interested in Scientology.

Sims has done quite well in the years since we were
roommates, as a radio station programmer and manager. We
both made the switch from rock radio to talk radio around the
same time. But Sims never hired me to host a talk show, even
when he was looking for talent. "Turi, I'll tell you the truth.
None of the female hosts I've ever hired has succeeded on the
air, so I'm not going to hire any more of them."

Because Sims and I have a history, I broke my usual "no
comment" policy, and told him what I thought about his
decision. "Sims, if you hire women because they are five-foot-
ten, red-haired models with sexy laughs, and not because
they're good talk show hosts, what do you expect? You hire
six times as many men as you do women. Ninety percent of
them fail. But you don't quit hiring men."

I've often wondered whether I should be ticked off that
Sims, with all the jobs he's had to fill over the years, was
never willing to give me a shot as a talk show host. But I've

decided that sometimes, people come into your life and do one great thing for you. That's it. That's all. Just one. The thing Sims did for me—finding me a job, bringing me to LA, and providing me with a roof when I was desperate and unemployed in San Francisco—was a truly good thing. He saved my career when it needed saving. Sims can hire all the redheads he wants. It doesn't bother me.

Weeks that I was not filling in for one of the full-time staff, I still lived with Ari in San Francisco, travelling to LA every Friday for my three Crazy103 air shifts. It was a heck of a commute. If I needed to be on the air for a week or more, I'd drive the three hundred fifty miles each way so I could have my own car with me. For short weekend shifts, I flew— buying two months' worth of sale-priced tickets at a time. It was a weird way to live. (I'd end up doing that same commute again, years later, for a talk station.) Even though my trips to work required two hours of combined flying and driving time, our traffic reporter pointed out that I still spent less time in transit than a lot of Angelinos with local commutes.

The flying itself had a surreal aspect to it. Most often, the Pan Am flight I booked every weekend was the first leg of an international trip to El Salvador, which was in the middle of a long and bloody civil war. From the moveable ramp as I deplaned in the fuel-scented evening glow of LAX each Friday, I could glimpse on the tarmac below, a small group of men gathered close together, and another couple of men wearing uniforms standing next to them. Eventually, I figured out that the first group stood close together because they'd been handcuffed that way. They were waiting to be deported. The second group was whatever law enforcement agency was in charge of making sure they left.

Every weekend, I'd look down to see another manacled group. I didn't fully grasp the significance of this at the time—the fact that many of these men were being sent home to nearly certain imprisonment, or death; but whenever I was tempted to complain about my commute or my bizarre travel schedule, the thought of those deportees silenced me.

Revenge of the Chihuahua

If only talent and character were handed out in equal amounts. While Zeke Sada, Crazy103's morning man, was a world-class jerk, at least he was not physically dangerous.

Hash Henderson owned evenings in LA rock radio. On Friday nights, my shift followed Hash's show. It was my job to make my way into the studio about a half hour before I started, to get the music and commercials I'd need, read the program log, and settle in. For some reason, on this particular night, Hash was wearing a pair of white pointed jazz shoes with his usual bomber jacket and jeans. I noticed them right away, because they were extremely white. Hash and I had engaged in some good-natured joshing over the months that I'd been working at the station, so I didn't think before I said, "Nice shoes. Planning to take up dancing? Tap or ballroom?"

Perhaps Hash interpreted this as an assault on his masculinity, but in light of later events, I'm more inclined to believe that Hash was simply in a bad mood. He sprang out of his rolling chair, taking me completely by surprise, grabbed me by both arms, and shoved me. I backed up. He came at me again. This time, he physically slammed me into the "snooper" tape deck that, along with other sound enhancing equipment, occupied one wall of our studio. It was probably the worst thing in the studio I could have hit. The massive, slow-running, reel-to-reel tape deck continuously recorded everything that went over the air on a giant metal reel of "logger" tape. Its purpose was to make sure that anything the disc jockeys said on mic was preserved for management and the company's lawyers, in case we were threatened with an FCC action or a listener lawsuit. It would have been far better for me that night if the snooper tape were recording what was going on inside the studio. The minute my body came in contact, at rather high speed and force, with the recorder, the reel sped up and started rolling up my hair, along with the logger tape. While I was trying to break free of the equipment, Hash ranted, directly into my face, over and over, "you dirty fucking kike." Hash didn't seem to have any other material—just that one phrase. Later, it occurred to me that having only one phrase with which to curse me showed a distinct lack of creativity; surprising for Hash, but which might have been the result of not letting top 40 radio air talent talk for longer than twenty seconds at a time. Mostly, though, I was disgusted by the fact that Hash was sort of spitting into my face, and I was in a slight panic about how to get free of the logger, which had stopped rolling, but was still in possession of a big chunk of my hair. After what was probably less than a minute, by which time I'd loosed myself both of Hash and the tape recorder, minus a sizeable handful of long brown hair, I was able to flee the studio.

From the production booth down the hall, with shaking hands, I dialed my friend, the station's production director, and relayed my situation. The production director, a Tulsa, Oklahoma native, hadn't actually known any Jews when he was growing up. Nevertheless, you could tell he was sympathetically horrified. I didn't think I'd be able to go on the air and cover my shift. "You need to do your shift, and you need to tell Scorch," he advised in his mild, off-air Midwestern twang. "You need to tell him right away." I wasn't too eager to phone Scorch at eleven at night and give him the story, but I left a note under his office door, took a few deep breaths, and, after Hash left the studio, made a quiet entrance and played music and jingles for three hours.

The next day began my education in the big dog/little dog approach to station management. I doubt things are much different in any business. No matter how many human resource hotlines, surveys, and anonymous reporting programs are established to give the average employee recourse against illegal or unethical behavior by higher-ups, it's still a fact that if you're a feisty Chihuahua, almost any pit bull with an appetite can have you for lunch.

As my friend the production director had predicted, Scorch, too, was outraged. He called me first thing Monday morning. "This behavior is unprofessional, unacceptable, and will not be tolerated," were his exact words.

"All I'd really like is an apology," I said, mentally applauding myself for my graciousness. But by two on Tuesday afternoon, it was clear Scorch had had a conversation with his bosses, who must have said something along the lines of, "Are you kidding us? Hash Henderson makes money for this radio station by the Brink's truckload. He's got fantastic ratings. The female demographic loves him. You can't seriously be thinking about disciplining him because some weekend chick says he wasn't nice to her?"

Hash and I were ordered to appear in Scorch's office the next day, which I could do because I was on the air all week, filling in for the overnight host. Hash took the only seat. I noticed he was not wearing his new white shoes, but chose not to comment. "I'm very disappointed in both of you," intoned Scorch; who, despite his now-obvious lack of spine, still had a working jaw. "And I expect better behavior in the future." We both nodded. That was it. The meeting was over, and Hash left the office. I stood a moment longer. Hoping, I suppose, that at least my boss might express privately something along the lines of "If it had been up to me..." But Scorch was stirring some music research data sheets around on his desk. He had nothing more to add. I left the office, contemplating how many weeks it might take me to land another job—something I felt sure would be required of me very soon.

Since the media conglomerate for which Hash and I worked was not going to discipline Hash, I felt I was entitled to some sort of score settling. So I resorted to more clandestine tactics. It happens that a lot of people in broadcasting jettison their birth names. Giordanos become St. Johns, Polaskis turn into Parkers, and Levinsons become Lewises. Hash Henderson, who actually *was* a Henderson, had recently been hired to host a music countdown show. He was hoping to syndicate it to radio stations nationwide. Within days of the "dirty fucking kike" incident, several former Levinsons, Rosenbergs, and Silversteins in the business—in particular, the ones running trade magazines and radio stations—were made aware of my experience. It's always best to have a champion in these matters, so I gave the task of distributing this information to a formerly ethnic, now neutrally named third party, who was willing to serve as a source. While Hash's evening show continued to prosper, (even after another memorable night when he threatened his producer with a handgun), the infant countdown show sputtered to an end. I don't suppose Hash ever knew why it failed.

The Trouble with Palm Trees

My act of sabotage didn't really help with the feeling that, as a part-timer, and a female one, when it came to workplace safety, I wasn't a priority. Even outside of work, LA was a rather dangerous place—especially if you had no idea how to tell whether you were in one of the city's islands of well-patrolled safety, or in one of its drug- and gang-infested, all-night shooting galleries.

When Ari's Scientologist friends had had enough of hosting me, they let me know I'd need to find an apartment of my own. So without realizing what I'd done, I rented a studio in a truly terrible section of LA. What fooled me were the palm trees. Having been raised in the Midwest during the TV era of the *Beverly Hillbillies*, I assumed that any neighborhood with palm trees and flowers must be high-class. Little did I know that palm trees and camellia are to Los Angeles what dandelions and maples are to Illinois. In abundance, they signal nothing so much as a lack of an enterprising gardener.

Returning from my overnight shift one Sunday morning before dawn, I noticed the light over my doorway was out. As I looked up, I felt a hand cover my face, and a knife at my side. What bothered me most, I remember, was the smell of that hand: a cross between something chemical, like grease cleaner, and mildew. Without thinking, I turned, threw my keys as far into the camellias as I could, and screamed into the air, several times, in a voice that probably carried farther than a fifty thousand-watt FM signal, "HELP! RAPE! CALL 911! CALL THE POLICE!"

It is my belief—or perhaps my mania for micromanaging people—that even in urgent, emergency circumstances, it is best to issue specific instructions. As the man with the hand and the knife tried to drag me around the corner of my building, and I kept screaming, three windows simultaneously flew up, three heads emerged, and an elderly woman with her hair wrapped in a scarf leaned out and called to me, "DON'T YOU WORRY, HONEY, POLICE ARE ON THE WAY!" It was enough to scare him off, and I escaped with minimal physical damage.

I moved out of the apartment days later. I called one of the few people I'd met in LA, a woman I barely knew. She allowed me to park my air mattress in a designated space on her living room floor. Leslie worked as a traffic reporter, as a producer, and as a news writer at a variety of stations, all under various assumed names. This is not unusual in radio. Since you can't see us, before we are known commodities recognizable by voice, we can be in a lot of places under numerous monikers. If you've ever wondered why Kaitlyn who does traffic on your favorite sports station sounds a lot like Susanna who reads overnight news on your favorite rock station—that's why.

I'd met Leslie on a visit to one of the stations where she worked in the news department. Howie and I had stopped by the station because his friend, Trace, had just gotten a job there as a talk show host. We were there to bring Trace cookies after his first show. While Howie and I waited, I noticed an interesting looking woman writing news copy. Even seated, you could tell she was tall. When she stood up, you noticed a figure that was part leggy ballet dancer, part buxom barmaid. Her nearly white skin and even features contrasted with extremely black hair plaited into two braids. The odd part was that both braids, against convention, originated on the same side of her head. They looked cool, but also like they'd present a challenge when wearing headphones; something that I needed to consider if I were going to try the style at home.

Just as I was trying to figure out the method behind the braids without staring, one of the station's phone screeners raced into the room. She had a secret to tell about a different talk show host. Desperate for callers, the host's producer was "planting" phone calls. That's where you have your producer, call screener, or your wife call in, pretending to be listeners. Most people consider planting phone calls to be cheating.

"I heard something in the producer's booth," the young woman said conspiratorially, "and when I looked inside, it was dark. Then, I heard his call screener, on the phone, pretending to be a woman who found out her husband is a cross-dresser."

"And you're sure his call screener isn't a woman who's married to a cross-dresser?" the braided woman asked.

"Pretty sure," the screener replied. "She's about seventeen."

Even though this was a juicy revelation, my attention kept fastening itself to the on-air monitor speaker on the wall of the newsroom. By now, Trace was off the air, and a man with a gorgeous voice was talking. This alone, to people who work in radio, means absolutely zero. You hear gorgeous voices from the minute you go to work until you're back home after your shift has ended. But this particularly warm and intimate voice was explaining that a lawsuit brought by a woman who was date raped was legit, because even though she had willingly been making out with her frat-boy party date, she had said "no" to having sex with him. "No means no," the voice said. "It doesn't matter if she stripped all her clothes off, danced around the room for you, and jumped on you in bed. If she changes her mind, man, it's game over."

I wanted to meet that voice. I liked what it was saying, even though I thought he was being a lot more forgiving than I would probably be of women who jump naked on top of men and then change their minds. I asked Trace, when he came into the newsroom, for the name of the host with the gentlemanly standards: Paul Hart. I made a note of it.

I casually made my way over to the newswoman and the gossipy call screener and introduced myself as a visitor who worked at Crazy103. Leslie gave me her real name. At some point in the conversation, it came up that Leslie was looking for an air mattress to borrow, since she had company coming. Since I had a real bed in my new place, I happily lent her mine.

In what we both considered her genuine professional life, Leslie had most recently held a far loftier position at a publication in the entertainment business, but it had ended when she'd refused an unethical request to write a favorable article on someone who absolutely did not deserve it. While she contemplated her next move, and I worked my final months in LA, we became one another's weekend dates.

I'd fly into LA each Friday, go to work overnight, then show up at Leslie's house at 6:00 a.m. She would make coffee as I prepared my camping spot near her couch. By Saturday afternoon, I'd be up, and she'd be in. We dined together, and then, as she headed for bed, I'd drive my rental car to the station and work another shift. Leslie never charged me a dime of rent.

Leslie's apartment was in Beverly Hills, where I was far less likely to be attacked at my front door after an overnight air shift. I relaxed a bit about coming home in the dark. However, I did ask Crazy103 for an indoor, secure parking space in their empty-at-night lot. They refused, leaving me to park on barren, and at the time, crime-infested Sunset Boulevard.

Even in elite and star-studded Beverly Hills, there can be sleaze. The unit above Leslie's was occupied by Dolly, an older woman, and Luke, her younger, drunken, paramour. Whenever he was demolished by alcohol—which was every Saturday night—Dolly would put Luke out, and we'd hear him wailing from the stairwell, like Marlon Brando in *Streetcar Named Desire*, "Dolllllie! Dolllllie! Please Dolly, I love you...Dollllie..." Not even the palm trees and blooming jasmine around the well-kept stucco six flat could absorb the sound of Luke's drunken despair.

The company's lack of interest in my welfare was matched by its dedication to its own bottom line. On one occasion, all the airstaff were ordered to attend a meeting on emergency procedures. I arrived at the conference room, expecting we'd be trained in earthquake preparedness, or at least shown a room where we could safely hide if a crazed listener barged in, armed and looking for hostages. Instead, the meeting was to show us a stack of plastic tarpaulins and explain to us how to arrange them over the valuable electronic equipment in the studio, in order to prevent water damage should the fire alarm and sprinkler system ever be activated. You may be appalled at the idea that a company would actually issue instructions to its employees to risk their lives for the station's broadcasting equipment, but I regret to this day that I never had the joy that could have been mine, if only Crazy103's fire alarm and sprinklers ever *had* been activated. I yearned to look over my shoulder as I ran for the fire stairs and catch a delicious glimpse of Crazy103's studio sparking away under a downpour of water and flame repellant.

Even with free lodging in LA and Ari making a small contribution to the mortgage in San Francisco, I couldn't afford to live in the house I'd bought. So we decided to rent it out and take an inexpensive apartment in the Bay Area. A couple of brothers signed a lease for my San Francisco house. I was jealous of their ability to afford it.

As poor as my decision-making had been in choosing the perilous palm tree palace in LA, Ari surpassed me by finding an apartment in a part of San Francisco so foggy, dark, and damp, it might as well have been a kelp bed at the bottom of Monterey Bay. The small, one-bedroom unit featured mud-brown carpeting and was located next to the building's rumbling elevator. The complex itself sat across from a skeet shooting range. Ari clearly did not consider my sleep or aesthetic sensibilities to be of great importance. This was a bad sign. But I still believed Ari and I could survive as a couple, providing I could find a job back in the Bay Area.

There's a lot of temporary dislocation in broadcasting, and the commuter relationship is often the prelude to the end. I'd spent the last year and a half being away at least three days a week. While I was gone, Ari had lived alone, except for our house rabbit, Martin Bunny, who had succeeded Velcro the guinea pig, and whose presence was mostly made known by his ability to clandestinely devour the edges of records, rugs, and furniture. For the first few months, Ari welcomed me home every week with a small bouquet of flowers on the table. As the week passed, the flowers would begin to disappear in an odd way: the stems would remain in the vase, but each day, a bloom or two would be gone. I thought it was a peculiar method Ari had of pruning the bouquet, but attributed it to cultural differences. There was something disturbing about watching your romantic bouquet vanish little by little, leaving only the drying stems in water, but I never thought of it as foreshadowing. Eventually I spotted Martin Bunny, atop the card table that served as our only dining surface, happily chewing a bloom.

I continued to hold on to the idea of returning to live with my boyfriend. I'd been tempted by some of the interesting and powerful men I'd met in LA, including one especially creative and successful producer who had asked me out several times and offered to buy me a Porsche in my favorite model and color—granite green. But I still considered myself to be spoken for.

The Zero Talk Hour

Permanent positions in radio are an oxymoron. It eventually became clear that Crazy103 and I were no longer simpatico. I was back to my former practice of applying to radio stations everywhere. Again, even though I now had three of the top five radio markets in my résumé, and legendary call letters on my air check tapes, I was running into that "we don't think women should say the things you say" problem.

In LA, actors often speak about their characters' motivations. Anyone who had been playing me at this point in my life would have had plenty of motivation for constantly pouring over trade magazines in order to smell out the faintest whiff of an on-air vacancy. Motivated by my run-in with Hash Henderson, and Scorch Brooks' unwillingness to make me feel either safe or appreciated, as well as a dim awareness that all was not going well with Ari in San Francisco, I was propelled to virtual job suicide by my desire to get away from what may have been the dumbest man ever allowed to run a radio station.

When I say I was working for the dumbest man ever allowed to run a radio station, that's saying something. Running a music radio station in that decade required less on the intelligence and creativity scale than, say…babysitting an energetic three-year-old without resorting to video. The company's research department would dictate the music, and the station would play four, five, six songs in a row, leaving a few segments (called stop sets) open every hour for the DJs to provide a little humor, information, or entertainment news before or after commercials.

Crazy103 employed some of the most talented, legendary names in contemporary hit radio, or CHR. You could give them fifteen seconds of an intro to a song, and they could tell you a complete story, or interest you in a contest, or let you know that your favorite singer was engaged to marry your favorite actor even though he'd just had a baby with his soon-to-be-ex-wife, before the singer at the end of that fifteen-second intro ever opened his mouth to sing a single note. But even these professionals were having the fun sucked out of their days by increasingly restrictive programming rules and time constraints. It didn't matter to management. You were going to get fifteen seconds, perhaps four times an hour, to create any content for your show. The rest was the hits, commercials, and the station's in-house promotional announcements.

Several of the jocks made their peace with it. They were earning executive salaries to sit on swivel chairs and say nothing. There wasn't anywhere else in town where things were likely to be better. One drank himself to death. Some left their on-air shifts to create promotional announcements and ads, doing creative work in sixty-second increments. A very, very few moved to talk radio.

I was one of those who switched to talk, but it didn't happen all at once. Like a battered spouse, I came back to music radio one more time, because even though it hurt me, I thought we were still in love.

The incident that made me truly desperate to leave Crazy103 happened at an airstaff meeting over brunch at one of the fanciest restaurants in Los Angeles. When a radio station's management team decides to take everybody out for a meal, it's trouble. Friends who do other kinds of work tell me this is not normal. In other businesses, when your company takes everyone out for a cruise on the San Francisco Bay, or a wine-tasting train ride through the Sonoma Valley, it's to announce a new product or bonus or that they're sending a team to be photographed enjoying the cuisine of France and "Who wants to go?"

Unfortunately, broadcast companies have a different tradition: they like to force people to act cheerful in luxurious environments while hearing bad news. I've been to a company Christmas party at an exclusive country club where the owner, giving the live band a break, took the stage to announce, to somewhat pallid applause, that there would be no company bonuses or profit sharing that year, because he had decided to invest in a new technology that would revolutionize the industry and pay massive dividends—to him. But—he continued—instead of everyone going home with a company gift and the traditional check, one lucky employee would be able to try out this revolutionary technology, free, for a year. I've also been to lunches where the staff has been told their station will be changing ownership in two weeks. This brunch, at the swanky Italian modern-chandelier-lit-wood-paneled Hotel St. Jerome, on the Sunset Strip, in the heart of Hollywood, was where Scorch Brooks chose to announce the advent of the Zero Talk Hour.

The announcement of the Zero Talk Hour was one of those situations—you may have experienced them yourself—where a bunch of people are listening to somebody in authority advancing some utterly absurd idea, and nobody is contradicting him or complaining or calling attention to the utter ridiculousness of what he is saying. The most horrible part of these events is when *you know you are going to be the one to say something.*

I always wonder how other, quieter, people manage. Do they have a secret code whereby they designate some dope like me to open up her mouth? Am I controlled by transmitters implanted by aliens? Is it a physical law of the universe, like gravity, that in every group gathered around a pompous idiot spouting drivel, there will be one fool who, in opposition to every instinct for self-preservation, points it out?

Scorch Brooks, the program director of our world-famous top 40 success story, staffed by legendary Los Angeles air personalities, stood before a microphone and asked for quiet.

Then, he announced that when we returned to the station, we would promote the fact that for one hour at a time, several times each day, none of the highly paid, well-trained entertainers employed by the station and presently eating their lox and bagels in front of him was going to say anything. On the occasions when we would be permitted a few seconds to speak on the air, we would be touting the idea that the best thing that could possibly happen to the listener was that we would shut up again.

After Scorch's announcement, the sound of chewing somehow seemed more audible, despite the plush lavender carpeting on the floor of the heavily-mirrored private dining room of the Hotel St. Jerome. Our boss and his boss were smiling, nodding, and laughing. The Zero Talk Hour was "New, new, new in the industry! It was gonna be the bomb! This was really going to take us to the next level!"

Here's a thing you might not know about radio: our management is obsessed with "the next level." Radio station managers spend an amazing amount of time talking to their staffs, trade publications, and clients about how they are going to "take it to the next level." Perhaps management is also obsessed with "taking it to the next level" in the trucking business, or the medical waste disposal business, but I doubt it. In the broadcasting industry, usually "the next level" means that they're going to see improved ratings. But managers don't like to say, "This is going to improve our ratings by 20 percent," because that would be an actual, verifiable number they would have to either meet or miss. So instead they go on about "the next level" as though they're making their way to the observation deck of the new World Trade Center.

Several seconds, which may have been minutes, which felt like an hour, after the Zero Talk Hour was unveiled, the room was still deadly quiet. The wet sound of masticated omelets continued, uninterrupted, until I couldn't stand it anymore. My boss' boss, Kitty, the general manager, was looking around the room for questions. Although I was just a lowly weekender, I swallowed, raised my hand, and was "recognized" by Kitty, who would not have recognized me in real life even if she'd had my company ID to help her. "So," I said, speaking out clearly and loudly in order to be heard at the front of the room over the racket of thirty-seven knives spreading cream cheese, "what you're asking us to do...is promote the fact that people will be happier if we aren't there." Everyone stared, first at me, then at the general manager. I continued. "What you're saying is that people would rather have a station that sounds just like sixty minutes of all their favorite songs on tape. In that case, why have us promote it at all? Why not just have all of us play music without saying anything, ever?"

Scorch did have an answer for that one. "That isn't true at all," he huffed. "People need the service elements, and they need you to call attention to the fact that we play the most music."

"Or they might not notice," I said. "I see." Then I sat down and looked at my suddenly inedible bagel.

During my exit interview, which occurred about two weeks after that lunch, Scorch gave me the reason he was letting me go. "I don't think you're happy here, Turi. I don't think you like me."

I wanted to explain to Scorch that asking LA's best jocks to be excited about not being on the air seemed about as reasonable as expecting prison guards to be excited about improvements in home confinement technology. Instead, I handed him a piece of paper on Crazy103 letterhead and said, "I do like you, Scorch. But I'm taking a full-time job back in the Bay Area, starting in two weeks. And right at the bottom of this resignation letter," pointing to the bottom of the letter I'd typed that morning, "it says thank you and how much I've appreciated the chance to work for you. I like you just fine, Scorch. It's Zero Talk Hours I can't stand."

Scorch remained on my list of top five PINWWAs until he passed away a few years ago. Possibly, he regretted his failure to stand up for me in the Hash Henderson incident. I suspect that was the reason he signed off on one of the most elaborate and enthusiastic letters of recommendation I have ever received.

It's true that the internet will divulge, for just a few dollars, the complete arrest records of anyone from your hair stylist to the person who cuts your lawn. However, you could be sitting in San Quentin Prison convicted of bank robbery and your employer would still be prohibited by its human resources department from acknowledging that you are anything less than an ideal employee. And that is why I write my reference letters myself. I don't mean I forge them; I mean I write the letter, and then give it to my soon-to-be-former boss to endorse. With a boss who has, at best, a limited attention span, and at worst, a burning desire to get rid of me, the DIY reference letter works well for all. I always have to write the letter a few times. My first-draft efforts tend to be overly enthusiastic ("Turi has been to top 40 radio in Los Angeles what Mozart is to classical music"), so I redo them, and tone it down. Then, I stand around the desk of my soon-to-be former boss, drinking coffee and talking about how much I've loved working for him until he signs it.

Points for Recklessness

You can be *too* creative. The program director of K-Star radio was a long-time Bay Area radio veteran. He'd worked at early album rock FM stations, the kind that first played the sound of Haight Asbury and were part of the whole musical history—Jefferson Airplane, The Grateful Dead, The Tubes, The Steve Miller Band, Huey Lewis—of the City by the Bay. This programming gig was a little unusual for him; a full service "Hot A/C" (Adult Contemporary) station with personalities and news in nearly every day-part. For air talent, this was a throwback to the stations that made us want to be on the radio in the first place. Artists stopped by for quick interviews and photo-ops; we played new records (though not terribly adventurous ones) early; and you could create as much entertainment between the records as your ratings could support. But I almost didn't get the gig. Benny Caine had the idea of doing a "competitive audition." He thought he'd get a bunch of female air talent in the room and ask us to compete for the job.

To be fair, Benny was a big supporter of mine, and fairly open-minded about putting women on the air, but I don't think he'd have ever considered trying a competitive audition with a roomful of men. It would have been an unthinkable act to ask male disc jockeys, with all their egos—and sometimes the physical aggression—that goes with airing your personality in front of the public every day. To me, the competitive audition sounded like a radio version of nude mud wrestling. When Benny told me about it, I looked at him hard for a moment, as though he were a maître d' offering me a seat next to a garbage dumpster.

"Benny," I said, "you know me. You know my work. You know the stations I've worked for. They're the best, most successful, most famous stations in radio. If you honestly think you can find somebody with more personality than I have, who sounds better on the air than I do—hire her. Otherwise, let's skip this competitive audition crap and just figure out when you want me to start."

I didn't plan a word of that, but it worked. Benny made up his mind. I was back on the air in San Francisco. It was a job so much the opposite of Crazy103 that I fell in love with personality music radio all over again. The station's airstaff were a pleasure—all grownups, none of them misbehaved—and they were happy to help each other succeed. To make things even more wonderful, the station had an award-winning news department, which had, in part, been built by my friend Leslie, before she'd moved to LA. A well-written newscast, and a reporter who knows his or her story well enough to talk about it on the air with you and your listeners, is one of the pure joys of radio.

Almost immediately, I began supplying comedy bits to the morning host, who was happy to use them. The first one I left for him, around April 15th, was a bit about how, if you were clever, you could figure out how everything in your life—from your cat to a can of cranberry sauce—could be a professional tax deduction. He used it right away. I imagined myself like the elves in the fairy tale who leave the shoemaker a pair of lovely boots each morning. I was sure this was going to be my ticket to San Francisco radio stardom.

I had hoped that my return to the Bay Area would allow me to resume my contented domestic life with Ari. That didn't go exactly as planned. Since I was hosting a show of my own again—from seven in the evening till midnight, five nights a week—a show that allowed me to attend concerts, write comedy sketches, and interact with listeners, I had less time for being sweet. He wasn't too happy with my hours, either.

No matter when you go to work, I'll bet you don't go to bed an hour after you get home. But Ari wasn't buying my argument that it was unreasonable of him to expect me to throw myself into my car, zoom to our hideous apartment directly from the radio station right after my show, down a fried egg or some leftover pasta, brush my teeth, and nestle into my down comforter for the night by 1:00 a.m. Since Ari left for work at six, I argued that it was more logical for me to simply tiptoe to the bedroom after he was sound asleep. But I just could not get Ari to give up on the idea of a single bedtime for both of us.

Two other women, friends of mine, also hosted seven to midnight on San Francisco's smooth jazz and classic soul music stations. So I had plenty of people with whom I could socialize after work. My girlfriend Becca, the smooth jazz personality, met me on one of those nights in an all-night Chinatown restaurant over mock-duck chow mien. Our conversation turned to how fortunate it was that we both had men in our lives who understood, if not our sleeping hours, at least our requirement for independence and the freedom to set our own schedules. We didn't rush our dinner. We each returned home at 3:00 a.m. to find our respective companions furious, frightened, and ready to phone the cops.

Ari and I stumbled along for a total of three years, including a trip to meet his parents in Israel, before he decided he'd rather marry an Israeli. The attraction, he said, was that "Every Israeli woman is connected to the ground." It's true I wasn't all that "connected to the ground," but I had planned on building a life with Ari, so the breakup was hard. I guess I thought that because he was a musician, he would understand the performance highs, the long bouts of unemployment, the financial peril, the weird hours, the bizarre bosses, the kind, entertaining, or scary listeners—but he didn't. Ari gave me my first glimpse of a normal life, but it hadn't been a normal time: He met me after my relocation to an empty house thousands of miles from my family, then watched me wait out a one-year contract that paid me for doing almost no work, followed by a second year of long distance commuting, followed by a third year of working the kind of hours most people don't keep. Instead of being connected to the ground, my life offered four-word conversations with the guy behind the counter at Clown Alley, a greasy, six table, all-night diner with bright red vinyl chairs and a lime green counter down the block from our studio, where you could get a burger the size of the nearby Transamerica building, and an occasional exchange of short greetings with the uniformed security guard in the station's front lobby. It would take another three years before I was able to drive past the not-at-all-connected-to-the–ground houseboat Ari rented after he moved out without hyperventilating.

I grieved over my lost shot at a normal life for about a year. The reality of finding a companion seemed completely incompatible with a life in radio. I was getting to the age where many women say they start to seriously consider IVF if they haven't had kids with their partners, and while I literally cried over the thought that I'd never have a spouse, it never occurred to me to mourn, as some women say they do, the idea that I would never be a mom. Strangely, while I had spent a good deal of time imagining being married to Ari, I had given absolutely no thought to having children with him—probably because I had given no thought to having children at all.

The Wart

Naturally, because everything was going so well at K-Star, management had to make a change. The whole station's numbers, including mine, were climbing fast. Benny Caine was promoted to some sort of corporate position. The general manager of K-Star announced Benny's new job at a specially catered lunch in the K-Star conference room. We all applauded and cheered. "And," continued our manager, "I'm excited to tell you that your new program director will be arriving next week." I recognized the name. He was the guy my friend Howie, who had worked for him in New York, referred to as "The Wart."

"Great," I mumbled to my fellow jocks. "Eat, drink, and be fired."

Over the next few days, we studied up on The Wart. In radio, usually one of your friends has worked for any given boss in the industry, because, as one program director used to say, "The broadcasting business is run by a total of seven people, each of whom you will work for twice before you die." The Wart was known for planting small microphones in the on-air studios of stations he'd managed; the better to hear what off-air spleen the staff might be venting about him. The Wart's talent for endearing himself to employees was exceeded only by his ability to succeed with women. The Wart was on his fifth wife. It was a mystery to many of us how attractive men with good hygiene, dental work, and jobs, were having trouble finding dates—never mind spouses— while The Wart, who looked like something out of a Tolkien novel, and who had neither a fortune nor a cabinet position to recommend him, came to marry and lose four wives. Eventually, we discovered that the previous four wives, and this one, too, were from Asia, and that none of them spoke English.

The Wart liked to play tapes of your show to you on a little battery-operated, hand-held cassette deck. He said that was how most listeners heard us. So The Wart and I would sit in his office full of high tech stereo equipment, with a cheap, toy tape player balanced on his desk while he vilified me for not sounding *likable*. "Likable" was defined as having a pleasing vocal tone of the sort that might put listeners in the mood for sex. The sessions would probably have gone more smoothly, though, if I hadn't stated right away that I was not interested in having sex with my listeners.

Here's how that meeting went:

"You need to sound more *likeable*," The Wart began. "Men should think you are *likeable*."

"How do you mean, *likeable*?" I asked, the picture of innocence. "Like, nice? Or maybe friendly?"

"You know what I mean," growled The Wart, his face reddening underneath his petite head of gray hair. "You need to sound more like that woman on K-Beach." The Wart named an evening show from Los Angeles, hosted by a woman who made James Bond's paramours sound like football coaches.

"I think maybe you should hire Cerise." I suggested. Cerise, a talented woman recently working in Washington DC, had a silken voice, although she didn't look at all like a Bond Girl. Cerise was proportioned more like two Bond Girls. "She's fabulous...and she sounds very *likeable.*"

"Cerise is fatter than a house," responded The Wart.

It took me half a second to believe what I'd just heard. I thought for another half second. I said, "Half the guys on this radio station are fatter than houses. You don't mind them."

"Don't you bring any of your feminist shit around here," The Wart exploded with indignation. My relationship with my new boss was not off to a good start.

The Wart also took two hours a day to close his office door and meditate, during which time the radio station could be overtaken by aliens, for all he cared. On any given day between eleven and one, a line of people formed outside The Wart's office door. Someone holding a computer printout, schedule, ad campaign, or other important document would take up a position at the rear.

"Is he done yet?" The person in front of the line would risk an ear to the door.

"I think I still hear chanting."

"What happens if we just knock?"

"He's levitating."

"You're kidding."

"Nope, that's what he says."

"Can you let me know when he lands?"

If only The Wart had been as adept at keeping a radio station off the ground. Alas, years before the disco revival, The Wart began adding old Donna Summer records to our lineup. Nobody knew why. The ratings sank, and The Wart added KC and the Sunshine Band. He also fired me, observing HR protocol by including the general manager in our final meeting. I was a little stunned to hear that the GM's reason for cutting me from the airstaff was that I was not a "team player." I'm not sure exactly what The Wart had told our manager to support this, but it must have been fairly unpleasant. I only realized it because a few years later, when I came back to visit a friend who still worked at K-Star. The GM, hearing laughter, stopped by the coffee room where a group of about six K-Star staffers, with whom I had worked, were gathered, catching up. From the look on his face, I could see him realizing that The Wart had played him. He looked ashamed. "Come any time," he offered. "We'll all be glad to see you."

Cerise, it turns out, was in one of her slender phases. I was delighted to hear that The Wart had hired her.

Three months later, The Wart's termination was announced. He "retired" to run his own radio consulting business based in a small town in the Northwest. Presumably, he continues to encourage any women he hires to diet and sound *likeable*.

Landlords are (Stupid) People Too

I **bought a** second house because I was a bad landlord. A good landlord doesn't let the tenants order her around. But when the men who were renting my San Francisco house asked me if they could stay for several years, I said that would be fine. So it never occurred to me to tell them, when Ari and I broke up, that I would not be renewing their lease because I was going to need somewhere to live. Instead, I looked for a house in the East Bay, which felt more like home to me anyway, for the principal reason that I've never really understood what anyone in San Francisco does for a living.

In what was becoming a habit for me, I closed on my Oakland house the week before The Wart fired me. Now I had two houses I couldn't afford. It was the first time in my life that I was not going to be able to pay my bills. I started looking for a roommate, or someone who would rent the whole place.

Leslie, with whom I remained in close regular touch, suggested I try talk radio. I was definitely *not* interested in talk radio.

"What if you could do it just like rock radio, only without the records?" she asked.

"Who does that?"

"I want to introduce you to a consultant I know," she said.

White Cake

White Cake got his name because one of my friends sat next to him at an industry awards dinner. After an entirely unremarkable fish entrée, the dessert course arrived: small squares of plain white sheet cake with vanilla vegetable shortening frosting. Every other person at the table thinned her lips, squinted, and decided to remain on her diet—except for White Cake. He looked up at the waitress, beaming. "White cake, with white frosting! My favorite!"

I'd been sent to White Cake by the station's new consultant, Burt Ingersol. White Cake was the general manager of a new talk station that was just getting signed on in Portland, Oregon. Again, it had been a top 40 AM station, but its ratings had disintegrated over the last few years, and while everyone knew its famous call letters, few actually listened. By this time, music radio on AM was considered by nearly everyone to be a losing proposition. Talk radio (and its *enfant terrible*, Rush Limbaugh) were hot.

At my first interview with White Cake, I answered his "How did you get your start in radio?" icebreaker with my story of creating a résumé out of nothing but high-cotton-fiber office paper, then tossing phantom call letters off my history list every time I acquired a new, genuine set. I concluded, not without a small measure of pride, that at this point every station mentioned on the résumé before him was absolutely bona fide. Instead of generating admiration for my dedication, creativity, and intrepid spirit, the guy was appalled. He would have tossed me back into the applicant pool like an out-of-season trout, but Ingersol intervened, and White Cake relented.

Have you ever had a boss who believes that, if the notion struck, he or she could do your job far better than you? White Cake was that boss. Sometimes your superior really could do your job. But in radio, those who can succeed on the air usually *are* on the air, and those who have other areas of strength are in sales, marketing, and management. Also, unlike working for a car dealership, where people who sell, for example, Jaguars, are also people who like to own and drive Jaguars, after the broadcasting industry's consolidation, more and more often, the radio station that's meant for the ears of twenty-four-year-old men is being sold to advertisers by forty-two-year-old women. The sorts of programs these two groups find listenable, never mind fascinating, are usually very different.

Still, it often happens that the off-air team members harbor the fantasy that it would be easy-peasy-no-trouble-at-all to walk into a soundproof room for four hours every day and create entertainment for everybody out of—and over—literally, thin air. Most people can talk, and, therefore, many feel they have an inner talk show host just waiting to be recognized. I'm guessing you don't find this sort of hubris among other managers. The manager of the animal shelter probably doesn't say: "Neutering. Nothing to it. I'd like to give it a try." The person running a pathology laboratory probably doesn't say, "Let me have a look at those cells. How hard can it be to pick out the cancerous ones?" Even the folks who drive the truck that paints the double yellow lines down the middle of the road obviously have a specialized skill. To protect yourself from these "do-it-myself-ers," when you are a radio personality out job hunting, you should probably interview your prospective supervisor in advance about whether or not he or she would like to do your job, or has ever done your job; and if so how that went. I wish I had had this advice before going to work for White Cake.

When you have a boss who believes that he is both funny and fascinating, he will feel compelled to demonstrate this regularly. To explain why I was suspended for doing something unfunny on the air, White Cake would point at a rubber chicken he had resting on the credenza near his desk. "I know what humor is, and I know what's funny. I brought that chicken to the company meeting last fall, and *that* was funny." I secretly wondered just how uproarious White Cake's rubber chicken would be if it were held up to a microphone attached to a 50,000-watt transmitter. You don't have to be a genius to figure out that when the guy who signs your paycheck is telling you a joke he thinks is hilarious, you should laugh. White Cake left broadcasting, I was told, for a speed-of-light brief career in stand-up comedy.

I'll be Suspended for Christmas

In some cases, it's harder on a broadcaster to be suspended than to be sacked. Suspensions almost always happen because you did something on the air that has caused a listener disturbance, and therefore a media and advertiser fracas, and there you are, shamed in the press, and waiting for the phone call you know will be coming. Of course, getting suspended, if finances are not a big concern, also has its good qualities. I should know. I ruined the Twelve Days of Christmas promotion.

I would be willing to bet my kid's college tuition that every commercial radio station in America has run a Twelve Days of Christmas promotion. The Twelve Days of Christmas promotion works like this: the station awards a series of progressively valuable prizes, every day, for twelve of the Advent days of Christmas. Usually on the twelfth day, if you win, you get some remarkably expensive prize, plus all the other smaller prizes. The world, and your listeners in particular, are convinced that no regular people will ever win the grand twelfth-day prize. The general public is absolutely right to be skeptical. It is unlikely they will win, because of the contest pigs.

There exists a substratum of people who play contests for a living. They fill whole houses with the minutiae of sweepstake-winning: sniping software, postal machines, mail-in entry forms, etc. They know when games will be played or numbers drawn. They don't listen to anybody's radio station, and they don't jump up and down and scream, "I won, I won, OMG I won" when they win because they win all the time and the rules of the contest, which they know by heart, don't say they have to. Promotion and marketing directors spend their lives trying to keep contest pigs from winning, but it's hopeless. I personally have nothing against contest pigs. I just wish promotions directors would state in the rules that if you don't sound like you give a rat's ass when you win something, we can go on and take the next contestant who does.

It is also true that playing the odds does not excite everyone. If you are a gambler, there are entire cities set up to cater to your every betting need. But if, as a kid, you always skipped those quarter-a-toss carnival games because you could plainly see that there was a pretty slim chance you would end up with the doggie on the stick; if it was clear to you that your quarter would be lying on the outside edge of the plate with all the other unfortunate quarters, whereas, if you gave the cotton candy vendor your quarter, you were certain of getting something in return; then you'll understand what happened when I was finally working my first morning drive shift, in talk radio, in the Pacific Northwest. The Portland station's prize for the Twelfth Day of Christmas was to be five hundred lottery tickets; or, as they put it in their promotional materials, "Your opportunity to win millions!"

Coincidently, Portland's media were having a field day with a sympathetic portrayal of a couple who had sent their kids to live with relatives because they could not afford clothes or school materials. But now this destitute family had just won a huge lottery prize. The angle of the story was, more or less, that this couple's purchase of a winning lottery ticket proved the existence of God.

I did not find the argument conclusive. I said so on my morning show.

"There are several relevant facts that the media doesn't seem to be much interested in discovering. Did this couple spend a couple of dollars every so often on the hope that the lottery would catapult them to a better life, or did they buy lottery tickets by the paycheck-full, spending amounts that might just as easily have fed and clothed their kids? You could send a kid to school in a nice outfit every day for about the price of a few lottery tickets, if you buy them all the time. Child-rearing should not depend on a game of chance." I went on to point out that I was skeptical of chance, namely the Christmas lottery tickets, as a gift. "A gift is a gift; a chance is a chance," I said. As a grand finale, I suggested this:

"If you are the lucky winner of the Twelve Days of Christmas prize of five hundred lottery tickets—which are not being advertised as five hundred lottery tickets, but rather as your virtual shoe-in at a million dollars—you might politely ask the sales department if you could just have the $500 instead—as a gift. If you win, you should try it. See if management will trade you for it. Offer them the tickets, in exchange for the five hundred bucks. Even though it would be waving goodbye to your nearly certain future as a millionaire, see what happens. I don't think they'll go for it, by the way."

That's exactly what the five hundred ticket winner did. For ruining the Christmas promotion, I got a week off with pay.

I spent a lot of my week off talking on the phone with Paul Hart, the man who had so impressed me with his "no means no" monologue when I heard him on my visit to his station in LA. At some point in the conversation, Paul decided to fly up to take me out for dinner. I hadn't had a real laugh in a while. Between the breakup with Ari, three moves, two job changes, the ensuing financial wreckage, and a boss who wasn't sure why I was on the air at his radio station, I needed someone who could make me laugh—and not by mispronouncing English.

As it turns out, Paul really meant every word he'd said about "no." We spent a long time getting to know each other. He's perhaps the most gentlemanly person I've ever dated, and still one of my favorite friends today. Paul also totally deserved the voice he got. He would want me to tell you he's sexy. He is sexy. He's also smart, creative, and now pretty famous. To this day, Paul can get away with complimenting my ass, which I find far more flattering now than I did then, considering my age and a remarkable lack of perkiness in that department. At the time, Paul was just about to lose his first major market, part-time talk radio job, and found work doing morning drive at a tiny radio station just north of Los Angeles. There, he created and voiced his own characters to make up for the fact that he didn't have any real ones calling in. In case you're wondering, that's not cheating. The difference between planting callers and creating characters to use as callers is like the difference between a video game of *Grand Theft Auto* and driving the Indianapolis 500.

Like me, Paul had been a major market rock jock. He was soon to be sleeping on the floor of a cheesy one-bedroom apartment very much like the one Sims had lived in in LA, where you could hear people complaining through the newsprint-thin walls that their toast was burnt. But envying those who could rent sturdier housing stock seemed like asking for too much. I confined myself to envying people who could afford toasters. What money Paul and I had was spent on plane tickets. It was my second commuter relationship. This time, we both had full-time jobs, but his paid almost nothing, and mine would soon end.

I had a direct boss in Portland. Wes Proctor was a small, bald, gentle man, completely unsuited for the hell I was about to put him through. I was the bane of his existence. I told him so myself. After that, he regularly referred to me as the bane of his existence. Much later, Wes returned to the Midwest to work for his former employer. He's a corporate executive now, and his salary, which was published in one of the industry trades, is staggering. If you amortize it, though, over the five months he had to deal with the drama and distress I caused him at the Portland station, it seems more reasonable.

Wes was regularly expected to run interference between the rubber chicken toting general manager and me; between the sales team and me; between the guys on the airstaff and me. Eventually, he just got tired. I don't blame him. Once, Biff the sales manager asked me for a meeting. Biff, a lovely, dark-haired, fit, and five-foot-ten, with a wardrobe of exquisite suits and even more exquisite ties, was proud of being an out gay man at a time when being an out gay man was not so common. But if I talked about anything involving gay people, whose civil rights I've long supported, on the air, Biff grew frantic.

"You can't say those things on the air, Turi. That thing you said about nobody wanting to really know what goes on in anybody's bedroom. You can't say that."

"Why, Biff? Why shouldn't I say that? When homophobes call and tell me the idea of gay sex is disgusting and I point out that the idea of your parents having sex is also disgusting, and I remind them that looking at any real couple having sex would probably not be a visually appealing experience, unless your friends are all porn stars—why is that a problem for you, or the gay community?"

Biff never had any answers to these questions, but one day he had a question for me. "Turi, I'd like you to write an apology. Will you do that for me?"

"Of course, Biff, if I've crossed a line or done something I shouldn't, I'll apologize. I have no problem doing that on or off the air. What's the situation? What did I do that you want me to apologize for?"

"I just think it would help."

"What do you mean you think it would help? With what?"

"With clients. It would help with them."

"Let me get this straight, Biff. Although you can't tell me anything specific I've done that one of your customers feels warrants an apology, you want me to write one anyhow, to give to clients, as what? A selling tool?"

"I just think it would help."

"No, Biff. I will not write you general letter of apology that you can use as a selling tool."

So Biff would complain to Wes. And all the sales people left over from the previous music format—who were kept on to sell talk radio even though they hated it and their clients hated it and the idea of having to go out and get new clients who wanted to advertise on talk radio was even *more* hateful to them—would complain to Wes; as well as the producer of the midday show, who complained that I embarrassed her when I pointed out—off the air—that the phrase "Jew them down" was bigoted. Even with all that, I think Wes might have hung in there, since the show was gaining ratings and generating tremendous press, if I hadn't gone after the United Way campaign.

Perhaps your workplace holds a United Way campaign. I've never really understood them. As it happens, I'm a big fan of charitable giving. My parents taught me that if you have enough, then you have enough to give. If not money, then time. But a lot of people who work in corporate settings don't make much money, so the United Way campaign, where employees are pressured into giving a fair chunk of a paycheck to charitable causes they might or might not want to support, has always seemed more like a tax, or a wage garnishment. Still, considering many station managers like to brag to each other, or report to corporate headquarters, how their United Way campaign is going, I probably shouldn't have spent an hour on the air getting regular working people to call in and confess how much they resented it. And they *certainly* didn't appreciate my saying that if some companies would simply pay their people a little better, a lot of the charities that the United Ways supports, like food pantries and medical clinics, might become obsolete.

I still had a big bouquet of flowers from Paul on my desk, which he'd sent me the last time I'd come back to work after being suspended, when Portland paid me off, and asked me to clean out my workspace. I'd learned a lot, and sincerely wished them well. Not that it helped. The whole format change to talk radio was abandoned within the year.

I had no reason to stay in Portland. I'd made a couple of wonderful friends, but there was no work for me, and the Pacific Northwest has always felt—as in fact it is—like the end of the continent and far away from the rest of my life. I'd rented a very dark apartment, purposely, because I had been working mornings, and needed to go to bed while it was still light out. So sitting around there was a bad idea. Both of my houses were leased to brand new tenants, and I couldn't afford to live in them anyhow. Paul flew up to help me load a truck and move back to Chicago.

Baby You Can Drive My Truck

Radio is a great way to see the country, if your dream has always been to experience America from the inside of a rental truck with a governor on the accelerator that keeps you from going over sixty miles an hour.

Here are some things you may have imagined about DIY cross-country moves:

Myth: You'll have fun learning to drive a truck.

Truth: Unless you are already a licensed truck driver, you will not be able to back your truck out of driveways, or turn around in residential cul-de-sacs. Pulling into anything that is not a truck stop will give you a short-term feeling of accomplishment. Then comes the moment you need to reverse, and, like a mouse on a glue board, you realize you are trapped. If you've ever wondered how a truck "jack knifes," backing up a rental truck with a car on a trailer behind it is a good way to find out. On one of my several cross-country moves, I actually managed to run into my own car, which was in tow, with the back end of my rental truck. My error proved both embarrassing and expensive. To this day, I am not certain how I managed to get the truck to do exactly what it did. To make matters worse, the handsome single friend I was visiting in this Cleveland suburb called his dad, the local carpet king, for assistance. The king summoned one of his professional delivery crew, who rode to the rescue like the cavalry, untangled the mash-up, and refused a tip.

Myth: Your Friends will all come over to help you load your truck, and then, after a magical few hours during which the cargo area gets perfectly stacked and secured, you will celebrate your immanent departure by treating the whole gang to a friendly pizza and beverage, just like in the beer commercials.

Truth: You or your partner will call in every favor you've ever done for anyone who is not in a wheelchair. The requested favors will not be cheerfully returned, since you are leaving town, and there may be nothing in the future you can do for them. This results in moving errors, like having your camping gear and wooden clogs tossed into a long, black, canvas duffel bag, along with your fine china, then hefted onto the truck like a sack of potatoes. If you are exceptionally lucky, you have one friend who stays till the bitter end, persevering with almost unnatural doggedness. If you are not married, you might want to consider choosing this person as a partner for life.

You might think that hiring experts would prevent the misery of loading, but even professional movers frequently screw up in the loading department. On my relocation from Chicago to San Francisco, I was persuaded by the moving company's estimator to put my new sports car on the truck, along with my household goods, which resulted in an insurance claim I'll bet has not been seen before or since: a collision between a Toyota Supra and a 1920s walnut wood wardrobe.

The loading effort will take all day, and likely well into the night. People will begin drinking beer long before the work is done, leading to disruptive ideas about carton stacking technique. The pizza will arrive just as people are leaving to go home, and you will end up eating cold anchovies and coffee for several days as road food in the cab of your truck. You will have indigestion, as well as motion sickness, when you navigate particularly windy stretches of highway.

Myth: You'll get to take your time, enjoy great scenery, and discover out-of-the-way spots you wouldn't get to see otherwise.

Truth: Your car, which you are towing behind your rental truck, makes it impossible to find a place to park that's "off the beaten path." So, it is unlikely that you will visit anything that's not a truck stop. Try not to feel too disappointed. Truck stops, while not known for their scenic qualities, still have many good features. You can buy a soft-serve ice cream cone and wander through the brightly lit displays, marveling at the fact that every kind of appliance used in the American home has been miniaturized so that it can be powered off a cigarette lighter. Admire shrunken air conditioners, coffee makers, microwaves, and sauce pots.

Also, it's amazing how many different types of stench-covering room scents have been created to mask the natural odors you would typically find in the cab of a truck. There are the ones you'd expect, like evergreen and rainwater; also, baby powder and apple pie. The only place I've seen more elaborate scents and flavorings is the Jelly Belly™ jellybean factory in Vallejo, California. Jelly Belly™ has also created a special kids' "gross-out" line, featuring flavors like baby diapers and farts. Now that I think of it, someone should suggest to the designers of the gross-out jellybeans the scent of "long-haul truck cab."

Myth: You'll have a rollicking good adventure, spending time with your great friend and designated co-driver.

Truth: It's complicated. After being in radio for a while, you know whom to call to ride shotgun when another DIY move is near. Mostly, you want to pick someone with whom you can fight without coming to tears, blows, or jumping out of the vehicle while it is moving.

Myth: All will be well.

Truth: Before all ends well, something will go seriously wrong. The first time Paul helped me relocate, we hauled my car "rear wheels down" behind the rental truck—a huge error. Somewhere in the middle of Nebraska, we came up through the fog in time to see the carcass of a dead deer in the middle of our lane, but not in time to avoid running over it a second time. We cleared it with the U-Haul, but the rear end of my car lost its exhaust system, and it took a long time before I could drive it without smelling venison.

Crying Uncle

You should give up. No one would blame you. It's not unreasonable to decide to do something else with your life after you've been unemployed for over a year. I suppose it depends on what else you can think of to do.

In the past, to prove that my mom actually didn't believe I had a real profession, I'd sometimes tell her I was considering law school. "Really?" she'd respond instantly, with the enthusiasm most people show when they have just been presented with one of those giant sweepstakes checks that turn up at your door with a camera crew. "You'd like to go to law school? That's an excellent idea! We could help with that." I never had any intention of going to law school. But it was fun, in a mean sort of way, to tease my mom with the idea that I might pursue what she considers a legitimate occupation.

After my first talk radio gig ended, it took me so long to find another job that I actually bought one of those "How to Study for the LSAT" books. I should be glad that, despite my history of doing remarkably well on standardized tests, I performed abysmally on the practice exams inside. Since I had sworn an oath, after hauling drinks and sandwiches around from the time I was fifteen until I finished college, that I would never again serve anything from a tray, that eliminated waitressing. What else was I qualified to do, with my English degree and my big mouth and my talent for making things up?

I always enjoyed the soothing task of organizing and filing papers, but computers made that work obsolete. I'd held exactly one retail position, at an Ups and Downs teenage clothing store in a suburban mall, and the sadism of my manager had given me no reason to try that line of work anywhere else. Corporate people, I already noticed, were required to keep their opinions to themselves to an extent that looked dangerous to my sanity. There really didn't seem to be anything besides talk radio that I could stand to do. When the Portland job blew up, I filed for unemployment, and started looking.

Shortly after my return to Chicago, with winter wrapped around the city, my tenants notified me they were leaving my San Francisco house. Using what remained of my severance pay, I flew to the Bay Area to see about renting out my house again. What greeted me was a cold, filthy mess. The refrigerator was full of food with the power turned off. The tub looked like it had possibly been used in a pet washing business. Someone who didn't have, or couldn't find, a house key had simply knocked out a window in the back, using it as an entrance. The lot next door had been purchased and built out, covering the master bedroom window and leaving the place cellar dark. I would need to renovate to cut a window into the gardenside wall. The rehab alone would take weeks.

I borrowed a sleeping bag, not quite enough blankets, and a coffee pot, and moved back in, with the goal of getting the place in shape and finding a new tenant—one with better housekeeping habits. Once again, my life consisted of cleaning, yard chores, listening to radio, and looking for work. I also had to find an inexpensive construction crew. Fortunately, one of my girlfriend's significant others was a contractor, and between jobs. He agreed to work with his brother to reconfigure the cave room for a modest price. They'd do it as a favor, and to have the chance to spend time together.

My circumstances at the house this time, however, were far less luxurious than on my first tour. Then, I'd had furniture, Ari, and a steady paycheck.

Not expecting the calamitous state in which I'd found things, I had not packed much in the way of clothing, and nothing at all in the way of household supplies. I also didn't have my car with me, so when I needed to buy more painting and cleaning equipment than I could carry on public transit, I would catch a bus into the Mission District. For a few dollars more than bus fare, I could "Rent-a-Relic."

A different bus, which ran up and down our neighborhood's rather steep hill on the street behind mine, would take me downtown, or to the train, but it also connected a rather notorious housing project with the city's courthouse and jail. Long before reality TV, you could get a dose of the concerns and conversations of San Francisco's underclass by hopping on the Number Nineteen. You could find out whose boyfriend was not making bail and why. You could hear children being disciplined in alarmingly inappropriate language. It was not the San Francisco tourists flock to see.

Paul, now back in Southern California and finding a measure of success in his new position as a full-time talk show host, did what he could to be supportive. I particularly appreciated his holiday gifts of flannel pajamas and three pairs of woolly socks. It's not that Paul wasn't romantic. He asked what I wanted for the holidays, and warmth was all I could think of.

Mornings in the Bay Area are frequently foggy, damp, and chilly. They are especially chilly if you are living in an empty, un-insulated, hundred-year-old house furnished with only a card table, folding chair, and air mattress. My house once had two heaters. When I first moved in, I called the gas company to set up service. While they were at it, they thoughtfully shut off the ancient floor heater, declaring it nearly certain to result in death by carbon monoxide poisoning. So my sole source of thermal assistance was now an aged wall furnace with a blower fan that sounded like a school bus screeching to a stop. It put out about as much actual warmth as a box of birthday candles. I began to appreciate wooly socks the way some women admire a pair of Louboutin heels.

To keep looking for work while my house was under construction, I installed a basic phone line, and had my résumés and audition tapes forwarded to me from Chicago. I also borrowed a ladder. Whatever part of the day was not used for painting, scrubbing, or stopping in at mealtimes at the homes of friends who could cook, was spent running to the post office with application packages.

Weeks later, I rented the house and made my way to Paul's tiny apartment. He was spending a lot of time at the station, working. I was so bored; I bought him a $4.00 yard-sale table and began stripping it of paint—by peeling off the latex with my fingernails. I also amused myself when Paul was on the air by wandering the coast. Paul did his best to entertain me during the time he wasn't working or preparing for his show. He planned terrific day trips. We visited the Channel Islands. We drove to Ojai. We saw a local theater company perform *Death of a Salesman* in Santa Barbara and fought like tigers on the way home because he rightly accused me of being a theater snob. When I considered leaping from the truck and walking Highway 1 back to Ventura over my strong views on the actor who'd played Willy Loman, it was clear I couldn't hold out for a radio gig much longer.

I'm not sure what possessed the consultant who had found me the Portland job to try again, but he persuaded his new client in the Twin Cities to meet me. I adored KTLP's station manager, and she was willing to take a chance on me. Once again, I was to be a Midwesterner, on the radio in a Midwestern city. I flew home, retrieved my few possessions, my pet rabbit, and my car, and moved to a warehouse loft with a view of the Mississippi River.

Take Your Dominatrix to Work Day

A lot of folks think talk radio requires nothing more than an opinion and a microphone. That's like saying being a chef requires nothing more than a fish fillet and a book of matches.

One of the best, and one of the worst, things you get to do in talk radio is "meet" your listeners; mostly on the phone, but sometimes in person. Being a talk show host, or, in years gone by, a DJ, was a free pass to go anywhere, meet anyone, do anything—*if* you had the ability to paint a verbal picture of what you were doing, where you were going, and whom you were meeting. I once flew over San Francisco Bay in a helicopter, alighting on the deck of a naval vessel via what seemed to me an extremely flimsy ladder, during Fleet Week (do not wear a very short skirt to do this), and hosted a live event from a tugboat on the Mississippi River (do not wear a very long skirt to do this).

Sometimes, as was the case with the Minnesota dominatrix, you could get your listener to come to you…and *then* go to work with her. I forget exactly how the subject came up. It was likely when a prominent East Coast politician was unmasked, in an IRS investigation, as the customer of a known New York City madam who supplied strong and exotic discipline in the form of spankings, paddling, confinement, and the infliction of pain by numerous creative and alarming methods, including clothespins and candles. I was puzzled.

Why, I wondered aloud, would somebody pay thousands of dollars for an experience that could be replicated by simply giving birth? Why all the paraphernalia? Why the fixation with leather and latex? And why would a woman whose job it is to inflict pain on *other* people wear four-inch heels and a corset? At which point the phone rang, and on the screen, I saw the bright white letters: "Mistress Katrina. Dominatrix. St. Paul." I hit the on-air button.

"I don't wear four-inch heels to work, unless I'm seeing a foot fetishist—because then I get to sit down."

"That sounds sensible. What *do* you wear on your feet?"

"Engineer boots."

"How about the corset?"

"That's for magazine shots. Have you ever tried to hoist a handcuffed and bound, one-hundred-eighty-pound man by a pulley while wearing a corset?"

Clearly, on the other end of the line, I had a woman who knew her business—and her clientele. Mistress Katrina offered me a lesson. As a sideline to her work as a professional dominatrix, Mistress Katrina explained that she gave lessons, which she advertised through the back pages of the city's free weekly. These lessons were to help any woman with a desire to do so learn the mechanics—knot tying, types of whips, safe caning methods—of the practice of domination; whether as a hobby, or a profession. She gave women a choice of either small classes or private instruction.

"Are you worried that you're creating competition?" I asked her.

"Not at all. There are far more clients than I can possibly see. I only do one or two sessions a day."

"Do you accept men as students too?"

"Absolutely not. Men are already dominant in our society. I'm not about to give them any extra help."

I decided I liked Mistress Katrina. She had principles. "I'm not ready for a class," I told her, "but if you'd like to come in and visit the studio, I'd love for you to be my guest."

Mistress Katrina agreed, and my producer booked her for the next day's show.

It didn't take long for word to get around the station that Mistress Katrina would be coming to the studio. By four the following afternoon, the station's small lobby had so many employees "passing through" on their way to the coffee room that it looked like the morning rush at Starbucks. The young, handsome, and married police officer who provided our security rattled his handcuffs nervously, then realized what he was doing and abruptly ceased.

Suddenly, we became aware of another sound...the sound of a roller bag and a pair of stiletto heels clicking through tiled the entrance way...and there she was: all five-foot-two, ninety pounds of Mistress Katrina. She resembled a slim and compact version of an *American Girl* doll (if they made a dominatrix version of the *American Girl* doll) with dark brown hair worn just below her shoulders, a petite mouth with slightly imperfect, small, white teeth, black leather pants, a silky cream-colored pirate-style blouse, and a pair of strappy matching cream-colored leather sandals. Her pedicure was sublime. When I remarked on it, after the initial round of introductions, she thanked me.

"One of my clients gave it to me. He's very good. If I tell him to give you one, he'd be happy to do it. Would you like one?" I told Mistress Katrina I'd think it over, but that the idea of a strange man giving me a pedicure for his pleasure made me nervous.

"You don't understand," she purred. "It's not that it would give *him* pleasure to give you a pedicure. It's that it would please *me*."

Over the course of the show that evening, Twin Cities radio listeners learned about Mistress Katrina's line of work. Her rolling bag contained a heavy and cacophonous supply of clanking chains, leather dog collars, pulleys, and duct tape. Nothing looked particularly exotic, or dangerous—except maybe for the duct tape, which I remembered had been featured in certain crime novels and TV shows—or anything like what I'd imagined I'd see. When I marveled at the apparent ordinariness of her accouterment, Mistress Katrina, being at heart a practical Minnesota girl, explained that while fancier versions of much of what she used could be purchased through specialty catalogs (adult internet sites were still new at the time), the majority of the "nuts and bolts" of her trade were literally just that: things that could be economically obtained at any hardware or pet store. I've never looked at the rolls of chain at Ace Hardware the same way since, and I can no longer walk down certain aisles at Home Depot without wondering who, exactly, is shopping next to me.

Mistress Katrina gave us an overview of her clients, whose outside lives ranged from an author to high-powered business executives, with a generous sprinkling of law enforcement professionals thrown in. My mind returned, just for a second, to our off-duty officer, still stationed, and presumably listening through the station's sound system in the lobby. Mistress Katrina explained that sex was not part of her job description. That if the client's pleased her, they might eventually be granted the privilege of pleasing themselves, but this was by no means certain. In fact, a fellow member of her profession had once prevailed in court on a prostitution charge by explaining that she never actually touched the private parts of any of her clients.

Mistress Katrina usually met her clients in some of the better hotel rooms of the city, but not always. Select clients might earn the honor of cleaning her house (although admittedly not while wearing what most professional house cleaners considered appropriate floor-washing attire), doing her shopping, and her cooking, too.

The life of a dominatrix was starting to sound extremely appealing. "Why wouldn't any woman do it full time?" I wondered on the air. It all sounded so spectacular, that when Mistress Katrina issued a parting invitation to me to entertain one of her clients with her the next week, I took her seriously.

"Will there be nudity?" I wanted to know. "Will anybody expect to touch me? I do *not* want anybody to touch me."

"The beauty of being a dominatrix," said Mistress Katrina, "Is that you don't have to do anything you don't want to do." All of a sudden, I wanted to be a dominatrix almost as much as I wanted to be a talk show host. I accepted her offer—not for myself, of course, but so I could tell the listeners about it later.

On the day of the appointment, I met Mistress Katrina and a well-toned male assistant in the lobby of a reputable upmarket business hotel. "I have a reservation," she told me, obliquely, as we rolled past the front desk with her clanking bag in tow. The first part of the afternoon was a demonstration session, just for me. Her aide, who by now had stripped to a pair of gym shorts, but who didn't particularly seem to be enjoying the experience, modeled the results of Mistress Katrina's various lifts, pulleys, and ropes, culminating in his literal suspension from the hotel's closet door. It took a good bit of knot-tying, engineering, and physical strength. Gradually, the dominatrix business began to look like what it was—a lot of hard work. When I mentioned this, Mistress Katrina reacted with surprise.

"Well of course it is. Did you think it would be easy? And not only that, I have to plan each session so that it goes smoothly. The client must feel I am totally in control. I have to create a new experience each time. I have to remember what each client likes and doesn't like. It's demanding and time-consuming. Why do you think I only see one or two clients a day?"

It was pretty clear by this point that the price of having my house cleaned by a man wearing a leather harness or a frilly white ballet skirt was actually higher than it had seemed a few days ago. But by then, it was time for the real client to arrive. Mistress Katrina's assistant departed, and we heard a timid-sounding knock at the hotel room door. An unremarkably dressed man of middle age and average appearance—brown-ish sport coat, brown-ish hair, inexpensive sport slacks, likely also brown—made a quiet entrance. When Mistress Katrina gave him permission, he dropped to his knees, and greeted me, eyes downcast, as "Miss Turi, friend of my Mistress." Mistress Katrina explained that "Bob," her submissive client, enjoyed feet. Mistress Katrina's feet were his special delight. "Bob" was allowed to say that he had asked his wife whether he could worship her feet, but that she had told him that she was absolutely not interested, and that he was so grateful to have found Mistress Katrina, whose feet were, he believed, exceptionally beautiful. I wondered what kind of nut I must be when it crossed my mind that my feet weren't all that bad looking and simultaneously realized I was now mentally competing with Mistress Katrina in the "most beautiful feet" contest.

I had done a small amount of research by consulting with some of my more adventurous girlfriends, prior to my date with Mistress Katrina, so I believed I knew what I'd witness that day. I fully expected to watch as Mistress Katrina's feet were used in an elaborate self-gratification ritual. I felt a little queasy at the prospect of having to witness anything involving heavy breathing and body parts, even covered ones. But for my listeners, I steeled myself at the prospect, and resolved to practice deep breathing, in an even and calm manner, as one does to prevent motion sickness. I had hoped that the hotel room would at least have a window that opened, in case I found myself in need of restorative fresh air. There was not. I was now more than a little nervous as the moment approached when Mistress Katrina and Bob would begin...whatever it was they were about to do...involving Mistress Katrina's feet and some part, I had no idea which, of Bob.

I calmed down a little when Mistress Katrina explained she would be getting a foot massage, though my pulse shot up again when she asked whether I would like one as well. Normally, a foot massage, in the context of a nail salon, which was the only place I'd ever had one, was a relaxing, costly treat. But there's something odd that happens in your head when you are offered a foot massage from a stranger whom you *know* is deeply serious about feet and is paying for the privilege of touching yours. It's a little like vertigo. There's this abyss that opens between what is usually a fairly commonplace form of contact, and the other side, where the same exact activity or contact has changed to something completely different. And all you have to do to be part of that *other* activity, in this case, is take off your shoes and socks. I don't think much about foot massages one way or the other on an average day. It never occurs to me to imagine that the person at the nail salon who is oiling and rubbing my feet is getting anything from it, other than a tip. But I didn't want my listeners, or Mistress Katrina, to think I was a total prude, so I said yes.

I sat next to Mistress Katrina, whose shoes were already off. I allowed Bob to remove my cowboy boots and socks. I waited. Bob didn't take off any of his clothes, and he didn't seem to be breathing heavily. He looked content.

"I have a game for you," Mistress Katrina told Bob. "Close your eyes." Then Mistress Katrina entwined her feet with mine. "With your eyes closed, feel each of our feet, and tell me whose are whose, and how they are different."

I'm not sure what I expected, but as Bob closed his eyes, bent forward, and rubbed our feet, kneeling low, with his face close to them, nothing especially weird happened. I will now admit for the first time that in the interest of research, and my own genuine curiosity, I tried to sneak a surreptitious glance at the place where I thought the level of Bob's personal interest in feet might reveal itself. Since he was on his knees on the floor, with his body angled over all four of our feet, I could not.

Bob complimented Mistress Katrina on having fresh polish and slightly longer nails, which is how he said he knew which feet belonged to her; and within minutes, or so it seemed, it was all over. Bob kept his clothes on. We kept everything above our ankles on, and I assume Mistress Katrina received her appropriate remuneration. Bob thanked me for the special treat of additional foot worship, and Bob thanked Mistress Katrina for *providing* this extra treat. I thanked Mistress Katrina and left.

That evening, on the air, I relayed the experience to my listeners, including how odd it felt to be performing in such a very personal way, for their very public benefit. We talked about what I'd seen, and what I'd expected to see, and how fascinating it was that you could make a living allowing someone to spend quality time with your feet. I had to give Mistress Katrina official credit for the hard work some of her other clients obviously required for their sessions, and the listeners called in creative suggestions for common household items like wooden spoons and cat toys that could be repurposed if any of them wanted to try a few of Mistress Katrina's techniques at home. I told the listeners that I was convinced, as I still am, that most people have some interest that might be considered unusual, even kinky, if discussed in the clear light of day in a room full of strangers. We talked about whether or not Bob's wife should have allowed him to worship her feet, seeing as feet clearly made him so happy.

We talked about what, if anything, we owe our partners, and how much you should *pretend* to enjoy something that only one of you *actually* enjoys. After about an hour, I felt that we had said about all there was to say on the subject. That, I figured, was that.

About a week later, a package arrived at the station. It contained a letter and several science fiction books—the paperback pamphlet kind that hard-core sci-fi readers collect. The writer of the letter wanted me to understand that he was a successful science fiction creator. I assumed the package was a listener who'd mentioned he'd be sending me something he'd written, but that I'd forgotten it was coming. It was halfway through that evening's show when I realized that, while the nom de plume was not one I had heard before, the letter writer was. He was Bob the foot worshipper. Bob wanted me to know him. He wanted me to correspond with him. *BOB THE FOOT WORSHIPPER WANTED TO BE PART OF MY LIFE.* Slightly panicked, I reviewed my options. I wanted nothing to do with Bob the foot worshipper. He had been an experience acquired in the name of show prep. I would not have cared whether Bob was a Nobel laureate in literature or the creator of *The Matrix*. I was done with Bob, even if he offered to clean my kitchen floor for a year.

On the other side of the equation, Bob could not be expected to understand the concept of "show prep." It would not be unreasonable for Bob to assume that I had a genuine need of attention in the foot department. It was dawning on me that perhaps Bob was not done with me. I took a deep breath. I remembered what Mistress Katrina had said about being a dominatrix: "You do not have to do anything you do not want to do." I picked up the books and the letter from Bob. I put the letter in the file that I always keep in my desk: the one my producer and management know they should look at first in case something ever happens to me. It contained my research on threatening callers, stalkers, and, now, one foot worshipper. I took the books in my hand and, although it flies in the face of everything I hold sacred about books, literature, and reading, I threw them in the trash. It occurred to me that perhaps I should alert Mistress Katrina to Bob's behavior, which even I could see would be considered something of a betrayal—if not to Mistress Katrina, then to her feet. Then I remembered Mistress Katrina's collection of whips and canes. I could only guess what kind of punishment might await a client who tried to use his mistress' "treat" as a device to create a connection with somebody else, and her feet. I took pity on Bob, or perhaps I punished him. In any case, I never told.

You Don't Say

I **must admit,** I hired the woman. Serena was educated, well-spoken, and, with a year of flacking for our sister station's TV magazine show on her résumé, albeit as an unpaid student intern, she seemed to be motivated to work hard. She didn't have a lot of experience, but I thought that meant that I'd be able to train her to do what I needed. I didn't stop to think that as a fairly recent recruit to talk radio, I really had no idea what I needed.

Serena, while bright, turned out to have absolutely no common sense at all. You may think I am overstating that for the sake of dramatic effect. How about if I tell you that in a state famous for twenty-two-inch snowfalls, Serena bought a tiny baby shoe of a car, designed for the sun-kissed roads of Japan, rated by every consumer agency as having a flawed electrical system and as a handling nightmare in good weather. Serena's new car ceased to move in any predictable direction the minute a dusting of powder hit the pavement. Normally, I'd say that was none of my business and her tough luck, but with a studio located in a semi-rural field at the transmitter site, far from any public transit, a car that seemed to be drawn as though by a magnet to every nearby ditch the moment skies were cloudy was not very useful for getting to work.

When she could make it to the studio, Serena slowly ascended the learning curve of producing a radio show. She began to master call screening, finding interesting guests, and suggesting timely topics. Unfortunately, although she was now officially employed as a talk radio producer, Serena continued to have trouble understanding that radio has sound, but no pictures.

For this reason, Serena's creative contributions, like holding up strange photos during the show, often went unappreciated; except, perhaps by the newsperson, a sweet but aging veteran who, every day, gave away the punch line to Paul Harvey's *The Rest of the Story*. (His specialty was the pre-commercial spoiler: "In a moment, you'll hear how the sickly little school boy grew up to be Ray Charles, the famous musician." I half wondered whether the radio station's security guard was there in the event that some furious Paul Harvey fan showed up one day to punish the newscaster for wrecking Mr. Harvey's carefully constructed surprise endings.) I could not make Serena understand that it didn't matter how funny something looked in the paper, or in the studio—if the audience couldn't hear it, or a description of it, coming out of their radio speakers, it didn't exist. She'd cut out paparazzi shots of celebrities caught in breast-lift to ample-breast-lift catfight confrontations on the beaches of Malibu or New York and give them to me as show prep material. "Serena," I would remonstrate as gently as I could, "this picture may be worth a thousand words, but only if the audience can see it. If what you want is for me to describe to the listeners what I'm seeing, then you need to include the caption with the photo, so I know the name of this action star who is handcuffed for bar fighting while his girlfriend's toy poodle bites him in the crotch. I cannot recognize him from this grainy black and white shot in the *National Enquirer*." Serena would nod soberly and continue leaving piles of photos clipped from magazines and supermarket rags on my desk. I still had hope, though, that the concept of the radio as sound without images might come to her eventually.

Sound was problematic for Serena in other ways, too. Her aptitude as an engineer was not the reason we'd hired her, but operating an audio console is something most people can get the hang of in a few weeks or less. Serena, though, seemed to be struggling. Music started and stopped. Commercials were played at the audio level of either a moth flying past your house, or an air raid siren. The one thing I had control of from my side of the glass was my own microphone—when she remembered to turn it on from the main mixing board on her side of the glass.

Three months into the job it became clear, once and for all, that I was lousy at training producers. It was my birthday. I don't remember having told anybody at work that my birthday was coming up, but I must have. Suddenly, in the middle of the show, with the subtlety of a garbage can mechanically dumped into a truck, the Diana Ross disco hit "Upside Down" boomed through my headphones and over the airways. Serena announced, over the air, that we had a "surprise guest," and a young, heavily muscled man bounced through the engineering side of the studio door—the side where Serena sat. He was wearing a policeman's uniform, which he began to remove in time to the music, about three feet from where Serena was now standing, directly on the other side of the soundproof double-glass window from me.

If you are someone who likes surprises, then you may not understand my initial reaction to having my show unexpectedly hijacked. I was stunned to silence, but only for a moment. "There's a man in my studio," I narrated, over the *whoomp whoomp* beat and the sound of the Supreme Diva of Motown as she sang, "And he's taking off his clothes." But something was wrong. I could hear the music in my headphones, but I couldn't hear myself. I checked. My microphone control for my side of the studio was on. The music continued to *thump thump thump* in my ears, but nothing I said was going over the air. Serena, as part of her surprise, had turned off my microphone. Fifty thousand watts of radio were now broadcasting disco to my talk radio listeners, who had absolutely no idea what had just happened to my show. For all they knew, this was some sort of emergency fill-in music while a technical difficulty was resolved; or perhaps a tornado was bearing down on them, and we had mislaid the emergency warning buzzer. I couldn't narrate, or explain, that by this time there was a sunlamp-tanned, leather-thong-wearing, baton-caressing male stripper in the studio, because Serena continued to override my microphone in the control room, leaving me with no way to say anything audible to anyone.

I had never before attempted to scream loudly enough to be heard through the soundproof wall, but I still can't believe nobody in there heard me. Or at least got the point of the hand gestures. "Turn my microphone on!" I shouted. "Turn it ON."

Serena, with Buddha-like serenity—if the Buddha had been interested in watching a crotch-fondling frat boy unbuckle his fake gun and holster from his oiled, shaved torso and twirl it around his head like a lasso—was smiling, oblivious.

"Turn the mic on, Serena! None of the listeners knows what the heck is going on! THEY CAN'T SEE ANYTHING! THIS IS RADIO, DAMMIT!" Serena looked pleased. She had created the image of me she'd dreamed for herself. What fun! What a birthday surprise!

On my side of the glass, I felt like a toddler, suspended in mid-air by an adult who's just picked her up by the back of her shirt for trying to run after a fleeing-but-pretty skunk. Three months of training, and my alleged producer still didn't understand that what was important was WHAT THE LISTENERS HEARD. I threw my pencil at the glass. I was still in enough control not to throw something heavier, but by now it would have been impossible for anyone to mistake the look on my face for anything other than pure fury. I was not enjoying myself. I was not looking at the stripper. I was listening to the third long minute of Diana Ross singing over a heavy bass line, "Instinctively you give to me the love that I need, I cherish the moments with you." As the final chorus of

"Upside Down" began to play, I forgot the piece of advice that I gave Serene on her first day of work—a piece of advice that should have been as much a part of my professional persona as breathing. *"TURN THE FUCKING MICROPHONE ON!"* I bellowed, just as Serene turned the fucking microphone on.

The next day, in the station manager's office, I tried to explain, and apologize. After listening to me for ten minutes, my kind and long-suffering boss looked me in the eye and said quietly, "I own this radio station. But you can lose my license."

I do not know who first assessed the potential for unintended disaster when in the presence of any microphone. It might have been a broadcaster. It could as easily have been a head of state. I'm pretty sure that whomever it was, he or she lived through a version of my stripper-in-the-control-booth experience. My two-day suspension from KTLP gave me plenty of time to remember:

The microphone, you must assume, is always, always, on.

Part II

Therapy Works

By your mid-thirties, most women know pretty well what level of quirkiness they want, or can tolerate, in a partner. It's not like I figured it out all by myself, though. Freudian psychotherapy was taken at least as seriously as religion in my childhood home. It practically *was* a religion. In some families, if you have a problem, your mom might sit you down for a talk in the kitchen, or take you shopping. Your dad might offer a fishing trip or a walk. But in my family, if you were cutting class, or crying in your room, or staying out till three in the morning—you didn't get grounded. You certainly didn't get a new pair of shoes or a bucket of bait. You got therapy. When you're thirty-three, and every man you date seems only a slightly more functional version of your tried and failed models of years past, you see a therapist.

My dad, Harry, had this to say after my breakup with Ari, a relationship that had lasted over three years: "Well, Turi, he was better than the last one. So you're making progress." Harry, who scores off the charts at doctor-picking (although he also insisted I have my ears pierced by a surgeon) helped me locate a therapist, Dr. Kestrel. I told Dr. Kestrel my goal: to not be bored by a nice guy, should I meet one. "We can do that," said Dr. Kestrel.

Dr. Kestrel turned out to be an extremely gifted therapist. When, for example, I asked her whether I would hear my mother's voice in my head giving me a hard time about not being a lawyer for the rest of my life, she said, "Oh, you'll keep hearing her. But you'll learn to ignore her." That seemed reasonable. It also seemed reasonable that if my hormones were set for guys who either had serious problems or anger issues, then I should look for a guy who filled other criteria on my list, and wait for my hormones to catch up.

So when I met Save the Planet, I tried not to let it bother me that he was unshaven and in need of a haircut, badly dressed, and hunched over a box of pamphlets for Dan Dribbens, a terrible candidate who was running for mayor of St. Paul. I was in the middle of regretting that I'd offered myself as a speaker at a rally for Dribbens—a man who a few weeks before, had given a press conference to announce that at the age of thirty-seven, he took his clothes to a laundromat; a man who had actually said during an interview on my radio station that he smoked pot because it was impossible to go to a party where there was no pot being smoked. He answered this question on our radio station's midday show, and I could just imagine the ladies of the Upper Midwest asking each other:

"Jean? When you go to bridge club, do the girls smoke that marijuana?"

"No, Bernice, I don't think so. Maybe he's talking about Gert Johnson's quilting circle."

Unfortunately, Dribbens' opponent was even worse: Nils Nelson. I'd been introduced to Nelson socially several times, but he'd barely acknowledged me. That changed the day he was placed before me at a community event where my radio station was broadcasting live. When he realized I hosted a talk show, he expressed the sort of avid interest in me that a dog shows for its favorite toy when you hold it just out of reach. When Save the Planet, on leave from a US Senate office and on loan to the candidate we'd come to call Dan "Doobie" Dribbens, was told of my feelings about Nils Nelson—feelings I'd expressed by walking, just as any other voter would, into the local party office and asking what the heck the party was doing to stop Nils—Save the Planet called to ask whether I could come out for a rally to introduce his candidate.

"But I really don't like your candidate all that much. I just detest Nelson," I demurred.

"That's fine. You don't actually have to say anything about Dribbens. You just have to get the crowd worked up and introduce him. The senator will be there, plus our other candidate for US Senate." That was tantalizing. I'd heard Save the Planet's senator speak before. He had a real southern tent-revival style; not surprising, considering his Virginia roots, and that was refreshing, and rare, in our buttoned-down city.

"Okay. I can come on a personal basis. Not representing the station."

"That would be fine."

I found out later that Save the Planet didn't listen to commercial radio, so all he knew about me was that I came into the local party office to complain about the scatterbrained Dribbens campaign. The party volunteers had recognized me. They'd been to the state fair a few months earlier.

I must tell you a little about state fairs, in case you don't attend them. In some states, nearly the entire population attends the fair, every year. You may never feel the need to visit a "crop art" pavilion, or cheer at a pig race; though if you go through life without having seen Elvis Presley and Ronald Reagan portrayed in collages made of corn kernels and lentils, you have truly missed something.

If you live where everybody goes to the fair, then you may have experienced the phenomenon of feeling as though you've met everyone who lives in your entire state—because you have. If you have to perform your four-hour show live in front of anyone, fan or foe, who shows up at the fair, five days a week, for almost three weeks, then pretty much everyone in the state *has* seen you. You will discover this when you are swimming laps at your local Y, with a cap and goggles on, and can't possibly look less like yourself, and somebody calls you up on the air the next day and thanks you for making room in your lane for him. What kind of savant recognizes someone wearing swimming goggles and a latex cap? I can't even pick out my own kid in a little league uniform.

You start to feel like the entire state is creepily stalking you, but really, it's just the fair. I had no anonymity among state fair patrons.

"Where is this rally going to be?"

"It will be at Holy Temptress College, in the Chapel, Sunday, October 30, at eleven."

"Won't we get in the way of the services?"

"Holy Temptress isn't that kind of college. See you there."

On Sunday morning, at 9:00 a.m., an hour at which night people are seldom awake, never mind washed and dressed, I tossed a light, rayon, art-y coat into the back seat of my shiny black sports car, even though it was nearly November in the snowbelt. "You don't want to be schlepping a heavy winter coat around a hot chapel," I reasoned. "You'll sweat to death."

I noticed, when I pulled into the Holy Temptress parking lot, that a rather strong wind was blowing a few flakes of snow, sparse, but the size of quarters, horizontally toward the chapel. I followed the flakes. There, not inside the chapel, where they were supposed to be, but *outside*, where the flakes were swirling in a small, localized, tornado-shaped formation, was a table with posters, fliers, and what looked suspiciously like a microphone. This did not bode well. With evident concern, I approached the table. "Which one of you is Save the Planet?" I enquired politely, not wanting to start out on the wrong foot. Four hands belonging to four separate volunteers pointed to a scruffy figure in not-too-clean-looking polar fleece, who was, at that moment, crouched over a box of Dan "Doobie" Dribbens campaign literature. He looked up. I noticed that he had nice eyes, but he wasn't really my type. I liked the type who looked, at minimum, clean.

"You're not going to be indoors, are you?" It was part question, part stating the obvious.

"We thought we'd move the rally outside, to attract more people," the scruffy stranger admitted.

"No wonder this party is always losing," I said, in one of those voices that isn't quite loud, but which carries quite a way in a courtyard. "You don't know enough to come out of the cold." I watched to see what my host would do. He continued to gaze up at me with eyes that were even bluer than they'd looked at first, and I realized that, under the beard, he might be rather attractive. "I'll bet you don't have any coffee, either."

"No, but I'd be happy to go get you a cup," offered the blue-eyed, now rather interesting looking, stranger. "There's a coffee shop down the street."

Dr. Kestrel and I, I remembered at that moment, had agreed that I should pick a guy who was not my type. This guy with the dark, sleep-deprived circles under his eyes, who looked like he'd just spent three weeks in the wilderness living off berries and wild game, was definitely not my usual type.

"I'll go myself," I said, "and you may come with me."

In the block and a half walk to the coffee shop, where I bought Save the Planet (STP) a cup of coffee for which he forgot to thank me, I ascertained that he had a house and a dog, but no wife or children, and that he was not a full-time Dan "Doobie" Dribbens employee. Rather, he had been leant as a "hired gun" for the obviously troubled Dribbens campaign by the office of the aforementioned senator, for whom he served as political director. I'm not sure what information meant more to me: that he might be available, in a state with a noticeable lack of single men, or that he was not one of Dribbens' true believers.

I don't remember anything about the actual rally, except that it was very, very cold. This memory was later confirmed by the candidate for the other seat in the United States Senate, who also attended, and who also froze. She was wearing a wool coat. STP offered me his polar fleece, but it looked like it might harbor pests or thorns. Also, it would not have worked with my outfit. Even though it was freezing, I certainly wasn't going to be caught in a skanky winter coat, even wearing makeup. I thanked him for his chivalrous gesture. He pointed out that it was in his self-interest not to have a hypothermic speaker.

After fulfilling my commitment to whip up the troops to go out and vote, I fled.

Then, I did something completely out of character: I called STP at the Dribbens office. "Do you need any more volunteers for anything?" I asked.

"Well...we're about done here, but we are going out tonight to put flyers on doorknobs and car windshields." I must have been really, really, invested in my new stratagem of dating someone who was not my usual type, because normally any guy who asked me to go around in the dark and spread political litter on innocent peoples' doorsteps wouldn't have gotten as far as giving me the address of headquarters. But I told him I'd volunteer for it, if I could volunteer with him. What I actually said was, "I'll go if I can go with you, because you're nice."

When I picked up my box of fliers the next day, Dribbens' headquarters, in a vacant storefront, was a manic, desperate scene. The candidate recognized me and swooped in for a chat, hoping perhaps for some word of optimism, which I absolutely did not have. I managed to detach myself for a few moments, to speak with STP.

"I'm heading out. It looks like you're too busy to leave," I said.

"Yeah. Looks like it. Would you like to come to our victory party?" he asked.

"What makes you so sure it's going to be a victory party?"

"Well, I kind of have to say that."

If you asked me to pick one moment, that was when I realized there was something special about STP, a political operative with a significant track record of electoral success who could nevertheless admit he was on a sinking ship. That's the kind of honesty that a person who is inundated daily with press releases and who hears a snootfull of talk radio, appreciates. Candor in a man is like driving a reliable car. It may not turn heads, but it won't leave you stranded at the side of the highway with high-speed traffic blowing the contents out of your purse as you search for your towing insurance card. If I were really looking for a reliable car kind of guy, as I had told Dr. Kestrel, then it appeared I had found one.

"Anyhow," he said, "we're having a victory party, and you're welcome to come."

I left by myself with the box of fliers. Unwilling to dig through shoveled crusts of ice to leave Dribbens lit on peoples' snowy car windshields (the flakes of yesterday's rally had turned out to be the early stages of a record-breaking Halloween blizzard), I drove home and fliered the heated hallways of my apartment building instead, tossing the remainder of the literature into the building's giant blue recycling bin. Fortunately, Dribbens lost by a huge margin, relieving me of guilt.

The Dribbens victory party was held at the most historic and grandest hotel in town. To the surprise of no one who could read a poll, it turned out to be a "consolation party," which meant that a lot of people were drinking heavily. I dropped by after my shift ended, at about 10:30 p.m. As the women of the campaign doused the last sparks of hope for victory in local beer, I noticed how many of them seemed fond of Save the Planet. In fact, I was having trouble getting near him, as woman after woman threw her arms around him, and avowed that working with him had been the best thing about the election. I was not sure I had ever dated a man who had a lot of women friends, but it seemed like something I should report back to my therapist. I would also let her know that STP was a generous tipper of waitresses. As a former waitress, I found this to be an excellent predictor of personality.

The evening dragged on for far longer than I wished to be there. I was looking forward to having a few minutes alone with STP, but nobody was leaving, certainly not a healthy looking blonde woman with significantly more drinking stamina than I possessed. She seemed to have the identical goal of spending a bit of time with STP. I knew I'd never outlast her. Resigned, I congratulated the tableful of volunteers and supporters, paid my bill, excused myself, and walked, slowly, down the long chintz-pattern-carpeted, dark-wood-paneled hallway to the hotel's grand entrance. With seconds to go before entering the polished brass and glass revolving door, STP appeared at my elbow.

"So, I'd like to see you again."

"That would be fine, but you'll have to call me, and ask to see me again." (Dr. Kestrel had said nothing about changing my demanding behavior once I located a guy who was not my type.)

"I don't have your phone number. When I booked you for the rally, you didn't give it to me."

"I know, but now I might. To get my phone number, you'd have to *ask* for my phone number."

"May I have your phone number?"

"Yes." I handed over my phone number

"I haven't slept in three days. I never sleep before an election. So, I'll get some rest, and when I wake up, I'll call you if that's okay?"

"That's okay."

The next night, I met the Guatemalan clown pants.

Guatemalan Clown Pants

My phone was ringing with unusual determination. Or maybe it just felt that way. When I get home from work at 10:30 p.m., I have supper. Usually, I don't want to talk to anybody. I've been talking to listeners and callers for the last three hours. I didn't want to talk. I answered anyhow. Before there was caller ID, if you had a neurotic fear of hearing someone say, "She called you from her hospital bed, but you didn't pick up to hear her last words," that's what you did.

"I've slept," Save the Planet reported.

"That's great. How do you feel about the election results now that it's over?"

"It's over. Now I can go back to work in the Senate office and stop getting calls from people who want to know how to get invited to the kind of parties that Dribbens claims he goes to."

"Well," I said, remembering my deal with Dr. Kestrel that I would do things differently when it came to dating, "I'm about to cook dinner. And, if you'd like, you may come over to my house and join me for dinner. I realize that it is late, and some people might misunderstand this invitation, but there aren't any decent restaurants open in this town at 10:30, and now it's nearly eleven, and I'm hungry. So, you are welcome to come for dinner, as long as you are clear that dinner is exactly and only what this invitation is for."

It was a rather long speech, and it may have taken some of the romance out of being invited for dinner to the home of a person you've just met, and who presumably you find attractive and interesting, but it turned out there was a different kind of problem with my invitation.

Save the Planet is a teeny bit clueless at deciphering subtext, and it wasn't just that he was still tired. My initial assessment has borne out over the years. For example: once, in an effort to stop him from telling my friend Jason, an actor, about a newspaper review in which Jason was unfavorably compared to the TV pitchman for Sham Wow miracle cleaning cloths, I nudged Save the Planet gently, under the table. "Why are you kicking me?" he demanded indignantly. So to my offer of dinner and only dinner, he responded, "Oh, I've already eaten." This guy was definitely not my usual type.

"Well, if you like, you might want to keep me company while I have my dinner, and then you could have coffee and dessert." There was a pause. I counted to eight. Slowly. He got it.

"That would be great."

"Okay, let me give you directions. You get on the highway—"

"Sorry, but I can't get on the highway," he interrupted.

"Do you have a car? Are you afraid of driving on the highway?" I prepared myself for a tale of a traumatic auto accident; or, if not, to go back to my usual type, who had no problem driving on highways, often in conditions or at times when they should not.

"No, but I'll be on my bike."

You may remember reading that we had just experienced a record-breaking blizzard. The roads were still rutted with salty gray slush and ice. It was extremely dark, and freezing cold.

"A motorcycle bike, or a bicycle bike?"

"A bicycle bike. Just give me the address and I'll find my way. It should take me about twenty minutes."

Half an hour later, a very different looking man than the one I remembered seeing at the hotel knocked at my door. This one had a beard that was frozen into tiny hail-like ice balls, and he wore black Lycra bike tights with a padded crotch that made him look like a pervy high wire act. Thank goodness he seemed to realize the ridiculousness of the ensemble.

"May I use your bathroom to change?" he asked politely. I gestured toward the bathroom and left him to take on a normal human appearance while I finished the dinner preparations.

Moments later, STP emerged, wearing a pink community radio T-shirt, polar fleece black, red, yellow, and blue patterned socks, and a pair of striped ethnic Guatemalan clown pants. At least, that is what I assumed Guatemalan men would wear if Guatemalan men worked the center ring for Barnum & Bailey: brightly colored cotton sewn in the cut of baggy, shapeless sweatpants with an elastic waist. The look was Berkeley, 1978. I had seen it on album covers, and on panhandlers in San Francisco.

I struggled to keep my face neutral. People go to therapy, I reminded myself, because they want to change something about their lives. You spent a lot of time and money trying to change. You want *not* to be bored by a nice guy when you meet him. This seems like a nice guy. Are you really going to write him off after dinner because he is wearing an absurd pair of clown pants? Clown pants are a lot easier to change than a cocaine habit, or a need to suddenly leave the country for unexplained reasons, or a violent temper.

"Where did you get those pants?" I enquired.

"Guatemala. I biked through South America a few years ago."

"Did you bring back any other pants?"

"No, but I have a lot of jeans. That's what I mostly wear."

"Good to know." I considered the last three guys I had dated. One moved to Texas, after courting me for three months, the minute I seemed interested. Another had resumed his drinking habit after we'd been together about a year. The third had alarmed me by slamming his fist on the dashboard of his SUV hard enough to crack it during an argument over a production of *The House of Blue Leaves*.

"So," I asked, "would you like caf or decaf?"

White Out

A blizzard had immobilized the Twin Cities.

Even the intrepid newspaper delivery people were stuck in their trucks.

Because I had to be on the air, my boss—who was known on the air by this time as "The Queen," sent a huge black and shiny SUV to pick me up and transport me to the station's suburban studios. A trip that customarily took ten minutes consumed the better part of an hour, as we crawled through drifts and crunched across icy roadway.

Although I arrived well within business hours for my afternoon drive show, there was nobody in the entire building but the driver, The Queen, and a red-eyed engineer who had been on duty for nearly thirty-six hours. His hair looked like a pile of greasy bicycle chains. I was grateful for the soundproof glass between us, because on my quick visit to his side of the sound booth to check in, I'd been nearly overcome by the funk of unwashed David-Bowie-T-shirt warmed to maximum aroma by several thousand watts of broadcasting equipment.

Retreating to my desk, I rummaged around to see if any mail had come. Nothing.

With no newspapers, and no US mail, I grabbed a file of clippings and notes I'd put aside for a "slow news day" (though with over four feet of snow on the ground, and more coming down, life hadn't exactly been uneventful). A khaki-colored padded envelope slid from the overstuffed manila file, and from it rolled an old-fashioned steel reel, with actual half-inch tape neatly coiled in audiophile fashion, "tails out." Reel to reel tape, as opposed to the consumer product—cassette tape—was a tipoff that the envelope had likely been sent by someone in the broadcasting industry, so I took a second look at it, and stuck a finger into the envelope, rooting around for a letter or some clue as to who had sent the thing.

There was a note: "This is to thank you for the hours of listening and laughter. Your fan, Patrick Jacobsen." The note was on letterhead from the local new-age jazz station. Mystified, I made my way to the under-equipped back corner of the transmitter site that served as our station's production studio, where commercials and promotional announcements were created. Relieved to find a functioning reel-to-reel recorder, I rewound, cued up the tape, and pressed play.

Instinctively, my head whipped around, looking to confirm that the mellifluous voice I heard was actually coming from the studio's speakers. "Turi Ryder," was all it said. But how it said it! The voice was deep, warm, and confident. I'd never heard one more gorgeous, while less affected.

Next followed an artfully arranged montage of callers and pieces of monologue, culled from an assortment of my shows. It made me sound brilliant. It made me sound hilarious. It made me sound more interesting than anything I had ever actually done on the air. And then there was that voice again. "Turi Ryder. Afternoons on KTLP."

I sat still for a good ten seconds. Then I raced out to see if The Queen was still in her office. She was. "Come hear this," I grabbed her arm in excitement. "You have to hear this tape someone sent me." Dutifully, The Queen followed me back to the dingy production room. The Queen is tall. She practically had to stoop to enter. I played the tape again. I liked it even better the second time. I looked over expectantly at The Queen. She never disappoints me. "Well," she said, "can we hire him?"

Patrick Jacobsen, when I met him, turned out to be a six-foot-four, blond, long-locked, chiseled, extremely beautiful and very young man. He was quiet. He was funny. He was a proudly out gay man. I adored him. We hired him to be the voice of KTLP. The station voice is the voice you hear on all the promotional announcements created by your station, for your station. Patrick continued to create promos for me that made me feel someone was writing a love letter to my show every time I heard one.

Patrick's goal was to move to Los Angeles; so our Twin Cities consultant hooked him up with a radio station in LA that needed a production director, and Patrick moved to the land of permanent sunshine, and entertainment dissembling. It took him a while to catch on. His first Thanksgiving, he invited his new circle of acquaintances to a home cooked,

Midwestern-style turkey dinner. They all accepted. None showed up. Patrick, however, was a quick study.

Before long, he'd found a gym, bought a Jaguar, and fallen in love with a gifted and beautiful theater director who ultimately commanded stages in four coastal cities and Broadway.

Patrick's career ascended until he was one of the best known and consistently working narration and voiceover talents in film and television. Through it all, he lent his creativity, and his delicious sound, to the station back home in Minnesota. LA would eventually do its worst to him, but not for several more years.

The Way to a Woman's Heart

Radio still has a few good perks, though these have shrunk in size and impressiveness over the years. When you're on the air at a music station, there's still a never-ending supply of free promotional T-shirts, tote bags, and beer koozies. You used to be able to see a lot of concerts, car shows, and sporting events. Those have grown scarcer. But whatever format you work in, from classical to top 40, you can nearly always obtain the proverbial free lunch or dinner. Yes, there is such a thing.

Your gratis meals will vary widely, from gourmet restaurant scrip to whatever the Elks, Eagles, or Rotary clubs have on the buffet line when you volunteer as the master of ceremonies for their charity auctions. Food is constantly delivered to radio stations by grills, bars, and donut joints looking for a free plug. Management usually understands that if they are going to underpay their support staff, they had better not get in the way of a shout out to the establishment that just sent over pizza for twenty people.

The corollary to the "free food wherever you can find it" policy embraced by working radio personalities, is the "never eat anything prepared by a listener" rule. It's not personal, but all of us, from the most beloved, effervescent midday host to the most careless production director, fear the occasional psychotic listener armed with rat poison or a bottle of Ex-Lax™. Even overnight DJs, people who often forage through the coleslaw at the bottom of yesterday's conference room deli tray, looking for scraps of turkey and pickles, strictly adhere to this rule. In fact, the words "a listener sent it" can produce in someone just about to consume a yummy-smelling chocolate chip cookie a combination gag reflex and high-velocity throw that would make any major league pitcher envious.

My first meal with Save the Planet was scheduled to occur the same night I acted as the master of ceremonies for a charity bachelor auction. I could have feasted on the free hors d'oeuvres there: caviar on slices of hard boiled egg, smoked salmon, and some kind of spinach and cheese savory pastry, but I saved my appetite. STP had invited me to a personally prepared dinner.

Women are encouraged to distribute compliments about a man's cooking as freely as a department store gives out shopping bags—even when a man's cooking is less tasty than the bag's string handle. This is a terrible idea. Never praise the cooking of someone who can't cook. Food preparation is one of those subjects that should be graded on a pass/fail scale. While many men cook:

1. A man watching a football game is not paying attention to the pasta.

2. Beware of men who bake from their own "special recipes." It simply means they didn't follow the directions.

3. Nothing tastes good after you've waited three hours for it.

STP, for our debut dining date, had offered to prepare Mexican food. That sounded like an excellent idea, since Mexican food is warm, soft, and comforting. But there's no comfort, I now know, in the words STP said to me for the first time that night—words, time has taught me to dread.

"It will just be a few minutes."

For some people, any phrase with the word *just* in it, actually means *not*; as in "your dinner will *not* be ready until several hours after you would normally have brushed your teeth and gone to bed." So instead of saying, "I know you are waiting in your sexiest nightgown for me to clean up the kitchen and come to bed, but I think it's really important that I check on the status of the compost pile and bring a few pieces of sporting gear in from the yard before I watch a rerun on TV," some people's boyfriends might say, "I'll be right in. I'm *just* going to take care of something in the garage."

This use of the word *just* is also common in sales pitches. There, the phrase, "Just $9.99 a month, plus shipping and handling," actually means "The sixty-cents worth of exercise

DVDs we're sending you will cost you $9.99 a month for the next ten years, and there will also be a charge of $14 each month for ten cents worth of bubble wrap, an envelope, and bulk postage."

I waited for my Mexican food. Save the Planet had prepared nachos as an appetizer, in advance. Well in advance. These nachos were ready for their three-thousand-mile oil change. The grease from the cheese had soaked into the undercoating of chips. What was left of the cheese resembled orange shoelaces. Little strings of cheese tied the greasy chips into a solid mass. There were no beans or avocados, but there was some homemade salsa the taste and consistency of spicy, watery tomato juice. Poured on the chips, it reduced them to oily cornmeal dough, with those floating cheese strings as dental floss at the top.

None of this boded well for the rest of the meal, but I optimistically hoped this was because the chef had been devoting his energies to the main course. The dish of the evening would be black beans with rice and tortillas—salad on the side. What eventually appeared on the plate were, in fact, black beans. Unfortunately, they were still in much the same condition in which they had been put into the pot: hard, raw, and without discernible seasoning of any kind.

When you go through the bulk bin section of the supermarket, many things may tempt you: the rice crackers, the sesame sticks, the candy corn, chocolate-covered peanuts, even the gummy worms. But you've probably never once been tempted to dip your hand into the bulk black bean bin and pop a few into your mouth. Cooking time is the key factor here.

The salad did not compensate. There's such a thing as "seven layer salad." There's also "seven layer dip." You can buy it around Super Bowl season at warehouse stores and supermarkets. The idea is to cut down through the salad, layer by layer, so that each person eating gets a serving of all the goodies. However, it appeared that the salad on tonight's menu was being served one layer at a time, and this salad had an entire layer no less than two inches thick comprised entirely of purple onion. That was the layer I got. Giving STP the benefit of the doubt, there may have been other layers to the salad. I observed some lettuce on his side of the salad bowl. He had an awful lot of onions, too.

"Hope you don't mind," STP said sweetly, "I just had a few pieces of broccoli left, so I put them in, even though they aren't quite as fresh as the other ingredients." What other ingredients? It would have been fine if the rest of the salad were carbon-datable, if only there *were* a rest of the salad. The onion pile on one side of my plate was growing quite large. And there was the bean problem. I now had a huge bowl of them, and underneath my portion, the size of which would have made a Dickensian orphan moan with joy, I had previously noticed an equally frightening dollop of rice. Perhaps that was where the flavor and spices were hiding? I began an excavation project—Journey to the Center of Your Dinner. Rummaging about for a bit of rice, I came up with some more of the barely cooked beans. I mouthed the forkful.

It was about as chewy and comforting a process as bringing one's teeth firmly down on a piece of tinfoil.

Save the Planet watched for approbation. He had a dear and concerned expression on his face. I have seen the look before, on dogs, when they bring in a particularly well-decomposed specimen of wildlife. "How is your dinner?" he asked.

When you come to one of these moments—usually early in the dating process—you often end up resolving questions far greater than the simple query that's been laid before you. The bigger question, figuratively and literally, on the table was: Is this worth it?

Let's just say this turns out to be the partner of your dreams, and this is the cooking—of which he is so proud—that you may be eating for the rest of your life. Perhaps he will be talking with a therapist about his need to nurture and sense of rejection if you are not delighted by the repast. On the other hand—actually, on the plate in front of me—was really, truly awful food. I decided I was not going to eat it. I couldn't have eaten it if I'd tried, because it was nothing more than raw onions, uncooked beans, and flavorless gummy rice.

I have dated men who were alcoholics, who cheated and lied and were neglectful fathers and rotten ex-husbands. But I have *never* dated a man who starved me and then offered silage for dinner. I also wasn't going to put any more of the beans in my mouth if I could help it. So I said, "Thanks for the invitation, and for doing all this work."

"But how do you *like it*?" he asked again.

"It was really thoughtful of you to do all this," I parried.

Under direct attack, I made a calculation: man of my dreams, plus thirty years of crappy food, plus lying about it, equals...somebody else. My recent months of therapy with Dr. Kestrel, however, had made me strong enough to offer him a final chance at escape.

"I am glad that you made all these things for me. It was truly nice of you."

Tact quota exhausted, I unwittingly took another bite of the beans, and realized that there was a whole pressure cooker of them on the stove. Plainly, this man thought that this food was good enough to eat for several days. So when he asked one more time, "But what about the meal?" I just figured, the hell with it. So what if I am thirty-four-years-old and stuck in Minnesota where all the men except this one are married at twenty-three to women they have known since they were in high school. So what if the last guy I dated here was more interested in picking out tile for his bathroom whirlpool than having sex in it. So what if he sent his kids to a religious camp where the pamphlets advertised that activities included tennis, hiking, and converting heathens. So what. At least I ate well. And then, out loud, I told Save The Planet:

"Obviously, you have not adjusted to the fact that here in America, we are in the enviable position of being able to eat for pleasure. We, who have the good fortune of being able to walk to the nearest supermarket where we can purchase any ingredients we wish, should take advantage of our luck. Just because one chooses to make a meal from the simple staples of a third-world country does not mean that that meal should taste like it fell off a Red Cross truck. I have seen late-night pleas for international aid where children drinking filth next to the family water buffalo seemed to be enjoying that mixture better than they'd like what's on my plate. Salt has not been a symbol of the evils of the feudal system for several hundred years now, and can be easily found both in drive-through restaurants and on pavement in winter. So what health or political point are you attempting to make by leaving it out of dinner altogether? You couldn't fool me into liking this meal if I'd been lying on a cot for days, with flies buzzing around me and a physician from Doctors Without Borders making an impassioned request for penicillin standing nearby. And while we're at it, have you ever heard of the concept of the multi-vegetable salad? If it doesn't have at least three items in it, it is not salad. It is a raw vegetable. Don't even ask about the nachos. Nachos are not supposed to be the Mexican equivalent of day-old refrigerated French toast. I would have been better off eating downstairs with Mickey the dog. His food is probably tastier."

My chef was stricken. "That's not true. Mickey loves my cooking, dontcha Mick?" Much tail wagging from under the table.

"Dogs don't eat raw beans," I said. "They have more sense."

"He loves my cooking." The gauntlet was down.

"Okay," I told him, "put some of the beans in Mickey's bowl. Then we'll watch him not eat them." My host scooped beans into the dog bowl. Mickey approached, sniffed, and returned to wagging his tail. STP tried to coax Mickey to take a bean. Mickey politely refused. STP made a desperate move. He picked up the bowl, cleverly submerged a nacho globule as a "come hither" to Mickey, then replaced it on the floor. This time, Mickey was interested. He circled the bowl twice, delicately used a side fang to extract the nacho clump from the beans, almost simultaneously making a dash from the room, and down the basement stairs. My prospective future life partner was visibly shaken.

"Mick, Mick," he kept saying. "How could you do this to me, buddy?"

I am not gracious in victory. I gloated. Crestfallen, STP looked at me carefully, as though he were making a deal he might later regret.

"Would you like to go out for dinner next time?"

I stopped gloating.

"Tomorrow night," I said. "That would be nice."

A Head Made of Butter

I judged the belt sander races. It was confusing, but it looked like the guys racing belt sanders down a homemade track had a good time. We held a party on a barge on the Mississippi River, and a garage sale in a giant suburban movie theater parking ramp (booth fees to charity). When a fire burned down an apartment building in town, we daisy-chained a whole bunch of microphone cords together, and I broadcast and fundraised live from outside our studios.

But no personal appearance can do to your life or career what the state fair can do. The state fair runs for twelve days, at the end of every August. If I'd stayed in the Twin Cities, my funeral would likely have been held on day thirteen, just as the cream puffs and magic dusting cloth supplies dwindled to an end.

The first year after I was hired, our station owner proudly informed her KTLP staff that she'd been able to secure, by trading commercials for materials, our very own small state fair studio, from which our entire airstaff would be broadcasting live. We'd be seen and heard by all fairgoers, from the Future Farmers of America, who raised iridescently green and gold show chickens, to the town ladies who bake pies with fillings brighter than nail polish and make hot corn relish that can peel lipstick—and possibly your lips—right off your face.

For me, the live afternoon broadcast meant lining up three weeks of clothes, outfit by outfit, in my closet. I learned the hard way that after day four, I could no longer think about what looked good with what. Arriving at corporate headquarters, fully prepared, two hours before my show, I hopped the station's minibus shuttle, press credentials prominently displayed on the windshield, to the fairgrounds. Then, in ninety-degree heat and nearly 100 percent humidity, I would perform for the assembled fans and hecklers inside a shed the size of your average refrigerator carton, until the claustrophobia rising in my chest like an inflating beach toy forced me to venture outside to the studio's little deck. There, I could sweat with the listeners, and perform live monologues, tell new and old stories, and greet Minnesota's citizens, senior and junior, until my voice ran out, followed by signing autographs until my hand froze into a stiff claw.

The off-duty police officers who provided our security on fair days, and at the station, had an even tougher time than we did. Several of KTLP's air personalities attracted stalkers and sworn enemies; both because of our political views, and because—it is my opinion—something about a disembodied voice gives people who already *hear* disembodied voices just the push they need to take manic, dangerous actions. One of our protectors also confessed to me that while he'd loved coming to the fair as a kid, going to the fair as an adult was ruined by walking among so many people he'd arrested for everything from shoplifting to child abuse. A few free milkshakes were not going to make his day any easier.

Year two of my contract, I tried everything I could think of to get out of performing at the fair, which by then, I had renamed the state F-word. I offered to visit the dairy barn before opening day and do a photo-op with the Dairy Princess while she had her head sculpted in butter. I promised to show up incognito and give out free plastic bags with the station's logo on them. I volunteered to switch places with Serena, and let her host the show as a gimmick, while I ran the main board back at the studios.

The Queen remained unmoved. On the third day of the second year, I accidently discovered the only way out of hosting my show live from the Minnesota State Fair when I stopped for a late bite at a sushi restaurant on my way home. By day five, there was no argument about whether or not I could broadcast. I was lying wrapped in towels inside my bathtub, into which I had crawled to minimize the impact of a rather severe case of food poisoning. Even as a feverish, shaking, leaking mess, in the moments between chills, I believed I'd been spared worse. As I showered for the twelfth time that morning, I gratefully prayed. "Four fewer days of state fair broadcasts! Thank you, unsafe food handlers of the world."

Tough as it was, the state F-word taught me a few valuable things. It was at the state fair that we could really gauge the impact that the station was having. Our first year, a small but loyal group came out to greet us. By my final summer appearance, the crowds had grown so large, for all of our air talents' shows, that we couldn't tell where they ended and the line for the bungee jump began. I saw with my own eyes the connection between the audience and me, which before I had only sensed. To watch people listening, instead of just imagining them on the other side of their radios, was powerful and affecting. It made me want to do better work. I also learned that, according to one farmer, my show, when played in the dairy barn, made his cows give tastier milk.

Your Zone of Cheapness

I **started to** believe that I might not be living at the edge of financial ruin for the rest of my life. Not that I wasn't prepared to continue walking on the fragile crust of solvency that passes for terra firma in the broadcasting business. Most radio veterans would admit that one of the qualities needed for success, one that's nearly as important as talent and hard work, is the ability to survive on almost no money at all.

That is why, even if you didn't have one before, radio can make you end up with a bigger than average "zone of cheapness." Your zone of cheapness, also known as your "Inner Scrooge," does not disappear when you find success. It stays with you for a lifetime. Fortunately, my Inner Scrooge was, thanks to KTLP, now partially balanced by an "Inner Kim," as in Kim Kardashian, the celebrity known for, among other things, buying a Swarovski crystal-encrusted freezer costing over $300,000.

Some kids are raised with parents who, household budgets permitting, encourage their children's Inner Kims; cheerfully honoring requests for electronics, makeup, trips, lessons, and clothes. In Harry and Eva's house, Scrooge ruled. The stock response to requests for any of these was "No." So it took a long while for me to liberate my Inner Kim. But even if you are not in radio, have money, and are usually a generous person, it is still highly probable you have a zone of cheapness.

Save the Planet revealed his zone of cheapness about three weeks after we started dating. His zone of cheapness is parking. STP believes all parking should be free, just like water and air and seats on the lawn at Chicago's Pritzker Pavilion. I am not inclined to toss my keys to a valet at every restaurant in town, but three to six bucks—depending on your area—on a metered space at the curb does not strike me as profligate. Save the Planet will look for a side street, even if he's running fifty minutes late.

The first inkling I had that STP was parking-fee averse was on a winter night in Minneapolis. It was the kind of cold night where your car engine makes a sound, if you can get it running at all, as though every pot and pan in your house were being thrown down a flight of stairs, and at the bottom, ground into metallic hamburger. It was the kind of windy, freezing, cold where, if your scarf unwinds and accidently blows off your face, you have exactly thirty seconds to chase it down the street before you lose sensation in your nose and lips.

As we drove to the hip little concert venue in downtown Minneapolis where John Hiatt was playing, past the heaped gray salty snow piles barricading the sidewalks of the nightclub district, my new sweetheart suddenly seemed to levitate an inch off the driver's seat with excitement.

"Look! There! Right there!" he cried out, his voice gleeful. "A parking space!"

"Yes," I agreed, peering through the sleet, "that is a parking space. But there are also parking spots available in downtown Joplin, Missouri, and Armonk, New York. And none of these locations, our present one included, is close enough to where we're going to be relevant. Please keep driving."

"No. This is good," he said, sliding his car confidently into the spot. Since it was early in our relationship, and I was trying to be agreeable, I swallowed the obscenity-laced tirade I would normally have given as I stumbled across gravel salt and ice for the nine-block walk to the club, by which time I could feel none of my extremities.

I was wearing "club attire." Club attire, when I was thirty-four and not married, included knee-high black leather boots with three-inch heels and a short leather jacket with red snakeskin inserts. There was nothing warm about it.

Save the Planet must have heard me say something under my breath, but since he was hearing it through his wool ski cap and my twice-wound-around-my-face alpaca scarf, what he seemed to have understood was that I was not willing to wear high-heeled boots in the wintertime anymore, and that was fine with him, since it gave him a chance to stop in at REI to check out mountaineering boots he thought I might like.

REI is the direct line to Save the Planet's Inner Kim. The proof was in his basement. A visitor to STP's basement could not help but notice that every form of camping gear, bike equipment, and fishing wear was stacked, suspended, or piled up under the entire floor plan of STP's modest bungalow. The REI seasonal brochure was as titillating to him as the Victoria's Secret lingerie catalog is to many other gentlemen.

Before KTLP, I lived for so long in my zone of cheapness, that I'd quit noticing it. My first job in radio at WVPD still left me qualified for food stamps. But when I finally turned the corner and landed my first salaried position at Drivin' 99, I experienced an epiphany in front of the dairy shelf at the neighborhood supermarket.

Clutching my shopping list, I stood absolutely still before the cottage cheese case, feeling guilty and ashamed. For months, I had been buying the generic brand—grim little curds, swimming in what looked like gray skim milk. Thanks to my new job, I could afford the Breakstone's premium cottage cheese, which cost fully twice as much and spooned up like ice cream, if I wanted it. As a compromise, I was ready to buy the store brand, priced in the middle, but not as tasty. It took about twenty minutes for me to make my peace with the spendiest spread, but I did it, and have never looked back. My Inner Kim also loves lox.

My Kim is also known to engage in retaliatory and compensatory emotional purchasing—frequently in the form of art or antiques. These purchases usually happen at the end of a particularly horrible day at a radio station.

Years ago, I worked for a compulsive and sadistic boss. He used to do things like order me to show up at my desk two hours before my show...just because. Then he'd say things like, "Are you sure you were at your desk at 1:00 p.m.? Do you want to bet your job on it? Shall we call the security guard and ask him to look at the security sign-in log to see what time you signed into the building?"

Since I'd taken this job on a trial arrangement basis, my contract was only short term. I hadn't moved my stuff to this large but distant city yet. Instead, I sublet the apartment of an aspiring actress friend in an area that turned out to be right next door to a major outdoor trysting spot for gay men. The hiking trail was thus off limits to anyone wanting a simple walk in the woods. Instead, the woods had come to my apartment in the form of fleas, which feasted on my friend's resident cat when men were in short supply. The leaseholder had taken her tabby with her, but not her furniture or the insects that were silently hiding in the cushions, waiting for a suitable new tenant to arrive. The fleas discovered me all at once, in the middle of the night. I woke up to find myself the blood supper of vermin.

After locating the building manager, who had a standing deal with a pest exterminator, I arrived at my workplace, an LA talk radio station, for three hours of broadcasting, followed by an hour of abuse at the hands of management. By the time I left the office, nearly in tears, I needed the kind of solace only a major Kim move could provide. Meandering home slowly, to allow the bug bombers time for their poison to set in, the window of an Oriental rug shop drew me like a magnet. Inside, seated in the middle of a red-themed Kerman, surrounded by the beauty of a traditional artwork in a design hundreds of years old, I felt nourished. The credit card flew out of my wallet, and the bill, when it came, was paid without complaint. My Kim was satisfied.

You don't always know where somebody's zone of cheapness lies. A friend of mine has been accused of being a tightwad. He dresses modestly, drives a mid-priced sedan, and lives in a small townhouse. A mutual acquaintance often accuses Ted of having the first nickel he ever earned, but I've always found Ted to be more than generous. He's happy to send plane tickets to less fortunate family members so that they can visit. He gives of his considerable expertise on computers with infinite patience. He insists on buying dinner, though he loves it if you offer. But it is true that Ted doesn't spend a lot on himself. He buys his clothes from catalogs, and he has one pot and one pan in his kitchen. Ted can't stand the idea of "wasting" money on things he considers unnecessary—like furniture—so when you visit him for computer lessons, you'll be working on top-of-the-line equipment while your back aches from the metal folding chair.

Ted's decision to forego some familiar American luxuries, like a spouse and a living room sofa, means he is free to lock his door and move to France for two years. There, he can stay in hotels that look like Masterpiece Theater sets, indulge his passion for visiting World War II battlefields, and collect amusing stories about French plumbing and the women who use it.

At the other end of the spectrum is my girlfriend Elise, a nearly full-time Kim. Elise delights in the retail experience, complete with gift-wrapping and fancy shopping bag. She considers business class airfare a necessity of life. But even Elise was appalled by the prospective cost of shipping a package of books to a friend in Africa. She uncovered, at last, her zone of cheapness: postage. Instead of simply mailing the books, Elise arranged to carry them by hand, in a large suitcase, to a friend in Sweden, who was planning a visit to Africa. The process took about six months, but saved Elise about $150. Elise steadfastly denied the existence of her Inner Scrooge, even when I pointed out to her the ridiculousness of schlepping a suitcase all the way to Europe to save on postage to Africa. Elise also once asked me why I tend to mention the prices I've paid for things. "It's the thrill of the hunt. The price is the trophy, the score. Without at least one markdown, I just wouldn't enjoy my purchase as much," I tell her.

Thanks to quite a bit of therapy, I have managed to shrink my zone of cheapness. As a broadcaster, however, it's still a fact that jobs, while occasionally lucrative, are seldom stable. So even if a decent paycheck has been making a regular appearance in my bank account for months, there is a small voice in me that always remembers I could be back to hunting for quarters in the glove compartment tomorrow.

Write it on my tombstone: She never paid retail.

Beautiful When You're Angry

Having made it through the inedible introductory dinner and the high-heeled, freezing forced march, Save the Planet and I settled in as a couple, working opposite ends of the day. STP showed up at his political office somewhere around nine in the morning, and I turned up at the station for show prep in the late afternoon. I made it clear that I would soon be leaving the city where Save the Planet had successfully lived and worked for the last fifteen years. Thanks to courage imparted by Dr. Kestrel, I'd also let him know that I was not dating for the fun of dating, but rather for marriage. I wasn't very subtle about either of these plans. In fact, I announced them, in almost those exact words, before our first date.

The Queen, almost unique in all the broadcasting world for her extraordinary kindness and generosity, let me know that my contract would not be renewed. I couldn't blame her. The sales department was in open rebellion over being asked to sell my show, and while the ratings were passable, the broadcast, which had already been moved to a later shift, in order to give air time to a much-loved local radio host who had become available, had not taken off as quickly as we both hoped. I could try to spread around the blame for this, but I think I'll skip it and just say it was All My Fault.

It's All My Fault became my stock answer for everything. Media in the Twin Cities had blamed me for the end of the town's renowned civility. I was accused, rightly, of mocking the city's beloved institutions and events. (Well they'd asked me to cover, in play-by-play style, a mid-winter parade featuring local beauty pageant winners; all of whom were slim yet mysteriously well-endowed, had teeth visible from four blocks away, and who wished to be taken seriously as scholars although they were wearing bathing suits in -20-degree weather—what did they expect?) I was also getting a reputation for saying things that were not nice about humorless politicians and blowhard radio hosts. Eventually, I began my show every day with the words, "I'm Turi Ryder. Blame me for everything."

The town's radio listeners, and its newsprint writers in particular, seemed to either love or detest me. There was no middle ground. I was nominated by two different media critics in two different publications as both one the "Best Of" and one of the "Worst Of" the city—in the same year. My boss spent a lot of time fielding angry calls from listeners and trying to calm down the sales people. The account executives expected to be able to pitch prospective clients without having to hear that the advertiser's wife was offended by my speculation on the dubious marital status of a certain public figure whose spouse had suddenly moved six states west of him.

While I mostly made trouble for management, I occasionally committed the personal faux pas as well. There was the hapless, deeply religious producer of the midday show. He objected to my Planned Parenthood poster featuring a curvaceous woman wearing only a chastity belt. There was the morning man. He hated everyone, but especially me, since the station had allowed him to host both drive time shifts before hiring me. He'd always felt he should have been allowed to keep both shifts and salaries; which, it turned out, he desperately needed, since, by his own later admission, he had a serious gambling habit. We also had a new general manager. He liked me slightly less than he'd like anyone who'd sunk his powerboat to the bottom of a deep lake.

If I was requested to name anyone or anything beyond myself that might have contributed to a less-than-brilliant run at KTLP, I would have assessed only one additional contributing factor: things about my show kept changing. One of the industry clichés about successful programming is that it takes "Product, Permanence, and Promotion." Permanence was definitely a problem. I like everyone who has a reason to appear on my show to be part of my show, but a rotating cast of characters constantly whirled around us. Most of them were completely beyond my control.

News anchors are an important part of my show. They are effectively your source of real time "fresh meat" for the table. With rare exceptions, I've been lucky in the news people department. The reporters and anchors with whom

I've worked have usually been smart, serious—but not so serious about themselves that they can't have fun—and fans of radio.

From my starting day at KTLP, I explained that I was not too keen on management's plan to require the TV anchors to read the news on the radio station. It sounded like a good idea, unless you knew that TV people are famous for wanting to look good. By that, I don't mean just their physical appearance, though they have to care about that, even if it's not in their nature. What I mean is that most TV news people fear, more than low ratings, looking silly. It is my belief that if you are really a professional, at news or anything else, you can separate your professional gravitas from your personal sense of the amusing or absurd. As you might expect, the less competent the TV news anchor, the more he or she fears looking foolish.

At first, it seemed I lucked out with the TV anchor assigned to me. Smart, quick-witted, and a true news-fiend, Guy eventually went on to successfully anchor the evening news in a far bigger city. Guy used to say that working on my show was the most fun he had all day, and generated the most positive feedback from his viewers. But to punish me for making fun of the two other anchors on the company's TV station, Guy was removed from my show.

To this day, I'm not sure I could have treated these women any differently. They couldn't answer a single background question on any story—even one they'd covered just days before. I considered them timid, stupid creatures—

possibly brain damaged by excessive use of hair spray—and they knew it. If you asked, for example, "Wasn't that legislator in that story you just told us the same fellow who got arrested last month while wearing nothing but a raccoon cap and wading in Lake Henrietta with a stripper?" they'd just re-read whatever story they had read the minute before, like perky blow-dried robots. It drove me nuts.

Because the city where Save the Planet and I both lived was actually more of a small town, word got around pretty quickly among his friends and co-workers that we were spending time together. I'd be over at his house, and the phone would ring, and we'd let the answering machine pick up the call. Then, often enough that it stopped taking us completely unprepared, we'd hear, "Hey, man, I hear *you* are Save the Planet. Cool. Call me back."

I figured that giving STP a "nom de air" would protect him from the embarrassment of anything I might reveal about him on my show. (My previous boyfriend, whom I called "Chia Pet" on the air, was known to have won my affection because, in the middle of winter, his car had been equipped with what was at the time a novelty feature: butt warming seats. After he dumped me—a period my listeners remembered as "the month you lived on orange juice and mashed potatoes," it turned out the butt warming seats were the thing I really missed about him.)

Then one day, STP did something that annoyed me enough to talk about it on the air. Except that I couldn't *really* talk about it on the air. It involved recreational herbs, which I do not use, and which he used to use. Our agreement was that I would never have to be around these items, not even if they were put away, innocently, inside a plastic bag in a roll of his socks, which I'd picked up because my feet were cold. Not even if, as he claimed, they belonged to someone else. To discuss this with my listeners, and ask them if I had handled the situation well, I had to use a "fer'instance." So I had a little chat with my audience about how Save the Planet had a nude boat party on the Mississippi River. I explained that I thought STP and I had agreed on no nude boat parties, and how he used the most tired and unacceptable technicality: "it's not my boat." The listeners and I had a good time, sharing stories of blaming other people for your misdeeds. I wasn't that angry, and it wasn't the end of the world, but two people who knew STP called him up and told him I was furious. He remained panicked until I innocently phoned to find out what time we were getting together that evening. By then, at least on his end of the line, the scene was not a good one. That is how we came up with our rule for coping with life as the partner of an air personality who puts a lot of her private doings out for public consumption. STP does not want to find out that I am upset with him over the air. I may be as incensed and as dramatic as I like, but he does not wish to be surprised by the information. That seems fair.

Quirky

It's probably a little unusual for a man to bless the plan of his fiancée to travel several thousand miles across the country in a Jeep with her ex-boyfriend, but I go for quirky. When Paul called to say he'd landed a full-time talk show in Minneapolis, I wasn't sure what to make of it. We'd mutually decided to give up on our romantic relationship just before I moved to the Twin Cities. Radio, and our egos and tempers, had made our assignations fraught and our arguments volatile. I told Paul I was glad he was coming, which was true. He rented a warehouse apartment with scary tan carpet about two blocks away from my St. Paul loft. Paul worked when I slept, so we didn't see much of each other, but I liked knowing he was nearby. If there'd been any idea of us getting back together, it was soon clear that phase of our relationship was as over as yesterday's emergency broadcast system test.

Paul's new station, one of the most traditional of the old line talk formats, wasn't really a good fit for his creative wit and the ingenious characters he still creates to accompany him on the air. He almost gave them up—which would have been a disaster for him professionally, and a loss for listeners. Paul's new program director seemed to have hired him with the idea of changing him into a traditional talk show host.

"Why do you have to be so *out there*? Can't you just do a *normal* show?" When your boss starts to treat you like you're the subject of a *What Not to Wear* makeover show, your job is now a grenade. With every air check-session or hotline call, the pin is pulled out a little further.

There cannot possibly be a talk show host with any longevity who hasn't, at some point, tried to refashion herself for a job she desperately needed. It's a trick that can be managed short-term, but if you really have original thought, traces of your actual personality begin to seep through. (When people ask me "Does insert-name-of-host-who-can't-possibly-be-that-mean-spirited *really* believe that stuff s/he says on the radio?" I usually mumble something about the emptier the soul, the easier to fill it with any convenient persona.)

It didn't take long for Paul to get a better offer, from a Miami station known for its controversial and original hosts. Guess who volunteered to drive down with him?

A professional moving company loaded most of Paul's household goods onto a van. We figured this would make an easier trip, and once again, had high hopes of "seeing the country." Save the Planet, by then my official fiancé, was willing to lend me out as a co-pilot of Paul's four-wheel drive vehicle, with just one request: that I return with Key limes from Miami, the city where Save the Planet had grown up.

I was more than willing to undertake this mission because I like Key limes. Key limes are one of the few kinds of fruits and vegetables that don't sport individual labels at the store. I take the presence of labels on individual fruit personally, since I resent spending part of my lunch hour, or cooking prep time, picking and peeling labels off peaches, plums, and pears. It used to be only bananas that had labels, and nobody ate the banana peel anyway. But the microdermabrasion process required to eat a pluot or a pepper puts nail-biters at a real disadvantage. So the request for Key limes—a humble, non-labeled fruit—seemed reasonable.

Somewhere in the middle of Tennessee, Paul and I stopped to gas up his Grand Cherokee. I had to use the bathroom, but Paul wanted to peruse the merchandise in the souvenir shop. A glance at the inventory as I sped toward the women's room let me know exactly where we were. One wall was lined with what an African-American friend of mine refers to as "Negrobelia." There were salt and pepper shakers, dishtowels, and teapots featuring Aunt Jemima and Uncle Tom—the 1950s stereotypes of Southern subservient household help—and black lawn jockey ornaments in a style this Northerner had assumed became obsolete with the advent of the Voting Rights Act. Every other surface and knickknack in the shop, from pocket knives to potholders, featured the Confederate flag, with the largest rebel banner taking up most of the wall above and behind the cash register.

I emerged from the ladies' room in time to witness Paul, solidly built, bald, Irish, and nearly impossibly pink and Caucasian, marching purposefully toward the checkout counter, clutching an Aunt Jemima saltshaker in his hand. "Do you," he asked, carefully placing the six-inch-high figurine next to the register in front of the cashier, "have any of these with white people?"

Our arrival in Miami was fairly uneventful. We followed the oceanfront down Collins Boulevard to our hotel. The radio station that had hired Paul had bartered, in exchange for advertising, a double room for us at the Fontainebleau, a four-star towering art deco palace on Miami Beach. We did notice as we turned over the keys to Paul's dusty 4X4 that the hotel's valet seemed a little overdressed, but it wasn't until we entered the lobby that we recognized the unmistakable look of the US Secret Service: shades, blazers large enough to cover an assortment of weapons, and the telltale ear piece. Moments later we were informed that the President of the United States would be speaking at a fundraiser in the hotel ballroom that night. Our car had been impounded.

I wasn't going to let the Leader of the Free World get between me and the Key limes of South Florida. We set off on foot, hunting the elusive small green orb; a fruit best known to many Americans as the flavor in the pie that bears its name. Until I met Save The Planet, I'd assumed Key lime was the name that manufacturers gave to regular dark green grocery store limes when the limes had been juiced and poured into little glass bottles. Then again, I was in college before I realized lemon juice didn't squirt out of a yellow plastic squeeze toy with a bright green screw-off cap. Save the Planet had explained that Key limes were special, not like regular limes at all. They were smaller, sweeter, and named for the Florida Keys, where they grew in abundance.

We began our search by hiking through Miami's humid, eighty-seven-degree heat to a local supermarket, about two miles away. The neighborhood there was not nearly as fancy as the area around our hotel. It looked much, much grittier — literally. There seemed to be a layer of broken bottles coating the parking lots of this supermarket and every corner bodega and mini-mart we saw, like the seaweed that remains after low tide. Trash blew in waves down the sidewalks, tumbled into the gutters, and scooted down glittering Miami streets. But the President had effectively sent me here.

Inside, the produce clerk seemed baffled by our request. "Key limes? Like the kind you put in pie?" he wondered. I was surprised he sounded so surprised. To hear Save the Planet tell it, Key limes were as well known a Florida feature as beach sand.

"Yes. Where are the Key limes?" I repeated. The confused lettuce-stacker escorted me to the baking supplies aisle and pointed to a shelf of little green bottles.

"Those are the only kind of Key limes we stock," he told me.

"I thought Key limes grow here," I said. Paul, who had been trailing along behind me during this whole escapade, now gave me the same look he'd have given me if, instead of insisting that local produce must be available at the local food store, I'd just claimed to be Lady Gaga. We thanked the clerk and moved outside. Paul had a brainstorm.

"The station has a cooking show. Let's call the guy who hosts it and see where he buys Key limes." After a few failed tries, we located a working pay phone in a booth surrounded by an ominously large amount of flask shards and dialed the hotline to the radio station. The engineer running the show looked up the cooking host. We phoned him. He used the stuff in the glass bottle, too. Tired, hot, and sweaty, Paul and I retreated on foot, north and east to the swanky Bal Harbor Shopping center, to have dinner outdoors, and admire the luxury cars and limos creeping down Ocean Drive to the President's fundraising dinner at the Fontainebleau. In an effort to reassure ourselves that the Key lime was a real food, and not a chimera food, like zero calorie fudge, we ordered a drink featuring it. Then we asked to see the lime.

"Sorry," answered the waiter, "we just use the juice out of the bottle." We regrouped in the courtyard of the mall after dinner, and I unveiled my new strategy for locating the elusive limes.

"There has to be a neighborhood fruit stand somewhere. Let's find one."

"You want to take a cab to a neighborhood fruit stand?" Paul's patience had finally run out. "Or do you want us to walk into possibly the worst neighborhood, in a city we know nothing about, for your boyfriend's Key limes? You want us to end up on *Cops*? The Grammys are on. I'm going back to the room to watch television." He had a point. The sun was going down, Key limes appeared to be as easily located in these parts as ivory-billed woodpeckers, and we had just driven 1,800 miles in three days.

"But I *promised*. My fiancé has just supported my decision to drive across this country with you. He's been so easygoing about this whole thing. Don't you think he deserves to have his only, modest request honored?" It is probably not too smart, when you are travelling with your ex-boyfriend, to point out, even in passing, the qualities that made you choose somebody else. It certainly isn't a good idea after several nights of little sleep, combined with the anticipated anxiety of starting a new job, while his car is impounded in a luxury hotel where a hot shower, big TV, and bed await. Paul looked like he might easily grab one of the lovely tropical planters tastefully stationed around the mall's interior court and hurl it through the window of the cruise wear boutique.

"Fine. You want to go into the barrio and forage for fruit? Go ahead. I want to go to sleep, but I'll make sure I stay up late, so I can identify your bleeding body on the eleven o'clock news."

I capitulated, and skulked back to the hotel. As Paul watched Natalie Cole singing a virtual duet with her deceased father, I placed a call to Save the Planet.

"Hi. We made it in."

"That's great."

"Yes, but I have some bad news. We've looked all over the place. We can't find any Key limes. They're not at the supermarket. Nobody knows what I'm talking about when I ask for them. Paul is about to kill me. I'm really, really sorry."

A moment of silence followed. Was it possible, I wondered, that Save the Planet would flip from Dr. Jekyll to Mr. Hyde? Usually, this only happened when he was confronted with a recalcitrant appliance needing repair. His mother, who for the most part, assumed her four boys lacked any defects at all, had warned me: "Just stay away from him if he's fixing anything." Would my failure send him into a shouting-and-swearing temper fit? Could I marry him if it did?

"Well," Save the Planet sighed, "now that you mention it, I never actually *saw* Key limes at the grocery store. My mom just used the ones that grew on the tree outside our house."

I watched Natalie Cole sing with her dead father and flew home the next day. Paul resumed speaking to me about a month later, after I sent him a hideously racist vintage bottle opener featuring a black child eating a watermelon that I'd found at a St. Paul yard sale.

Swear on This Mink That You Love Me

I **always knew,** intellectually, that to some people, a fur coat is less welcome at a festive gathering than a suicide vest, but it never occurred to me that I had to worry about those people. So I wore the dangerous mink to Save the Planet's birthday dinner.

The birthday dinners were a tradition among STP's brothers. Three of the four lived in the Twin Cities, in Minnesota. Each year, for each son's birthday, their parents would send a check, with instructions to have a celebratory dinner together. The first time I attended one of these events, we'd been dating a little over two months.

STP was born in January, which is a good month for a party at home. You don't mind baking—it helps heat the house. Even though I had offered to make a cake and a birthday dinner to go with it for both of his siblings and their respective partners, Save the Planet preferred to exercise the restaurant option.

Because of the icy temperatures—another record-breaking low of -30 degrees—I figured I'd wear my fur coat. This was my second fur coat. The first one, I bought for $30 when I was in college, at a thrift store. It was the size of Mississippi, and the warmest thing I'd ever owned. A 1940s relic, with hugely padded shoulders and balloon sleeves; the mink enabled me, if I had wished to do so, to wear nothing underneath but lingerie. The fur concealed all, while keeping me safely toasty.

The resale shop mink also made it possible for me to drive to my all-night shift in a snow-drift-resistant, but completely un-insulated, rag-top Jeep, though it did make an odd fashion statement when paired with snowmobile boots. When the fur finally fell to bits like a child's over-loved stuffed poodle, I knew it would have to be replaced, somehow. The Twin Cities radio station where I was working by the time the vintage mink disintegrated ran ads for a local furrier. I convinced Robbins Furs I would be their perfect spokesperson. In exchange for rock bottom pricing on another, Winnebago-trailer-sized coat, with a monogrammed lining, I became the presenter of Robbins Furs live commercials. So a lot of people around town knew that I owned and wore fur.

In Minnesota, warming yourself outdoors in winter usually requires help from some kind of animal. If it's not wool, it's feathers and down, or sheepskin, or fur. Fur is not only what you wear to the opera. It's what you throw on to run to the supermarket, or while you pump gas. It was what I was wearing the night it hit thirty degrees below zero, and we stepped out of our car to walk the twenty yards from our parking spot to the restaurant where Save the Planet's parents were hosting, long distance, his birthday dinner. We were, as usual, late. STP's brothers, Drake and Ron, were both there, and one of their girlfriends, Kiki. The other girlfriend, Brenda, I was told, wasn't feeling well. I made my way to the party table, and draped my coat, folded in half, over the back of my chair. It stayed there until we got up to leave, when I noticed the big wad of chewing gum affixing a "Yuck your bloody fur" sticker to its sleeve.

Comprehension dawned slowly on me that the coat had been deliberately vandalized, since chewing gum is one of those substances I just assume accidentally winds up places it shouldn't. Then Save the Planet remembered a young man who had entered the restaurant shortly after we had. STP noticed the guy because he was wearing a coat that looked like it was made of canvas, and he was so cold; his nose was the color of strawberry preserves and running like a preschooler's. I remembered the frozen patron, but assumed he was picking up a to-go dinner. I was still having trouble accepting that there were people who kept stickers and gum around for people and coats they found offensive. Our waiter brought some ice, so I could take the gum off my coat. We sang "Happy Birthday," and left.

On the drive home, I was shocked to hear Save the Planet say, "It was an inside job."

"What? What was an inside job?"

"Your coat. It was an inside job."

"That's ridiculous. It's a coat, not a casino vault."

"Didn't you see that guy? Did you see how cold he was? That guy was waiting for us. He was waiting, because somebody tipped him off that you would be there, wearing your coat. He's in A-P-T with Nancy and Brenda. It was a planned action."

"Now you are being even more absurd. Who is going to tip somebody off about what I am wearing? I'm a talk host, not Jackie Kennedy. What's APT?"

"It stands for Animals are People Too. I know that guy was waiting. And I know who put him up to it. It was Brenda's sister, Nancy, and their whole group. Alec and Nancy were at another table at the restaurant tonight. Don't you remember? I waved to them."

I did not, in fact, remember seeing Alec, though we'd met before. A university biochemist, Alec was tall, blond, and athletic. He was a dead ringer for the boyfriend in *The Sound of Music* movie who turns out to be a Nazi sympathizer and hands his girlfriend's father over to the Third Reich. It wasn't really Alec's fault I didn't like him. I'm sure my *Sound of Music* problem would have died down after a while. But in the small pond of single Minnesota women over thirty, Alec had chosen to date Brenda's sister, Nancy, who had recently allowed a skin infection to swell her cheek up like a squirrel hiding walnuts, rather than take medicine that was tested on mice. This made me suspect both Alec's taste in women, and his academic credentials.

I was starting to feel uneasy. Not so much at the idea that there were mink coat stalkers wandering the streets of

Minneapolis, but because my boyfriend seemed to actually know these people. It was unnerving and upsetting—like discovering you have been hanging out with someone who sells gasoline to arsonists. I busied myself with locating my insurance card, in order to file a claim and get my vandalized coat repaired.

The phone rang shortly after we returned to STP's house. It was pretty late at night. He answered anyhow, and had, on his side anyway, an unusually brief conversation. "Okay. Okay. Thanks." STP hung up. "That was Alec. He swears Nancy didn't put the gum on your coat. In which case, how did he even *know* about the gum? Now I'm sure. Nancy definitely did it. And that's why Brenda didn't come. She told her APT group that you would be there, and she told them you'd be wearing the coat, and then she stayed home."

I felt a sense of vertigo. "Who dates someone who belongs to a group that spends its time planning to put gum and stickers on people's coats?" I demanded. *"That's* a movement? Gum and stickers? And people actually have meetings and plan to attack people's coats with gum and stickers? And you *know these people*? I'm going to be *related* to one of these people?"

"They're not married," Save the Planet offered, "and I think Brenda takes medicine."

I can't say it ruined the entire birthday, but it definitely changed the mood. However, as my friend John says, "Everything is material."

So the next day, on the air, I recounted the story of the birthday party, and my fur coat, and the runny-nosed guy with the sticker and the gum, and asked what kind of weirdo nut jobs have nothing better to do than attack people's property just because they disapprove of it? And does that give me the right to put sugar in somebody's gas tank if I think the mileage of that vehicle is unconscionably low?

Just as STP had predicted, the gum guy called my show. I knew it was him, because he still sounded like he had a really runny nose. He also sounded like he was working hard to overcome a natural shyness. Perhaps I should have taken pity on him, but I was angry. It surprised me *how* angry. In hindsight, I was probably more annoyed with myself for having taken up with a man who associated with fur assailants than with this poor zealot on the phone, who was willing to risk hypothermia to make what he considered to be a vital critical point.

I wish I were the sort of person who could have transcended my outrage at the injustice of falling in love with a man whose friends were likely nutcases at best, and dangerous at worst. Save the Planet didn't object to any of my friends or family, no matter how peculiar or annoying they might be. I just assumed my friends and family were better, less trouble, and a lot more fun. Clearly, I have an enormous capacity for self-delusion. But this is why some people are talk show hosts. We are under the impression that just about everything we experience, and every emotion we have, can be phrased and described in such a way that it can be fascinating. I'd say that's another example of self-delusion, were there not ratings services that measure these things.

Anyhow, it's good to have a microphone when your anger is genuine, and your target is just a little bit unprepared. I was aware that the audience waited for these moments, and while I never manufactured them, I didn't suppress them, either. I let gum-guy go first.

"Hi. I just want you to know that your coat is cruel and immoral. It's wrong to kill animals, just like it's wrong to kill people."

This, I decided, was going to be too easy. "No," I replied, "it may or may not be wrong to kill animals, but it is not just like killing people. Animals are not people. Out of respect for the fact that you feel so strongly about this, I'll give you my honest view on using animals. Would you like to hear it?"

The sinus-inflamed caller was not, to his credit, unwilling to hear my side. "Sure. Go ahead."

"I think if we use or kill or eat animals, that they should be treated humanely, because it makes us better. Cruel use of animals, by causing them unnecessary pain, makes us worse. But you didn't call me up to have that conversation. You just decided you had a right to make your point by defacing my possession while I was eating dinner. That's rude, and it's illegal. Since you took direct action, I am going to take direct action as well. But I am not coming to the next Animals are People Too meeting with a box cutter and ripping up your recycled fleece jackets. No. Here is what I am going to do instead: I am going to call my insurance company. You may not realize this, but you can insure a mink coat, because it is valuable, just like you can insure a car or a boat. And Free Country Insurance is going to pay to clean my mink coat. And, by the way, you and Animals are People Too are going to run out of gum and stickers long before Free Country Insurance runs out of money. So they will pay to clean my coat, and that will use chemicals and solvents with possible animal origins, damaging the environment. So that will be your fault, for attacking my coat. And then, with the extra money my insurance company is going to pay me for fixing the coat, I am going to have a mink stole made. It's going to be a long stole...maybe six or seven minks. And I will have the kind of stole that leaves the tails on the mink skins; so you'll know, when you see me, if you are still following me around the Twin Cities, that these are the minks you caused to die. The deaths of these seven or eight minks are on your heads. Each one of their deaths is your responsibility." I could have stopped there, but what I really wanted to know—and what I said next—was "Where does your political viewpoint give you the right to somebody else's property? And why is this idea that you do have a right to express your view by damaging somebody else's belongings, or research, or laboratory or business seem so common in the animal rights movement? And, by the way, are you really saying you believe a mink's life is equal to a child?"

After listening to me rant, and perhaps wondering whether he, the gum and sticker attacker, should maybe have delegated the hoped-for, on-air confrontation to somebody without a head cold, the caller decided to take my last question first.

"Yes. A life is a life."

"You really believe this?" I was truly incredulous. "You really, deep in your soul, believe that a mink's life, or a goat's life, or a mouse's life, is the same as a child's life?"

"Yes. All life is equal. Killing animals is murder. That's what I believe."

"Do you have any children? I hope I know the answer, but go ahead, tell me."

"No. I don't."

"Thank God. How about pets? Do you have any pets?"

"I have an animal companion. A cat. She's not a pet."

"Okay. You have an animal companion—a cat—and not kids. Now, I think I know the answer to this, but I have to ask you, because this may be new information to other people who are listening. Let's say you move out of your parents' basement, and into your own apartment. Let's say you have a kid and a cat, and there's a fire, and you can only save one. Which do you pick?"

"I would try to save both."

"Of course you would. But you're on the second floor, and the smoke is pouring under your door, and you can carry your three-year-old kid down the stairs and escape, and you have the cat under your other arm, but the cat is squirming and you'll have to put down your kid to carry your cat with both hands, which means the kid will die, and your cat will live. Or, you can abandon the cat, who will zoom under your bed, where she will die of smoke inhalation, while you carry your kid downstairs through the flaming wallpaper on the hallway walls and down the burning stairway to safety. Which do you pick?"

"Both. I would try to save both."

"That's very nice, but you can't. So what do you do?"

"Um. Um—"

"I think you have taught us a lot about the animal rights movement. Thank you for calling."

This is how I accidentally became the darling of the hunters and fishermen of Minnesota. Finally, some left-wing hippie talk show host from California was deposited into their midst to preach the gospel of fresh venison and duck, walleye and trout.

The mail came first: photos of seven-point buck strapped to the tops of trucks, jubilant fisherwomen hoisting strings of trout and walleye. Clippings on catch and release fishing arrived in my mail, along with invitations to the local gun show, the camping show, and an offer to outfit me in my own blaze orange hunting vest and accompany me on a perhaps not-entirely educational trip into the woods.

Next, listeners started dropping by the station to exhibit whatever they'd shot or snared or hooked. I was impressed. Word got around. The postal deliveries now included envelopes stuffed with Xeroxes of peoples' handed-down recipes for squirrel, opossum and, from an Inuit living in Minnesota, a method for preparing seal-flipper pie, along with a photo of the Inuit technique for preserving seal meat over the Alaska winter: sticking them headfirst down into the snow in your yard.

Then, the ultimate honor: I received an in-studio visit and demonstration from our hunting and fishing show hosts. The hosts, a pair of plaid-shirted, charming, and cheerful men, were local gurus of everything that can be harvested from land, lake, or air. They offered to give me a lesson on where walleye cheeks come from, and how to cook a fish called an eelpout ("You stew it with carrots, celery, and onions—drain off the broth, and throw out the fish").

Gunnar and George entered the studio a few days later flourishing of a four-inch-deep aluminum pan covered with plastic. Affixed, by who knows what means, to the bottom of the pan was the fish that served as a regular punch line to jokes on their Sunday afternoon show—the notorious "trash fish" of Minnesota—the eelpout. The eelpout, about a foot long, tubular, with a grimace on its fishy, eel-y face, wore a doll's dress and smelled like it had been outfitted this way for a couple of days. I was invited to gaze on the eelpout to my heart's content.

The doll dress was perfect—a red and white floral pattern, with lace on the bottom hem. The fish was about the ugliest thing I'd ever seen in a cooking vessel. Yet, I had an inkling its appearance could be improved. "What are you doing?" the fishing hosts asked as I turned from them and began rooting around in the bottom of my purse.

"I know I jammed something in here the other night...here it is!" Removing a disfigured white disc of sticky paper from my bag, I triumphantly affixed it to the fish's doll outfit. It read "Yuck your bloody fur."

Judgment Call

Exactly **what is** wrong with being judgmental? I prefer to think of judgmental people as people who have developed high standards—perhaps over years of experience—perhaps in twenty seconds—and then stick with them.

So I wasn't confused at all by the 1993 standoff between the FBI and a religious cult in Waco, Texas. (This was during the lead-up to the disastrous raid that left the entire compound in ashes, and all the members of the Branch Davidian sect dead.) Callers to my show about a week into the siege fretted about the wives and devotees of the compound's cult leader, David Koresh. They didn't have any problem with being judgmental, either.

"They are slaves."

"They're pathetic."

"They've been duped."

I didn't feel too great about the fact that there were kids stuck in there (only nineteen of them had emerged in the first days of ATF negotiations, before the FBI took over), but I didn't have any sympathy at all for the parents. They'd joined a cult, for Pete's sakes.

"If you're going to join a cult, you have to have something wrong with you in the first place. You had to be screwed up for a while before they took you. Maybe your parents had a hint about it, or had something to do with it? Because you don't just wake up in the morning and say to yourself, 'What I really want is to take orders from a creepy guy or woman who controls my every move and thinks he's the messiah. I want to live in filth, in a bomb shelter stacked with canned food in the middle of a jungle, or Montana, or behind a walled fortress, to wait for the end of the world. I want to wear strange clothing that is picked for me by my messianic leader, ideally in a noticeable shade of pink or saffron. I want to stand around on the corner in the freezing cold selling roses for $2 apiece. I want to hook myself up to a voltmeter and call it therapy. I want to live on rice and sell overpriced books and pamphlets at the airport. I want to sell a series of expensive training sessions where the leaders have decided on different meanings for words I used to understand—so I will have to take a class to find out what they are talking about. I like being told when I can and cannot use the bathroom. I want to get married to someone I've never met before in a mass ceremony because everyone who doesn't believe my supreme leader is God incarnate is going straight to hell."

Then I told them about my own cult experience, which, I felt, also entitled me to be judgmental.

Once I went to a cult meeting, with my high school boyfriend. We didn't know that's where we were going; we just knew that a friend of ours had joined this group of people who were chanting some Americanized version of a Buddhist chant, and we thought she sounded crazy and we should talk her out of it.

I remember the apartment. I still drive by the building now and then. It was right on the border of Chicago, in a very nice neighborhood, near Lake Michigan. As soon as we rang from the lobby, we were buzzed in. From the apartment's open door, we could hear a different, loud buzzing sound, which increased in volume as we climbed the carpeted stairs to the third floor. There, in the minimally furnished living room of a luxury apartment, a group of people was sitting on pillows on the floor. They were whipping through some sentence in a foreign language—which turned out to be, according to later research, a Japanese translation of a Sanskrit and Chinese phrase—over and over. They didn't seem bored, or tired, or let up at all, for what felt like an unbearably long time. I looked at my boyfriend with that look that says, 'I've had enough.' As if on cue, the chanting stopped. Our friend, who had ignored us completely up to that moment, introduced us.

The group's apparent leader explained that they were chanting what she called "the name of the universe." If you chanted the name of the universe, she informed us, the universe would give you whatever you wanted.

Since I didn't want to laugh in their faces, I confined myself to smirking slightly. I assumed that the adherents of the group were used to this from newcomers.

Even *if* the universe had a name, I reasoned, and they were somehow the one group in the world who had learned it, why would chanting anyone or anything's name over and over again make them or it give you anything you want—or even anything at all? (I admit to a bias here: I don't like people using my name a lot. Sales people do this. They've all been to the same seminar, where they are taught to repeatedly use your prospective clients' names. I like having my name used over and over in a simple conversation about as well as I like being poked in the chest for dramatic emphasis.)

Was this some religious version of "Rumpelstiltskin?" And why would getting everything you want be a good thing, anyhow? When I was a little girl, I wanted to not go to school, and to have my own candy store, so that I could have all the chocolate I wanted. Someone should have told me to chant when I was four, and I might not have a hot fudge sundae problem now. But before I had a chance to enjoy my righteous smirk, the testimonial portion of the evening commenced.

"I started chanting a few months ago," said one red-cheeked Dockers-wearing young man, "and my aunt died and left me $3,000."

Well, they had my attention. This was the first faith I'd ever come across where the idea was to get your close relatives to drop dead. I wondered whether having silently read the large scroll bearing a transliterated version of the chant that was displayed on the opposite wall might have any delirious effects on my family. A broken bone, perhaps? We fled the meeting and made fun of the group for weeks.

The schoolmate who'd joined the group kept chanting for a while, and then went on to join a series of other marginal groups. The last time I saw her, she was at a music festival, carrying a hugely obese cat in a baby sling.

That, for my listeners' illumination, was my fully formed view on cults. The buttons on the incoming caller phone lit up like Vegas. First, a woman whose daughter followed a preacher who predicted the end of the world would be coming soon. She told me she blamed herself for not locking up her daughter to keep her from leaving college and following her guru. The mother and her husband still had no idea where her daughter was...somewhere out west, she thought. Maybe Oregon?

Next, a man who had a college roommate who'd joined an Asian religious cult. "He always seemed pretty normal...just quiet. Then he started inviting me to these feasts. I always said no. I think he's still in. He finished college, but barely. Then I think he moved to Chicago to live with some other people in the church he joined."

Call after call. Most of the people were parents. They had no idea why their kids had joined various groups. One younger listener had parents who were members of a particularly restrictive church. "I think it's a cult. When I told them I didn't want to go to their church anymore, they kicked me out."

Weirdly, the parents who phoned in sounded almost unnaturally reasonable, even though many were obviously upset. I'd expected them to sound like the sort of people who preached fire and brimstone, or talked to tree spirits. My theory that poorly functioning parents were paving a path to their kids' cult membership wasn't holding up too well.

One of my friends agreed to tell me, on air, about her estranged brother. He was a former member of the David Koresh group, who had left the commune and was offering whatever help he could to the FBI in hopes that the standoff would end without bloodshed.

"The only thing I can tell you about Jonathan that fits your theory," my friend said, "is that our parents got divorced, and he wasn't seeing much of our dad. I think the idea of a father figure appealed to him."

The photos I'd seen of David Koresh, dressed as a struggling rock musician, didn't make him seem all that paternal, so I felt a bit skeptical. But that was all I had to go on, until Tim called.

"Turi, I love your show, but I have to tell you, you don't know what you're talking about on this. My brother was in a cult, and we had him kidnapped to get him out. It took two years. He still has nightmares that they're coming to take him back, or that he's going to burn in hell. And I can tell you that my brother was the most normal kid in the world. He's smart. He was going to the University of Michigan. I honestly think if they could take my brother, they can take anybody."

"You really think this could happen to anybody?" I responded. "I don't believe you. I think you could work on me for as long as you wanted, and I still wouldn't join a cult. I hate joining groups so much that they'd never even get me to their first meeting."

"Well, that would be about your last best hope. Because once they get you to your first meeting, or service, or whatever, they have ways to keep you. They all use the same basic tactics, and the tactics they use are the same things they do to prisoners of war. They can do what they did to my brother to *anybody*. You may be a rare exception, but I think they could do it to you, too. I'll send you some books on it."

I agreed to look at whatever Tim sent me. A few days later, a white shipping envelope holding two slim paperbacks was parked in the middle of my desk. The first was authored by a man who I'd seen on at least one famous TV talk show. His job was kidnapping and deprogramming young adults who'd joined cults. Cults, according to the book, were quite sophisticated at recruiting new members, and their methods came primarily from the kinds of destructive mind control used at prisoner of war camps. The list of tactics was horrifying, but standard.

They included keeping an eye out for anyone who looked lonely, then getting the person away from normal life and depriving him of sleep and proper food, all the while telling him great things are waiting for him; and later, that he's worthless without the group. Families and friends outside the group were mostly prohibited, and shaming and shunning anyone who'd left the cult was also required. Wallets, wages, bank accounts, and trust funds were all vacuumed clean in the name of the cause.

The book pointed out that the intake procedures were essentially a replication of the basic mind control techniques used against our armed forces in Vietnam and several other wars. If you think you can do better at resisting mind control than highly trained military veterans, the author implied, you are welcome to try.

I mentally paged back through the various cults that had made the news during my years on the air. I thought about the death cults, the doomsday cults, the racist and hate cults—and every person who escaped them (except for the kids, who were there because their parents had joined, or been born into them). I recalled all these people gave some version of this story when asked why or how they had joined in the first place.

Along with not being ashamed of being judgmental, in radio, as in life, it helps if you also don't mind admitting you are wrong. Clearly, I was wrong. It was still weeks before the final horrifying conclusion to the Waco confrontation, but the story continued to occupy the news headlines. I changed my mind, I told the listeners. We phoned Tim, the man who had sent me the reading matter, and put him on the air.

"It doesn't happen every day," I told him, "but I think you're probably right. You don't have to be a complete nut job before you join a cult. All you have to be is a little bit out of your element—maybe at college and away from home for the first time; maybe moved to a new city for a job; perhaps newly single; or just trying to figure out what you believe about the world for yourself—differentiate yourself from your parents a little—and that's all it takes. The people who recruit for cults have a system, and I'm not sure I could resist days without sleep, or adequate food, or masses of people who might keep me from my phone or my car or my family. But after reading this book, I still can't believe it's so hard for people to leave. They really think, months later, that something is going to happen to them?"

"I'm telling you, Turi, it's the scariest thing. I asked my brother straight out not long ago, and my brother still isn't sure that he's not going to be damned forever for leaving the group. They only had him for two years, and he was twenty when he joined, but they really did a job on him."

"I'd like to think I could resist them," I said to Tim. "I'd like to think I'd be the one they could love bomb and chant at and it would get them exactly nowhere, but I think it's probably better not to go to that first meeting."

"Yeah," Tim said. "Just skip it."

"Thanks for the good advice, and the books, Tim, and I hope your brother recovers."

"Yeah. I do, too."

You Owe Me

I seem to possess a remarkable ability to miss the signs that a man is interested in me as something other than a friend or professional acquaintance. I'm still not exactly sure that this is what happened with my attorney, but it may have been. Earl Rosen was of medium height, slender, with a large balding head, pale completion, and a pronounced, aquiline nose above thin lips. I have no idea what the rest of his physique looked like, because he always seemed to be wearing a suit. Even Earl's casual attire of polo shirts and jeans, when he wore them, somehow took on suit-like qualities—they looked rigid, structured, and formal.

Earl had represented me in legal matters since he'd been a union attorney. He twisted my arm into joining AFTRA at my first Chicago station, then left for LA to work for a movie production company. He didn't reveal his career goals; in fact, Earl didn't talk about much that was personal. Earl was a pretty buttoned-up guy. We'd hung out a bit in Chicago, and I was glad to have some company in Los Angeles during my weekends there, working for Crazy103.

One perk of being on the air is that you never have a shortage of free tickets to things. When we both lived in Chicago, Earl invited me to be his guest at opera and symphony performances. His tickets came through his union connections. I remember sitting front row center on opening night of the opera season and paying absolutely no attention to the music—because all I could think about was that the heroine, a buxom soprano, was going to heave her décolletage completely out of her costume during her melodramatic death scene. Sometimes, culture is just wasted on me.

When Crazy103 in LA hired me after my year of Bing Crosby and unemployment, it was my turn, and my pleasure, to invite Earl to be my plus-one for concerts, theater performances, and anything else that seemed interesting. Earl and I often had dinner at a local restaurant before these outings. He, with his attorney's salary, always offered to pay; and I on my part-time paycheck, always let him.

One day, as we left a Santa Monica Mediterranean spot not far from the beach, I thanked Earl in my habitual way for the lovely dinner. Without warning, Earl turned to me, practically snarling with suppressed anger and spitting garlic-y micro drops of the eggplant dish he'd just consumed directly at my face. "Nice of you to thank me, but you never pay for anything. I take you out every time we do anything. You just expect me to pay."

Though stunned, I managed to reply. "I just assumed my contribution was the tickets to whatever we are doing. In the future, I'm happy to pay for myself. Let's just go to cheaper restaurants." Earl seemed satisfied with this answer; or at least he calmed down, but I felt like I'd missed some kind of sign. Was I taking advantage of someone with more money and status than I had? Had Earl been interested in me all this time, and I'd never noticed? Did he assume that if I was away from Ari, I must be available?

For a while, I forced myself to continue inviting Earl to events. I paid for dinner. I felt like it was some sort of class assignment. Then, after what seemed to be a decent amount of time, I stopped needing him for anything that wasn't work-related. Eventually, we did most of our attorney-client business over the phone.

In conversation ten years later, I discovered that Earl had gotten married; had, in fact, been married for several years. "Congratulations," I told him. "I wish you'd let me know."

"Why?" he asked.

"I'd have sent a gift."

It was years before I got an encore performance of the angry, resentful Earl Rosen. Again, it may have been a result of mixed signals, but I'm more inclined to chalk it up to Earl not getting what he wanted from me. And, again, it involved money. This time, romance was absolutely not part of the equation.

By now, Earl's career goal was public. He had a young but growing talent agency, representing some of the youthful, edgy, up-and-coming talent in radio. Earl still negotiated my contracts—I briefly used someone else, who disappeared to have a baby (how dare she!) and, on return, speedily propelled herself to the top of a major LA entertainment law conglomerate. So when KTLP let me know I wouldn't be renewed, and an offer arrived from a new Chicago talk station, I came back to Earl, because he was good.

I wasn't trying to be difficult by resisting the constant pressure to sign on as a client of Earl's agency; it's just that I'd already had that experience with Bud. My conclusions were that there would be one on-air, full-time shift offered to a female talent, compared to five shifts for men, on any radio station that didn't use syndicated programming. If the station used syndicated programming, the number of opportunities open to women would go down, often to zero. Women could still be on the air, but *only* if they had male partners; never as the main, named, talent on the show. So, if an agent represented you to a station, he or she would likely pitch you for the "girl job:" half of, or sidekick for, a male-hosted show.

The way I've gotten most of the great jobs I've had—jobs where I am not the sidekick—is to personally reach out to a manager or consultant and convince him (or even her) that despite the fact that I'm not what they usually hire, it would be a good idea to hire me anyhow. No agent was going to do that for me. It would be too much work, far too time-consuming, and not cost-effective. You can spend months in an extended campaign to get hired by dropping in on program managers, bearing desk toys, bagels, and cookies, just so male programmers who have fixed ideas about what women in this business are like and what they can do will feel comfortable with you, and make an exception to their unspoken policy. (In case you think I'm going off the deep end on the baked goods, I know of at least one other successful female syndicated talent who has used pies to her advantage. I'm not a pie maker, but I did once bake a program manager a noodle and raisin kugel, with excellent results.)

It can take years before someone runs out of reasons *not* to hire me. So my answer to Earl's question about why I didn't come on board as a client of his talent agency was always, "I'll find the job. You negotiate the deal. I'll pay the bill."

Earl was an excellent entertainment lawyer. But on the third contract he negotiated for me—my return to Chicago— something seemed a little different. I put him in touch with Reese Roundhouse, the general manager at a cluster of stations. Reese was looking to put a talk format for women on one of its FM signals. Naturally, they were not planning to hire many women as program hosts—just one, and six male hosts. And that one female host would not be heard in any of the prime day-parts. But still…it was a huge market, one I already knew well, and it was FM radio, which was, at that time, where everyone assumed the future of talk was heading.

I sent Earl to do the deal. Although my prospective new employer was notoriously thrifty, their offer started far lower than I'd expected, and it didn't seem to be moving up in the way these things usually do in negotiations. In fact, nothing seemed to be happening at all, which made me especially nervous, since what my suitors did not know was that my current station had decided not to keep me after my contract ended, and I would be out of a gig within weeks. When that happened, I'd be changed, like the project of a reverse fairy godmother, from a princess they were courting into a scullery maid they could order around.

Earl called one morning, just as I was sitting down with my coffee and newspaper. "Do you know Fern and Domino?" he asked, somewhat breathlessly. I certainly did know Fern and Domino. They were the number one morning show in town, and they worked for the same company and management that was trying to hire me. "I've just signed them. Their contract is up this year."

"That's great for you," I said, as a dull headache began behind my right ear.

"And," continued Earl, sounding a bit calmer now, "I'm really getting to know Reese Roundhouse. We spent a couple of hours out on his boat this weekend. I'm building a relationship with him." Then, almost as an afterthought, Earl added, "That should help with your contract."

The headache sprang from behind by right ear to wrap itself with snakelike speed around my skull and squeezed my brain hard in a spiky, painful embrace. I suddenly knew exactly what was happening. Earl had used his position as my attorney as an admission ticket to spend time with my future boss, Reese Roundhouse. And I knew as surely as I also knew I could never ever prove what I knew, that Earl had done a little "horse-trading" with Roundhouse, giving him a discount on my salary in order to score goodwill points. Earl was going to cash in those goodwill points and do his fighting for higher compensation when Fern and Domino went into negotiations.

Why would he do that? Because, as their agent, Earl was going to get a percentage of what Fern and Domino earned, while I was only paying Earl for his time. As important as this deal was to me, I was goldfish food compared to the pond of big-name talent on the company's established stations in which Earl was now swimming as the representative of Fern and Domino. I got off the phone, took several ibuprofens, and braced myself for the conversation I knew would come next, after the terms of my deal were final. That took another week. Then, I called Earl.

"Hey Earl," I said, trying to sound casual yet professional. "I got my letter of intent from WMN today."

"That's good."

"And I looked over the union contract," I added, "which is all I'm going to need, even though they're going to want me to sign that crappy corporate agreement, right?"

"Yes. Correct."

"I'm not going to sign the crappy corporate deal, because they can't make me, since they've signed the letter of agreement already, right? So I'm going to need you to send me my bill. And then I think that will be it." I counted to five. Nothing from Earl's end of the line.

"What do you mean?" asked Earl, suspiciously.

"I mean I understand that you really want to work with talent you can represent as an agent. And I'm sure you're great at being an agent, but even so, I just don't *need* an agent.

So I think I'm going to look for someone who just wants to function as my attorney. It will be better for both of us this way. You won't be frustrated with me for not signing on for representation, since that's what you're really looking to do. And," I added, trying to placate him, although I had a sense nothing would, "it's perfectly understandable."

Somewhere in the middle of this little speech, I realized that, although I had not had this conversation before, I *had* had this conversation before: It was the "It's not you, it's me" breakup conversation. Only, I was having it with my lawyer, who had negotiated contracts for me for over fifteen years. For a moment, I was furious. Was this the only way a professional woman could end a professional relationship, by making it sound like she was doing her best to sensitively dump a sweet but boring boyfriend? But then I gave up fighting with myself, and simply executed the script.

"I'll be happy to pay you for the time you've spent, so please send me the bill." Which was said exactly the way you'd say to someone you've asked to leave your apartment after he's spent a whole lot of time there. "You can come by anytime to pick up your sports bag and your special coffee grinder, or I can send the stuff by mail, if you prefer."

It still amazes me that I didn't expect what came next. I should have realized that it would; because when you break up with someone for having done something rotten to you, even if you never ever mention the betrayal, the level of his or her outrage increases in direct proportion to the evil, shitty thing he or she did to you. Since Earl had traded away a good portion of my salary for the chance to earn a lot of money off of Fern and Domino, and had cultivated a relationship with Fern and Domino's employer, who was now *my* employer, on *my* legal tab, and he knew it, and he had a pretty good idea that *I* knew it, Earl was plenty outraged. In fact, he completely lost his temper.

For someone who had a reputation for being calm and soft spoken, it was a bit shocking to hear Earl declare, in a loud enough voice that if he'd been in my apartment, people doing laundry in the basement three floors below would certainly have heard him, "You can't do that. I've spent hours on your contract. You owe me. You owe me for all the work I've put into you and your career. You owe me your career."

Here's a thing about me. I'm a big yeller. When peeved or frustrated, I complain loudly. I get annoyed at high volume. I rave at my spouse and kids at a level that makes me realize, when I consider it, that for privacy's sake, I should close my windows and the storm windows, too. But when I'm angry—truly deeply angry—I don't yell. I grow calm, and very, very quiet. It scares the daylights out of anyone who knows me well. And it should. I get quiet because there's not any point in arguing with someone with whom you are truly, *permanently* done. When you're finished, there's only the matter of finding out where he wants you to leave his gym bag and special coffee grinder, and the inner calculation you must make as to whether he's so irrational and possibly violent that you should temporarily alter your route to work, or maybe buy a camera to monitor your front door.

Arguing—and yelling in particular—not only becomes a waste of time, it can divert you from the business at hand, which is getting out safely from a relationship that, like a building on a cop show, may soon catch fire and implode. You just need to find your way safely to the exit. So I repeated, quietly, as Earl screamed into my ear about how much time he had invested in me and how ungrateful I was and how I would regret what I was doing, and it would be the end of my career, "Send me your bill, Earl. I'm happy to pay you for every hour you've spent on this deal. Send it, and I'll pay it."

Then I said goodbye to Earl and hung up and it was over. Fifteen years. I'd learned a lot. I'd learned to read my union contract, because there's no point in negotiating for something you already have. I'd learned that once management put something in writing, they had to live with it—even if they hadn't realized the full implications of what they were writing at the time. I'd learned about ratings bonuses, and moving costs, and when it's better to get a severance package and look for a new position than to fight for what the contract says a company owes you. Lastly, I'd learned that nobody was going to represent me better than I represent myself.

It took a week for the bill to come. It was outrageous. It was about what I'd have owed him if he'd negotiated my contract with Reese Roundhouse over the course of a weekend cruise off the Virgin Islands, and billed for the plane fare, too. I sent a check for the entire amount the following day. No matter what Earl might say about me in the future, he would never be able to say I didn't pay my bills. I looked at it the way some men say they look at the cost of their divorces: it was the price of freedom.

Earl did very well for himself. Along with a couple of business partners, he built a successful entertainment agency. About five years after our parting of the ways, Earl approached a prominent broadcasting consultant to tell her about some of his talent, which he was certain she'd be interested in recommending to her client stations.

"I'm Earl Rosen," he began, extending his hand.

"Yes," said the consultant, "I know exactly who you are. Turi Ryder is a good friend of mine."

"He physically *backed up*," my friend, the consultant, who knew this whole story, said to me when she called to check in from the conference. "He actually backed away from me."

"Really?" I responded, a bit incredulous, "He actually backed up?"

"Yup. Backed up."

"Wow," I said. "Thanks for doing that."

"No problem. It was kind of fun."

A few years after that, my consultant friend and I were both at a different radio conference. I was part of a panel about using humor on the air. Exiting the ballroom where the session was held into the air-conditioned, deep-carpeted conference center hallway, I nearly ran right into Earl Rosen. We both jumped a little, surprised. And then, because it had been so long, and we both seemed to be in good places in our careers, we gave each other a small embrace, a little air kiss, and exchanged pleasantries for not-quite two minutes. Even though he still knows, and I still know. We have moved on.

Research Project

Advertisers and businesses pay oodles of money for research. If you have a talk show, you can host your own, completely non-scientific focus group. You can use your audience—who can be quite insightful, and who often pay better attention to you than most other people—to decide things like whether to dump the man you've been dating, or let your ex-bestie be your friend again.

I had the same best girlfriend all the way through high school, college, and for several years after that. Kristal had problems. I knew she had problems. She was raised to have problems.

Her father was a dictatorial refugee from a wealthy and privileged Persian family. He was used to servants, and treated his US-born children like property. Mr. Shah had married an American mouse of a woman, whose protests against his declarations, whims, and gratuitous rules were limited to things like surreptitiously spraying water spots onto his beloved Mercedes sports car with the lawn sprinkler and tossing dandelion seeds into his prized dahlia garden.

My friend was, predictably, a mess. So was her brother. There'd also been another brother, who died of crib death. Because of the actual intrusion of tragedy into their lives, you could never be sure whether Kristal's mother behaved weirdly—wandering their tiny yet prestigiously located home in her housecoat at four in the afternoon and serving Campbell's mushroom soup for breakfast, for example— because she was legitimately depressed, crazy, battered, or some combination of all three.

I put up with a lot from Kristal. If she consistently dropped out of every educational or career training program she started, from the University of Minnesota to cosmetology school, then complained about her lousy bartending job, what could anyone do? Staple her to her student manicure station? If she picked an alcoholic musician with minimal talent as the love of her life, it was her choice. When Kristal took a miserable wretch of a single mother, and her toddler, into her tiny studio apartment, and that single mother showed her appreciation by stealing Kristal's checkbook, draining her bank account, and sleeping with the aforementioned alcoholic musician boyfriend—who could stop it?

The first time Kristal disappeared, I was stunned, and initially petrified at the idea that something violent had happened to her. We were supposed to take a weekend trip, and she just never showed up. Phone calls and messages went unanswered. After several weeks of trying everything from the US mail to a knock on her door, then hearing from a mutual acquaintance that she was around the neighborhood, doing her usual routine, I resigned myself to having lost my best friend for unknown reasons. Until a few years later, when she magically returned—just "called to say hello!"

We eventually talked it through. Kristal knew I was right to disapprove of her choice of boyfriends, and she was embarrassed. The boyfriend was now officially history, and Kristal was in therapy. I could count on her again. She was certain of it. It all sounded reasonable. I was overjoyed to have my favorite person—smart, funny, and creative with everything from photography to a paintbrush—back in my world.

And then, a few years later, she did it again—just vanished, without explanation. This time, I heard an earful from her hysterical mom, who called to accuse me of ruining her daughter's life. I resisted the temptation to tell Mrs. Shah that she'd already given Kristal a running start on that, and simply listened to her rant for a full five minutes—which is a rather long time to rage to someone you don't know very well—wondering all the while how bad things have gotten when you phone your daughter's twenty-four-year-old best friend and blame her for your daughter's entire misspent life. That time, I didn't bother pursuing Kristal. I just let her go.

You can imagine my surprise when, almost ten years after Mrs. Shah had smashed her receiver down in self-righteous anger, my phone screener at WMN signaled through the glass that a special caller was on the line. I checked my screen, where the names of callers, the towns they're calling from, and a little about their question or comment were listed. It read:

"Kristal Shah. Says she's your friend. Wants to talk to you off the air."

Probably the worst possible time to tell me you only want to talk about something off the air is when I'm *on the air*. I don't surf, but hosting a talk show feels, in my imagination, the way it feels to ride the face of a big wave. There's an energy of motion that requires balance and concentration, and you do not want to get out of the flow. So of course, the first thing I said when the commercial break ended was "I'm going to change the subject. Because something has just come up. You have been listening to this show for a few months, and some of you have been listening to me for longer than that. But you would have to have been listening to me decades ago to have heard me mentioned my friend we'll call, 'Clara.'"

I told the entire story, and then asked the audience.

"So after all that, do you think I should actually call Clara back? And do I want to know why she disappeared the last time? Would you trust Clara as a friend, no matter what her reasons were? Would you want a friend like Clara?"

Apparently, a lot of people know a "Clara."

"Roberta from La Grange, you're on WMN."

"I had something like that happen to me. My best friend just left town one day. Never told me her plans or anything. She sent me a postcard saying she just had to *change her life*. It was mailed from Ohio. I'm not sure I'd call Ohio life-changing, but I figured she was on her way to somewhere else. I didn't hear from her for twelve years. And then she called to say she was coming to town, asked to get together."

"What did you say?"

"I decided to see her. I wanted to know what the heck had happened to her. So we had coffee. I couldn't believe, when I sat down, how angry I still felt. Angry, but mostly hurt."

"I can imagine."

"Which I told her, and she apologized, and then she told me she'd felt like she was stuck in the same place with the same people, and the only way she could change anything was to move someplace where nobody knew her, like New York. So she did."

"Well, you were right about Ohio."

"I guess. And the thing is, she didn't want to be the usual New York thing—an actress, or a comedian, or a writer. She just lived, like, a normal life. First she waitressed, and then she ended up getting a job as, like, somebody's personal assistant, and she had a bunch of roommates. And she just lived her life there, but with different people. She did some cool stuff, and some bad stuff—you know. While I was listening, I realized I'd quit being angry. It's not like she won the lottery and didn't share any of it, or left me for some glamorous life; she just needed to go. And I quit feeling like she'd rejected me personally."

"Why did she come back?"

"She decided she wanted to go to school, and live in a city, and she chose U of I Chicago."

"So are you guys still friends?"

"We are but we're not. I went on, and she went on, so we don't see much of each other. But we have a history, so I guess we are. I mean, if she needed anything..."

"So what do you think I should do about Clara?"

"Whatever you want. If your life is fine without her, then unless you're curious, what would be the point? Besides, she did it twice."

"Yes. Twice. Which I think is at least one time too many. Samantha from Peterson Park, you're on WMN."

"Do *not* take her back. You will be sorry. She'll do it again."

"Yeah, that's what I'm thinking."

"Well, you're right. You should listen to yourself."

"Or you. I could listen to you, Samantha. What makes you think she'll do it again?"

"Turi, people don't really change that much."

"I guess I can file that under my nutty-stays-nutty file."

"Exactly."

"Thanks, Samantha. Mick from Bridgeport, you're on WMN."

"Can her, Turi. Do not fall for it. She's gonna give you some excuse, and then she's gonna ask you for money."

"No, that she will not do. She's way too into being a victim. She'd rather live under a viaduct than ask anybody for money. She'd give somebody money and end up living under a viaduct, but I don't need any of her money, and I don't wish her any evil. I guess...I guess I just don't need to put myself in a position where she could do this to me again."

"Well, she's definitely listening, so now she knows."

"Yup. Now she knows. Thanks. José from Pilsen, welcome to WMN."

"I think you should just get it over with and come right out and tell her on the air exactly how you feel about her. That you don't hate her, but you just want her to leave you alone."

"You know, José, I think that's the best advice. Okay, here goes: Clara, you stuck it to me twice. You hurt my feelings more than you could possibly imagine, and I really don't need to expose myself to that ever again. I've got friends, I'm about to have my own family, and I don't see any way that having you in my life can be worth the potential agony of going through this whole dance again. So thanks for calling. I'm done."

"Good job."

"Thanks, José. Thanks everybody. And if you want to call and tell me how you broke up with your best friend, let's do that till seven, okay? Here's the number..."

Just out of curiosity, when I moved back to Chicago again, nearly twenty years later, I looked up Kristal. She seems to have moved around a lot. The last address I found for her on the internet was in Tulsa, Oklahoma. Her crazy mom is still living in the same house near the lake, probably teetering out on her walker a few times a week to toss a few invasive weeds into her raging husband's perennials.

I Am the Boss of You

Unfortunately, what had started out as a promising broadcasting opportunity to create talk radio for women on an FM station in my hometown, fast descended into radio purgatory. WMN FM had not gained an audience quickly enough to suit its corporate parents—a notoriously impatient group. The most important truth about launching a new talk station is that it takes, at minimum, a three-year runway to get the thing off the ground. The corporate managers, however, had expected results in six months. Just about the same time the boxes of promotional photos for the airstaff arrived, it was all over.

The newborn talk listeners we'd attracted would, it was declared, be absorbed into the company's older, established AM sister station. My still nearly new talk home would turn into a country format—but not right away. America was fascinated by the televised trial of former football, movie, and commercial star OJ Simpson for the murder of his wife and her friend. The story commanded headlines and round-the-clock Court TV coverage. I'd talked about the trial on my show. My bosses decided my passing interest in the case made me the ideal person to host our new, temporary, "All

OJ, All the Time" format. The dead radio station would continue, zombie-like, as a talk vehicle for OJ trial fanatics.

The rest of WMN's hosts were fired, but I was offered a choice: I could lose my job along with everyone else, or I could swap my evening talk show for days of "standing by" and talking OJ. Because I was recently engaged to Save the Planet, and was, by this time, deep into wedding plans, and because that wedding was going to happen in Chicago, it seemed like a good idea to keep working in any capacity. At first, it wasn't altogether humiliating; just boring and miserable.

My job was to spend all day, Monday through Friday, from the time court opened session till it adjourned for the day, standing by in the studio, listening to the trial, waiting to talk OJ. Whenever the lawyers called a private conference, I'd talk OJ, and take calls. I'd be on air during the court's noon break taking calls and talking OJ. I was not allowed to bring in guests, and I had no producer—just whatever notes I made for the day. To talk OJ, I made heavy use of a favorite talk show tool: a device I like to call "The Speculator." The Speculator is employed by most talk hosts, and also by regular people, when we don't have enough information to actually form a fact-based opinion. The Speculator generates results that start with words like "Maybe..." and "If that's so, then..." or "I wonder whether..." With the All OJ, All the Time format, I turned my Speculator up to eleven, and hoped my paychecks would continue through my honeymoon, or at least my wedding day.

The humiliation that proved that I'd sold my soul for a fancy wedding happened one typical trial day, April 19, 1995. If you're a connoisseur of heinous acts, especially homegrown ones, you'll remember that date as the most massive incident of domestic terrorism ever, up to that point, to have happened in the United States. Disaffected and disturbed militia sympathizer Timothy McVeigh and his co-conspirator, Terry Nichols, slaughtered one hundred and sixty-eight innocent people—many of them children in a daycare center—by blowing up the entire Alfred P. Murrah Federal Building and several surrounding structures in the middle of Oklahoma City. And it happened in the middle of the lunch break of the OJ Simpson trial.

"Take a look at CNN," the board operator barked into my headphones. I looked up and to the right, where, against a backdrop window view of the Chicago River, I could watch any of three TV screens. The soundless photos were horrifying.

"Take a commercial break," I ordered, and sprinted from the studio to find my boss, the program director. Then, remembering he was out of town for the week, I made a quick right into the office of his assistant, Delaney Bisquette. Bisquette, a barely qualified but loftily titled assistant program director, had limited experience, but a huge ego.

"Delaney," I breathed out the words on a rising tide of adrenalin as quickly as I could. "There's been a massive bombing of the Federal Building in Oklahoma City. I have to talk about it. It will make no sense to talk OJ with an

American government building on fire and people being carried out in body bags. We'll be a laughingstock if we don't switch to cover it."

"That's not what you're here to do," Delaney Bisquette sniffed in my direction. "Your job is to talk OJ. You will continue to talk OJ."

"You're asking me to give up any semblance of professional integrity and do something on the air that's actually wrong—a disservice to our listeners."

"They can talk about Oklahoma City on our sister station. You will talk OJ."

I could hear my commercial break ending. I bolted back to the studio, stuffed my headphones on my head, took another look at the smoking ruins of the Murrah Building on my screen, and asked myself whether I had any remaining professional self-respect whatsoever. I opened my microphone.

"If you haven't yet heard, a few moments ago, someone blew up the Murrah Federal Building. It looks as though a lot of people are dead. It's tempting to start jumping to conclusions, just as it's tempting to stick with our standard ideas about blame in the OJ Simpson case. Let's talk about your assumptions when you see crimes. Let's ask ourselves, 'What's my first idea about who blew up the Federal Building? Do I suspect Arab terrorists?' Does it occur to you that they could be American terrorists? Why do you make the assumptions you make? It's just like when OJ Simpson's wife and her friend turned up dead on the walkway of the luxurious neighborhood after a friendly lunch. You had assumptions, and ideas, about who was the most likely killer."

On the other side of the studio's glass window, between the TV and the view of the Chicago River, Delaney Bisquette charged into view. Delaney was a larger woman, with a pulpy body, pale skin, acne, and a dandruff-festooned head of short black hair. Her clothing choices ranged from unfortunate sweater sets to plaid skirts that may have been suitable as school uniforms, and she actually, sometimes, wore knee socks. But at this moment, what was most noticeable about Delaney Bisquette was her face, just outside my window. It was becoming quite red, and very sweaty, as she jumped up and down in fury, waiting for my next commercial break, when she could enter the room. I carried on giving out the phone number a few times, slowly steering the OJ listeners over to Oklahoma City.

"If your assumption that the smoking pile of rubble that used to be the biggest Federal Building in Oklahoma is the work of international terrorists, do you suspect Muslim extremists? And if that's so, is your assumption based on what has happened in the past? Don't you think that making assumptions is often based on what you've seen in the past? Maybe that's why I think OJ Simpson killed his wife. Not because he's black. Not because she's white. But because, most of the time, when a wife is killed in a low-crime area, and that wife has had a problem in her marriage with domestic abuse, and if that wife hasn't been robbed of a large sum of money or jewelry—or even if she has—typically, it's the husband. And just to show you how fair-minded I can be, I think it's unlikely that the Murrah Federal Building in Oklahoma City is the wreck that you can see, right this moment, on your television screens, because of Muslim terrorists. Muslim terrorists probably wouldn't bother with Oklahoma City in a million years." I gave out the phone number. We broke for commercials as I watched the lines light up.

Within seconds, Delaney Bisquette, sycophantic assistant to my actual boss, barged into the studio. The fact that she was in the studio didn't stop her poodle-like jumping motion. Rage had made Delaney into a bouncing ball of pure anger.

"You can't talk about this. You have to stop. You have to talk OJ. I am the boss! I am the boss!"

That is when I formed the belief, which I still hold to this day, that anyone who has to scream at you—even without jumping up and down—that she or he is your boss, is definitely *not* your boss. I looked at Delaney Bisquette. I said nothing. I waited for the commercials to end, and for Delaney to leave. And then...I continued talking about OJ and the Murrah Federal Building bombing. Together. It might not have been a natural pairing of topics, but for a couple of hours, I had my talk show back again, and realized that, wedding or no wedding, I still wanted to do real work. Which meant we'd be moving, again.

On the bright side of my WMN FM experience, I can say, along with very, very few other women, that OJ Simpson paid for my wedding. Because of that All-OJ paycheck, I could also buy a wedding dress.

Weddingland

A few weeks before OJ Simpson took over my life, I was still unaware that our talk station was not going to make it past infancy. Every weekday evening, I came to work at five. Every night, I got off the air at ten. In between, I planned my wedding to Save the Planet. We alternated driving or flying between Chicago and the Twin Cities, prepared to be together after STP completed his political work for the senator, who would be up for re-election in the fall.

One night, after my shift, I was working at my desk perusing some of the smaller local papers when I heard the on-air monitors play a commercial I'd been hearing all week: "Samples! All prices marked down dramatically at Weddingland! One night only!" Every person in Chicago who had operational ears could sing the Weddingland jingle in his or her sleep, along with those of the area's largest local furniture, flooring, and automotive dealership franchises.

As commercials tend to do, they swirl around in the atmosphere until they have something to advertise that you need. Then they smack you right in the middle of your brain. I could go right then, at 10:00 p.m., to get a wedding dress. It would be off my list. There would be no mobs of prospective brides. Brilliant!

I called my friend Syd, another radio night owl. "Wanna come look at wedding dresses with me? It should be a riot." Syd wasn't my ideal choice of wedding dress co-conspirator. His regular attire was a combination of old radio station T-shirts and clothes he'd had since prep school twenty years before. But for being up past ten, on short notice, Syd was my best option. Plus, I didn't think Syd would be the worst person to model in front of, since he wasn't exactly awash in female attention at the moment. Unfortunately, Syd had just ordered a pizza and wasn't going anywhere. Unlike multitudes of American brides, I wasn't going to shop for a wedding dress with my mom, or my girlfriends, or Syd the evening guy at the other radio station. I was going to shop for my wedding dress, in the middle of the night, all by myself.

On the way to Weddingland, I started my diet by not finishing the box of Entenmanns chocolate chip toffee cookies that lay on the passenger seat next to me. Naturally, I had decided I wanted to lose weight for my big day, just like they say to do in all the magazines. There are no fat brides. It is a rule of the universe. (Because of this, I still have a drawer full of fancy lingerie that I will never fit into again.) It's no accident that in Asia, white is the color of death. That's because you only look good in white after you've been wasting away for a few months.

Women are motivated to lose weight for their weddings because never in your whole life will you have so many photos of yourself taken and put on display, unless you start your own YouTube channel of pre-teen drunken beauty consultants. Your wedding offers you a chance to see what your body looked like, for ten days—until you began eating again—after six months of starvation.

Shopping for a wedding dress is the most humiliating process known to our gender, other than the pelvic exam. All your life, from little girlhood on, you think about your wedding dress and how you're going to look just like Barbie in it. It doesn't matter if in real life, you bear a closer resemblance to one of those giant goldfish in the waiting areas of Chinese restaurants. In her dreams, every little girl looks like Glinda the Good Witch of the North the day she gets married. This can be problematic when the time comes to meld fantasy with reality and actually come up with a wearable frock in a color and/or style you have never worn before. I pulled over and dumped the rest of the box of Entenmanns cookies into a corner garbage can. I contemplated spitting out the cookie that had somehow, mysteriously found its way into my mouth while I was thinking about my wedding dress, but decided that would be over-zealous.

One of the problems with losing weight and toning up for your wedding is that it's like showing your fiancé a house profiled in *Architectural Digest* and telling him it's your family's vacation home. He'll keep hoping you can go there and stay a while. If I'd known then what I know now, I would have prepared for marriage by gaining twenty pounds.

I had peeked at one of the many magazines devoted to brides and weddings that someone left at the place where I got my hair cut. That was a mistake. Those magazines have the same relationship to the wedding of an average bride as *Bon Appétit*'s recipe for seared ahi does to your mom's tuna surprise. If you look at those magazines, you will be sorry. You will ask yourself if there is any good reason why you should not spend $4,000 on a dress you are planning to wear for about six hours, and you will not be able to think of one, until you find out what the caterer costs. I realize that there are women who opt for $4,000 dresses and then serve their guests, who may have traveled for days to attend, finger sandwiches and ginger ale, but fortunately, I am not friendly enough with these women to be invited to their kids' birthday parties, never mind their weddings. Anyhow, it is important to shop for a dress with the same attitude one uses when buying a used car; i.e., there is probably a lot wrong with it that they aren't telling you, it will need maintenance, and the price is too high.

At about 11:00 p.m., I arrived solo at the big Italian neighborhood on the western edge of Chicago's near suburbs. It was a neighborhood renowned for banquet halls, bakeries that make their own cannoli, and, I hoped, generously proportioned wedding dresses. When I shoved open Weddingland's reluctant glass door, all four saleswomen— also apparently reluctant—were angled against the counter, smoking. Their makeup, which looked clay-dirt orange under the bright lights of the main showroom, was rubbed off in patches, giving them the appearance of chipped Mexican flowerpots. I think one of them had a false eyelash set coming loose. None of them was under sixty, and they were all leaning out of their high heels in an effort to temporarily level off their feet and restore circulation. I assumed the explanation for this was that it had been one heck of a sale, with brides practically snatching gowns out of salesladies' elaborately decorated talons. These women looked like they were not only former brides; they looked like they'd been married at least three times each, hated men, and weren't too fond of females who couldn't deliver a ten-minute monologue on what bastards their ex-husbands were. I said a little prayer, asking that there be a gown left for me, perhaps on the rolling rack marked "Sale—50-70% off."

I lurked by the sale rack next to the door for a minute or two, checking out five or six gowns while the saleswomen continued smoking. It seemed everything hanging there was labeled size ten, but they all looked so little, so much smaller than I remembered a size ten being. I certainly had a few size ten things in my wardrobe, all orders of magnitude bigger than these dresses, which also, naturally enough, smelled a bit smoky. It occurred to me that perhaps the owners of

Weddingland and the dry cleaner next door were related. Finally, one of the saleswomen took a long look at my left hand and asked if I needed any help.

"Are these all the sale dresses you have left?" I asked.

"They're in the back room," she responded, and blew a stream of smoke in the general direction of a purple painted door, adding in a three-pack-a-day growl, "on the left."

I threw my body against the lilac metal door. It swung open.

On the other side, in a fluorescently lit white room, the carpet changed from purple plush to worn mauve. The space seemed to be about the size of a high school swimming pool. The aisles were completely lined with iron racks. Each rack was packed with wedding dresses. It was blinding. I imagined the Amundsen expedition to the South Pole, complete with dogsleds, navigating the rows of gowns and becoming disoriented by chiffon and tulle. It was impossible to distinguish one gown from another. They were, or seemed to be, divided up by price and size, beginning with the $500 models and moving up.

You may think that $500 is a lot of money to spend on a dress. I certainly didn't have any other dresses that cost $500. In radio, before the introduction of the in-studio camera, fashion was optional. I once had a producer who liked to come to work in her pajamas when she was in a bad mood. My board operator and my phone screener each performed best in bedroom slippers. One time, we all went to the movies after our shift, and nobody thought of changing. But guess what you get for $500 in Weddingland? Something that looks like a "not tonight, Harry" nightgown, worn by a female impersonator under two inches of pancake makeup—an impersonator who allowed his wild and sweaty audience a free ride on his bodice. Additionally, there seemed to be an alarming amount of sequins and faux flowers attached to everything. Sequins were what I always wanted on my ballet costume as a child. Apparently, there are a lot of young women who have been waiting all their lives to do their own version of *Swan Lake* in front of a clergyperson.

From what I discerned that night, brides learn a lot about style from Disney. They also appear to obsess about their bridal look at a level more typical of the producers of Milan Fashion Week. I was not immune. Bad enough that I was willing to give more than ten minutes of consideration to the color of table linens, but the difference in mood created by pearl as opposed to pear-shaped beading did not deserve anywhere near the grip it was getting on my attention.

Here was the main thing I noticed: In Weddingland, simple costs more. Any gown devoid of plumage was going to be a few thousand dollars; and once I took hold of the fabric, I learned the reason why. You are not allowed to wear a natural fabric in a wedding dress until you have passed the price point that would get you a new Prius. Your guess is as good as mine as to whether this is because the excessive decoration is applied to camouflage bad polyester, or that only something as solidly woven as a *Saturday Night Fever*-era leisure suit can support six pounds of plastic seed pearls.

After several minutes of wandering behind the purple door, I was still waiting for the saleswoman to make an appearance. I wanted to stick my head out in the hall and yell for help, but gown blindness was overtaking me. Everywhere I turned, I was confronted by frilly, chiffon-laden overgrown doll dresses in sizes impossibly small. Their only distinguishing features were the stains that revealed they had been in at least one rehearsal, where it looked likely that the bride, the groom, or possibly both, had drunk themselves into a really good fight.

The interior side of the door was painted as white as the wedding dresses. It looked like I might be stuck in Weddingland's back room forever, or as long as it took for the salesladies to finish their Virginia Slims, until a voice called "How ya' doin?" through the forest of tulle. I jumped up and down and waved. When she arrived at my side, the saleswoman had just one question, and she seemed very serious about it: "Is price an object?"

Nobody had ever asked me that before. "Is price an object?" It was flattering, for a fraction of a second, to imagine I looked like the sort of person for whom price is no object. Then I remembered that, as a bride, I was expected to have taken total leave of my common sense and embraced with religious fervor the doctrine of "Because I'm worth it!"

Price, I told the saleswoman—specifically the advertised sale—was the reason I was shopping in Weddingland at 11:30 at night. It didn't seem worthwhile to point out that if price were not an object, I would simply have the designers bring

TURI RYDER 369

dresses to me personally, or have one made to suit my
fantasy. I listed my requirements: No sequins, bows, or other
"fruff" on my dress. Nothing over $500.

With perceptible lip tightening, dry throat clearing, and
other signs of scorn, the saleswoman retreated to a rack in the
back corner. The size flag on the rack read "fourteen." Now, I
have been heavier and I have been, infrequently, smaller, but
a size fourteen was about as likely to fit me as a bra built for
Kathy Griffin. Or at least, that's what I thought. "This,"
announced the saleswoman, as she thrust a dress into the air
like she'd just won the Stanley Cup, "is you."

From behind, it didn't look bad: an open back, a few
beads, and a very small bow. Then she turned the dress
around—to reveal a garment designed for Liberace, should he
ever return from the grave as Bette Midler. I didn't see
anything else in my size on the rack, but the saleswoman was
gurgling, "It's you, it's you," over and over like a murder
victim trying to name her assassin.

The coyly exposed sales tag showed a $7,000 price,
marked down to $3,500. I shook my head and pushed the
gown away. "No, too expensive. Even if you cut the price in
half again, it would be too expensive. So there's no need to try
it on." There was a moment of silence while the saleslady
considered her position. It was an hour till closing time, but
the store wasn't exactly packed with the young and the
dressless. She had the only customer in the place all to herself,
even if I was a fat, cheap customer. There was money to be
made.

If you were buying a car, what would the salesperson do right at this moment? Yes. This is the part where they go talk to the manager in the back room. Since Weddingland couldn't throw in power locks or a sunroof, they dropped the price. All of a sudden, this $7,000 dress was, for me, for one night only, $500. Well, I owed it to myself to try it on.

Even if you have never shopped for a wedding gown, you quickly realize that dressing rooms at bridal gown establishments are like nothing you've ever been inside before. These dresses are too vast to jam into just any old dressing room. We're talking *Gone with the Wind* style hoop skirts here. That Halloween costume you wore when you were the back end of a horse? It was more navigable than these dresses. Attempt to get even one of these frocks inside an old-fashioned dressing room, and your first dorm room starts to look like Kansas prairie. The dressing room was also decorated in what was probably your favorite color scheme when you first learned to crayon inside the lines: pink and purple. And in the middle—the bride stand, a larger version of what you may have used to display your dolls when you were a kid. If you had a Cinderella wristwatch, it came with a porcelain display figure on a stand just like this. While on the stand, I started noticing a number of areas where the dress looked like it needed a bit of improvement. But I didn't have a chance to say so, because I was engaged in a physical tussle with the saleswoman. She was trying to shove me into a dress that, numerically speaking, should have fit me through my second trimester. For some reason, though, I was not fitting into this dress. The effort of zipping it up the back was like opening a package of soup crackers after you've accidentally removed the cellophane pull-tab.

Finally, I could truly assess the horror before me in the giant mirror above the bride stand's purple shag carpet. The front of the dress was a shocking expanse of see-through lace. There was also the matter of the pasties. These were, I suppose, designed to cover my breasts in the event that, after purchasing the money-is-no-object-seven-thousand-dollar bridal gown, the wearer has no funds to buy a slip. A series of pearl strands were suspended from the pasties, which looked as though, given enough practice, they could be skillfully rotated in opposite directions simultaneously while soliciting tips. In this dress, I would be well equipped, at least on top, to be the next contestant in an amateur wet T-shirt contest at a Las Vegas brothel, or a pole dancer. The dress also featured sequins and fake flowers, not to mention padded shoulder epaulets, and bows. It looked like the demonstration kit for the design section at Michaels Arts & Crafts.

The garrulous saleswoman was continuing to shove my flesh into the dress much as one would maneuver a king-sized comforter into a double sized duvet cover. That completed, she hoisted the zipper up my back as far as it would go. "It's perfect, just *perfect* for you. You might have to alter it just a little bit…"

I realized that while I was already on a diet, the dress made me feel not like a bride, but more like a suckling pig, missing its apple. "You'll be able to get this tonight, at the sale, for this price for just a few more minutes," the saleslady reminded me. "Remember, we'll be closing soon, and tomorrow it'll be right back up to $7,000 again."

When that threat didn't produce the desired effect, the saleswoman abandoned me to wriggle out of the dress on my own. With the desperation of a game show contestant nearing the "time's up" buzzer, I struggled out of the dress in just under five minutes. As I fled the store, the saleslady, who was back in smoking position again, called out across the gargantuan, purple carpeted salon, for all to hear, "GOOD LUCK WITH YOUR DIET!"

I avoided bridal shops after that.

The next day, I retold the story of Weddingland on WMN FM. It was amazing how many women had similar experiences, or worse. Sometimes, a talk show is the most personally cathartic thing in the world. I was so grateful I was not at the wedding where the jealous sister-in-law deliberately put an open lipstick on the bride's chair during the preparatory makeup session, and that I didn't have to drive an hour round trip in a snowstorm right before my ceremony while convincing the local police, over the phone, to meet me and open up the shop of the recently deceased gown alterations person. I wished I could have invited all my listeners to my wedding. I just loved them, each of them, that day. They had such good attitudes…and all of them had also thrown out boxes of cookies.

As it turned out, a local department store carried a simple, silk, pearl gray-white party dress. It cost $300, but I signed up for a department store credit card and got 10% off. It was more than I usually spent on a dress, but I figured I could wear it to parties later; forgetting that, in the years before you have children, you don't wear a party dress with cake smeared on the front.

You may think I'm a little too practical about the whole wedding thing. Not true. If I were entirely without a spirit of romance, I would have been married in a chocolate-colored kimono that could later be used as a bathrobe.

The Wand of Greed

The OJ Simpson trial continued at tricycle speed while my wedding planning surged ahead. I knew my days on the air were numbered. The trial had to end sometime. The rest of the station's airstaff were seeking other opportunities or had found them already. WMN FM had come and gone, with a certain amount of fanfare, in less than half a year. Why so fast? The people at corporate headquarters who issue edicts about these things were disappointed that the station wasn't "doing better" in its new format. "Doing better" translates as generating ratings and making money. If you've ever wondered why there are so few new talk stations, as opposed to music radio stations, or why most of the talk radio programming heard in major cities is identical from town to town, and hardly ever local, my short-lived FM talk station provides a textbook example.

The corporate format "deciders," to borrow a phrase from a former US president, are typically focused on rapid return on their investment. News and talk talent is often, though not always, more expensive than music radio DJ talent; the exception being morning show hosts, who are essentially talk show hosts, only with a few songs thrown in.

The more money corporate has invested in a station, the more money they need to get back in their self-allotted time frame.

But corporate management tends to omit this line item from their calculations: Talk radio works differently than music radio. A Taylor Swift record sounds the same on whichever radio station is playing it. And you, the listener, don't need to have a relationship with the station that plays Taylor Swift in order to enjoy her music. It takes about five minutes with a new music format to decide whether a station is playing songs in a genre that you like. If you like Taylor Swift, and within twenty minutes of landing on the station's frequency, you hear Taylor Swift, then you'll likely become a regular listener. Talk radio, on the other hand, at least talk radio at its best, is deeply personal. Its success or failure depends on listeners developing a relationship with a particular host or show over a period of time. You want to know what your host thinks, for example, of your town's decision to hire former gang members as school crossing guards (no, I did not make that up). Or whether your host has decided to ask her landlord to fence off the underside of her front porch because a homeless person has been sleeping (and doing a lot of other things) there, even though it's a relatively sheltered spot and it's the dead of winter and the homeless person isn't harming anyone. In a way, the relationship you have as a talk show host with your listeners is like any other friendship: you may not always agree on everything, but over time, you come to respect and enjoy one another. You find each other good company, and you look forward to spending time together. It is actually a personal relationship.

As an example, several of my listeners are also Facebook friends with me. They recently had a discussion amongst themselves, on my Facebook feed, as to whether I would actually show up at their hospital bedside if one of them were ill. I was pleased to read that most of them felt I might.

But now, instead of hosting an evening talk show, I practiced a form of escapism known to many: planning my wedding. Having a wedding to plan was like having a painkiller prescription. Monday through Friday, as I "stood by" in the WMN FM state-of-the-art studio waiting to host my All-OJ lunch talk segment, while the jury ate sandwiches, I planned my wedding. Every Friday, I planned my wedding as I commuted the four hundred and eight miles to the city where Save the Planet was still working. I had chosen the caterer, the venue, and the band; but so far, I had avoided the gift registry.

Why had I not registered for a movie-house popcorn maker and a full size portable wine cooler? Because, as one of the oldest brides I knew, and a frequent wedding invitee, I had more than my share of time on the purchasing end of a high-tech device I call "The Wand of Greed." The Wand of Greed is handed to every bride and groom who announce to a store's wedding sales specialist that they have come to assemble their wedding registry. The Wand scans any bar code on any item in the store, and magically adds it to the couple's wish list. You may say, "Turi, that's not a Wand of

Greed. That's just a bar code scanner." To quote the Wicked Witch of the West, "We'll see about that."

I once worked with a fiery and chaotic air personality, heiress to a small real estate fortune, and the ex-wife of a man who held a high state political office. Their daughter's registry contained, along with the standard Cuisinart's and carving knives, dozens of far more *outré* items, like twenty-four-carat gold shower hooks, and a thousand-dollar tablecloth. When revealed in the local newspaper's gossip column, the registry provoked several hours of not-very-nice commentary by other talk show hosts, and a lot of eye rolling from listeners.

I never really blamed the talk host's daughter for her lengthy and luxurious list. I knew what had happened. She got stuck, like a first grader's tongue on a frozen lamppost, to the Wand of Greed. The Wand of Greed works like this: Your friends, let's call them Gordon and Allison, are getting married. They're thirty-something, professionals, and each has a fully furnished condo. (It makes no difference, by the way, if your friends are high school graduates living in their parents' basements—the attraction of the Wand of Greed is nearly universal.) Gordon and Allison decide to register for gifts at Department Store Xanadu, a Large Discount Chain called Marpet, and because they're outdoorsy, The Trout Emporium.

Before they make their first stop, Xanadu, they've already discussed what they'd like to receive for their wedding. My friend Jerry, who is from the Bronx and has an accent that sounds like something out of *Guys and Dolls*, recounted this conversation, which I believe is typical, to me:

"How's the wedding planning going?"

"Okay, I guess. Jessica tells me whad she wants. And den I say fine. And den we fight aboud how little I cayuh."

"Is there anything you actually *do* care about? I mean, about the wedding?"

"Yeah. I don really cayuh about the flowuhs, oah da invitation papuh, oah anything like dat. Jess can do whadevuh she wants. Fine. No problem. But I wanna have some artisanal beeyuh."

So Gordon, having already secured Allison's promise that there will be the artisanal beer, enters Xanadu planning on helping Allison choose what Allison wants: formal and casual china, bedding, and towels. As soon as they arrive at the housewares department, a salesperson assesses their status as soon-to-be newlyweds, and makes his way over. He gets the couple's basic information: name, wedding date, place for gifts to be sent, and then hands the innocents a small electronic device. This device will keep track of all the items Gordon and Allison will select for their bridal registry. All they have to do is point the little infrared beam at their prospective targets' bar codes, and voila! The store's computer does the rest. Well, it all looks fairly straightforward, but something happens when normally polite, modest, unassuming people get the Wand of Greed in their hands. They turn into whirlwinds of material desire. Suddenly, a set of everyday dishes becomes a set of bone china and casual dishes, plus stainless steel and sterling cutlery, serving platters, Lazy Susans, martini barware, kitchen tables and carts with foldout chairs, bagel toasters, bagel slicers, chef's knives, Dutch ovens, blenders, panini presses, $700 espresso machines, steamed milk carafes, and a full set of unbreakable—as well as crystal—wine glasses. Did I mention the plate warmer and nested mixing bowls? And that's before they hit the linen section, where they can wave the Wand of Greed at ultra-plush bath mats and wall mirrors from France.

When the list is printed up, you have to wonder how Gordon and Allison have been living up till now. Have they eaten their morning cereal crouched over an old plastic cafeteria tray while seated cross-legged on the floor? Have they been subsisting on canned peas that they open with Swiss army knives and heat on the radiator of their car? I happen to know they have not. It's all the fault of the Wand of Greed.

Now, here's how it works on the other end of the Wand: When confronted with the electronic wedding registry, it's easy to simply pick a dollar amount and pounce. I say "pounce," because if you waffle around with these things, by the time you make up your mind between the individual egg poacher and the hand held mini-mixer, the registry may have been picked through by somebody who has less trouble with decisions, leaving you with a choice between either sterling silver soup tureens, or gilt-edged bath towels. I am using bath towels not as some random example, by the way, but because the idea of buying "bride and groom" bath towels strikes me as being odd in the way that it would be odd if the couple registered for a year's supply of contraceptive devices. Bath towels are just too close to the body for me to comfortably buy them as a wedding gift. Same for sheet sets. That is why, as soon as a wedding invitation shows up in my mail, I race to the closest computer. While I know that in many cases, I'm simply buying chits in the form of barware that will be exchanged later on for a giant wine cooler and bath towels, still, I believe, it matters what you pick. While I'm perusing, I check to see whether any local celebrities have registered for anything amusing. In this regard, the Wand of Greed is like truth serum. Read the registries of random semi-famous people and find out more about them than perhaps they would like you to know. That shiatsu massage chair, for instance, can tell you a lot about what a couple does and does not do for fun.

I didn't allow myself near the Wand of Greed, for the same reason I've never been interested in taking drugs. The Wand of Greed, in my hands, would, I can guarantee with absolute certainty, cause me to do things I would deeply regret later on. The $700 espresso machine might be something I could explain, but there's just no way to look your friends in the eye when you've let them know you secretly desire a $400 digit-endangering vegetable guillotine called a "mandolin." Although, if I had one, I'm pretty sure it's scary enough that it would guarantee I'd never get divorced. I could just brandish my mandolin in any domestic argument and win instantly. And who is going to go before a judge and say he can't live with a woman because her weapon of choice is a giant vegetable slicer?

When the time came for me to register for my own wedding, out of fear that the Wand of Greed would lead me straight to perdition, we chose a set of dishes. Period. We asked the sales person to enter it in the registry for us. I was still a little shocked, and found it a teensy bit disturbing, when a sports reporter I'd turned down several times for a date, and to whom I had not spoken in years, sent me a full place setting.

Chicago Clout

"You can't get married at the Chicago Cultural Center," said Gwen, the woman in charge of booking the Chicago Cultural Center. "At least, not in a religious service."

I had wanted to have my wedding in the building that had once housed the Chicago Public Library ever since I was a little girl. It is historic and gorgeous. The entire interior is made of Tiffany glass, brass, and marble, with grand staircases and elaborate chandeliers. The structure was saved from the wrecking ball and converted into a palace for the arts. Inside, glorious gemlike colors of abalone, stone, and glass are arranged in mosaic inlays spelling out great literary quotations in a world of languages. The exterior is a graying neoclassical edifice that belies its extravagant domes and walkways. I needed to get married in the Cultural Center the way hamsters need to chew through cardboard tubing.

"You're telling me that if I want a ceremony performed by a Justice of the Peace, I can have my wedding in the Cultural Center; but if I want my ceremony to be performed by a priest or a minister or a rabbi, I can't?"

"You can still have your reception there," offered Gwen.

"That makes no sense," I answered indignantly. "And it's insanely expensive to book two places. Why does it matter to the City of Chicago who does my wedding?"

"You are not allowed to use a city facility for a religious service. That's the policy."

"What about the Gospel Festival in Grant Park every summer? That's religious, and it takes up a whole park."

"I don't manage Grant Park; just the Cultural Center. And if you want to get married in a religious ceremony, you'll have to do it somewhere else. Do you want me to reserve a night for your reception?"

"Not until I figure out where I'm going to get married. There wouldn't be much point in having a reception for a wedding that didn't happen."

I had just finished repeating, with a pretty good impersonation of Gwen, this conversation to my friend Nile, a jazz writer and radio host, who called to see whether he could bring a date to my wedding. I was getting, I told Nile, mighty sick and tired of running down places where STP and I could actually take our vows. Everything near the Cultural Center had turned out to be either an ancient hotel ballroom with stained wallpaper that smelled like smoke, or a stark, new, windowless hotel meeting room that gave the impression that a corporate presentation was about to start. (The Cultural Center, which now overlooks Millennium Park, at that time had a tremendous view overlooking the railroad tracks, and if you had really good vision, the armies of rats that patrolled them. You could also see Lake Michigan in the distance, if it wasn't raining.)

"What do you mean you can't get married at the Cultural Center?" asked Nile.

"I mean the city says you can't use public buildings for religious services—which, by the way, is a lie, since Grant Park hosts the Gospel Festival every year. That's religious. They practically offer baptisms at intermission."

"Don't pick on the Gospel Festival," advised Nile.

"I love the Gospel Festival. But unless I'm really missing something, it's religious."

"I was at a religious wedding at the Cultural Center last week," Niles mused, sounding puzzled.

"You were? At the Cultural Center? Are you sure they weren't married in a civil ceremony, by a Justice of the Peace? They told me I could do that."

"No. It was definitely a religious ceremony. Lola Weizengrad's son, who's a friend of mine, got married in the Cultural Center last week."

"Ha. That explains it. The son of the Cultural Affairs Executive Board Chair of the City of Chicago can have his ceremony wearing roller blades while standing on the Mayor's desk. Nobody will say anything about it. But in case you have not noticed, I'm not Lola Weizengrad."

"But," offered Nile helpfully, "you *are* a Chicago media personality."

I hadn't thought about that. When Gwen had filled out my application, I'd coyly given her my legal name rather than my "air name," and the name of the holding company that owned my radio station instead of its call letters. As a consequence, my hopes of being married under a canopy with a world-class view of Chicago's urban wildlife were vanishing. I called Gwen again.

This time, I made myself sound so much like a radio personality, I thought I might have to read a commercial announcement before saying "hello."

"Gwen speaking."

"Turi Ryder speaking. Hello Gwen. You may remember a couple weeks back; you told me there were no religious ceremonies allowed at the Cultural Center? I haven't been able to give you a date for my reception yet, because I'm having a tough time trying to find a place to hold my actual wedding. But I do have one question for you: What's the difference between my religious ceremony and Lola Weizengrad's son's religious ceremony?"

There was a pause, perhaps while Gwen racked her brain to see whether she could answer her next question without asking me…"What did you say your name was?"

"Turi Ryder."

"Ah. And where do you work?"

"I host evenings on WMN FM," I announced, in my best DJ voice.

"You know," said Gwen, more energetically than I'd heard her speak in our first conversation, "I thought you sounded familiar. My boss is out of town, but she gets back on Friday. Let me check with her. What time can you be reached?"

"I arrive at the studios at five, and I'm on the air at six every weeknight," I answered. "You can reach me at my desk, before the show, till about 5:45 p.m."

At 5:05 p.m. the following Friday, my phone rang. It was Gwen. "No problem about your ceremony," she said. "You just need to hold it after public hours and hire three off-duty police officers for security."

"It will be my pleasure to have three off-duty Chicago cops all to myself on my wedding day. And, they're welcome to have dinner. Thank you."

I hung up. I stared at the phone, feeling momentarily famous, and impressive, and all those things that truly famous and impressive people must feel every day. I thought of legendary newspaper columnist Mike Royko, and his descriptions of Chicago clout. I thought of other radio personalities I knew who really *did* have clout, like Len Grossman, sports director at The Big Rock, who had sprung my car out of the impound lot for free after it had been towed when I got off the air late one morning. *That* had been the most impressive piece of clout I'd ever seen—the Chicago impound lot being famously inflexible, even if you begged. But now, it seemed I had a little bit of clout of my own. I danced around my apartment with joy at my miraculous achievement. Then I remembered that I had just spent my Chicago clout—probably all of it. But I would have my wedding where I wanted. I owed Nile, WMN FM, and the blessedly clout-loving City of Chicago for that.

Searching for the Hoary Marmot

You should not find out you are not having a honeymoon from one of your fiancé's sports buddies. My listeners were with me completely on this. Several offered to explain the operational aspect of the honeymoon, and the planning that goes into it, to Save the Planet. I should have let them.

I was picking up Save The Planet from a soccer game, when one of his sweaty, purple-shorts-clad teammates jogged up to congratulate me on our impending nuptials, and to thank me for being such a good sport about holding off on my honeymoon so STP could play in the Thunder Chickens over-thirty soccer tournament. My future husband jumping up and down and making a cutting motion across his throat didn't get the message across to the enthusiastic teammate that perhaps I was not aware that my honeymoon had been postponed in the name of middle-age jockdom. Naturally, the minute I learned of the scheme, I put an end to it.

There'd been hints that my fiancé's planning was not going as well as I'd hoped. Someone would ask us where we were going to honeymoon, and I would say, "I don't think we have enough money for a honeymoon," and he would say,

"That's right." About the fourth time this happened, I had to explain that the "we can't afford a honeymoon" line was a red herring, concealing the fact that I was secretly hoping he had been planning our honeymoon.

When STP asked where I wanted to go for our honeymoon, I said Spain. We really couldn't afford Spain. That's how we got to Glacier National Park, the last place in the world I really wanted to visit, for a honeymoon or anything else.

When I am in the country or, heaven forbid, the wilderness, I spend a great deal of time imagining how I can get to an emergency room. I doubt that the dogsled captain who treks the Arctic Circle every year spends much time thinking about this. My emergency room obsession is also the reason I don't ski. Skiing, for me, is solely an extended contemplation on how long it would take a cosmetic dentist to replace every one of my teeth.

I'm not sure which got to me first: the virus the Rabbi who performed our ceremony was suffering from, or the aging Moroccan eggplant salad left over from our wedding dinner. I was out of commission by the second day, but I hung on to the fantasy that we would have a romantic honeymoon, together.

I had done a little advance wildlife research. According to the National Park Service website, we were likely to see mountain goats, bears, and perhaps the hoary marmot. I was particularly intrigued by the idea of the hoary marmot;

mostly because of its name, but also because it reminded me of a giant version of my first pet, Velcro the guinea pig.

In the park brochure, the 400-year-old glacier sounded pretty special. From the photos, I was able to imagine a thick platform of ice, combining the feeling of a moonwalk with a BBC nature special. But a honeymoon, as you know if you've had one, is not a brochure.

The disappointment didn't really start until I was over the Moroccan salad incident, and we were about two hours up the trail. The long trek is supposed to be enjoyable because of the fauna you can observe...with binoculars. If you don't have your binoculars with you, you can still easily spot any exotic wildlife; because wherever there's an animal, a group of tourists is pointing and looking through *their* binoculars.

I found it more interesting to watch the tourists. They get terribly excited. If they are looking at a bear, they all ask each other if it's safe, as if they believe that at any moment, the bear will come charging down the mountain and devour every one of them. Mathematically, this is not likely. It has to take at least a little time to eat a whole person, even if you go for one of the morsel-sized children on the trail. By then, everyone else can run to safety. Statistically speaking, you could pretty much walk, as a group, right up to the bear and most of you would make it through intact, except maybe for dropping your binoculars. So it's a mystery to me why there is all this worrying that you are going to be the Big Mac of Glacier National Park. You have a better chance of being interviewed by the Weekly World News for channeling the spirit of Amy Winehouse. But there it is: people will believe anything you tell them, if you put the National Park Service logo on the front. I did.

If anyone has spotted any mountain goats, the goats will be very high up on the mountain. Unless they are hanging out within Dixie cup-throwing distance of the ranger station, as many of these animals like to do. When the mountain goats turn up, you are supposed to call everyone else from two hundred yards up or down the trail. You do this in hopes that someone will have a better pair of binoculars than you. From where you are, the mountain goat looks like a Q-tip bopping along on a sheer face of rock. But with a *really good* pair of binoculars, you can see that it is actually a cotton ball bopping around on a sheer rock face. The fact that you could go to any major metropolitan zoo and see these animals from three feet away, and even smell their breath, does not seem to occur to anybody else.

The berries I stopped periodically to pick along the side of the trail turned out to be another of the honeymoon's disappointments. The park literature specifically mentioned the famous indigenous huckleberries as a treat for all who visit. But in our urban ignorance, we had consumed something called "serviceberries;" so called because they were of service to the Native Americans. The huckleberries were out of season. Jars of huckleberry jam cost about $9 in all the little National Park souvenir stands, but we soon understood why there were no little jars of serviceberry jam for sale anywhere. The original population of the park, both human and animal, probably ate a lot of stuff because that's all there was, and not because it tasted very good. The serviceberries, for those of you lucky enough never to have eaten them, taste a lot like a berry-colored velvet shirt that has been worn for several days by an NFL linebacker at a dance club.

I felt a gradual sense of relief as we approached the glacier's summit. You probably will not be surprised, although I was, to learn that going down requires re-traversing the exact same path as going up. The mountain has no hidden elevator in the back. At the top, there was a rest area, where I was certain I would see a hoary marmot. That's where the park guide said the hoary marmots liked to hang out, because they are secretive, and shy, and live very high on the mountain. Also, the guide mentioned an outhouse, which I was looking forward to seeing nearly as much as I wanted to meet the hoary marmot. I was intrigued by a sign inside the privy discouraging users from leaving the door open, as this would allow hoary marmots entry, to pillage through whatever can be found on the insides of outhouses. I decided that hoary marmots must not have acute senses of smell.

I have nearly forgotten to mention it: the *glacier*. The glacier was also supposed to be at the top of the mountain. Unfortunately, the glacier was out that day. Some remnant of the glacier was supposed to remain nearly all year long; but for most of that summer, it was only slightly smaller than the pile of dirty snow at the end of any conscientious Chicagoan's driveway around the twenty-eighth of February. Not only that, but if you wanted to see whatever bird-toy sized shred of glacier was left at the end of August, yet another ten-minute hike was required. I was not planning to make it. Save the Planet thought this was silly, that we had hiked for hours and hours to get to the glacier, and that therefore, the glacier must be seen. I pointed out that it might be more courteous to leave the glacier alone, since it was clearly not at its best. I also remind him that I was tired, recovering from what—for all I knew—was diphtheria, and generally not in a good mood. If he wanted to see the glacier, he was free to go on, and I'd just sit on a bench and amuse myself. Once I was alone, I discovered the extra special wildlife found at the top of the mountain—the only wildlife I actually saw close up on my entire honeymoon.

Keep in mind that the starting point for this glacier was the melting pool of water, warmed by the sun, and high mountain air, that had yet to begin its descent to the lakes below. This made it an ideal breeding environment for mosquitoes. These Glacier National Park mosquitoes seemed to have reproduced in as much profusion as the famed wildflowers so well known to many of us by their appearance in postcards sent by friends who visit the park. The Glacier Park mosquitoes were hungry, and I was the only resting, warm-blooded animal in sight. Resigned, I wrapped my polar fleece camping coat around me as best I could, sat myself on a log positioned for this purpose, and waited for the hoary marmot. The afternoon became a mix of bird songs, punctuated by the sound of me slapping myself. I figured that at least with less blood, I'd feel lighter on the way down.

Save the Planet returned. He had seen the glacier. He was content. I remembered hearing that in marriage, one is to take a part of one's joy in the happiness of one's partner. I also decided to book, for our first anniversary, a trip to Spain.

I'm Going to Disneyland

In theory, my job of hosting the OJ Simpson commentary should have been waiting for me at the end of my honeymoon. I wasn't surprised, however, to hear that the vacation relief person would be kept on until the trial ended. I bought a new computer, a printer, and some office supplies, and made my apartment into a radio employment bureau. Again.

Before I could launch myself into full-time job seeking mode, I got a call from a station in Los Angeles. The same company that had launched WMN FM was taking another stab at the "Talk Radio for Women" format, only this station would be on the traditional home for talk: AM. I knew the launch runway would be short. The company had just demonstrated how impatient it was for ratings and results. On the other hand, Save the Planet was now in full campaign mode back in Minnesota, and here was work. So I said yes to a three-month trial period, locked up my apartment, drove Fiona, my mini-lop bunny, up to Minnesota, and arranged to sublet the apartment of a friend who was deciding whether or not to give up on her own Hollywood dreams and return to her home in the Midwest.

Fun with Quitting

There's a huge amount of divorce in broadcasting. More than a handful of broadcasters have left radio when their spouses announced that the next move would not include them, their children, or the family savings account.

Not only do radio people tend to live transient, temporary existences, but there are a lot of people in the business who have moved so many times, they've given up on home life altogether, and dwell in expensive, but sparsely furnished, apartments with not much more furniture than a bed, TV, microwave, and recliner. I know one guy who had the relocation thing down to such a science; he actually constructed his furniture from the moving cartons he was too wise to unpack. People in my business know, almost as well as the salesforce from Mayflower Movers™ or Allied Van Lines™, the price of a dish-pack, and the cost of unprinted newspaper. Broadcasters look at people who own houses with a mixture of awe and fear. The law of our universe is: buy and be fired. You know you are a radio veteran when some charity's packet with four pages of free return address stickers arrives in your mailbox and you think, "Two pages. That's all I'll need."

When reading the online radio trade publications, you cannot always be sure whether a particularly spectacular fire-able incident is the work of the talent, management, or the PR department. Sometimes, as in a publicity stunt that goes horribly awry (like the one where a woman died by drinking insane amounts of water and then not peeing for hours in a contest to win a relatively inexpensive electronic gizmo), the answer is: All of the above.

When I leave a miserable job, I am not vengeful; unless you count this book, and the fact that I once used the office Xerox to print out copies of my grandmother's entire handwritten recipe book for every member of my extended family before I gave my notice.

Sometimes you really, really want to be out of a place, but you just can't afford to quit. In these cases, it's good to figure out ahead of time where you can go to pound on something and yell. It can't be the restroom. Somebody always comes into the restroom when you are hiccupping and blowing your nose, and wants to cheer you up.

A lot of people advocate shopping as a coping mechanism for horrible employment situations; but every time I've tried making purchases to take my mind off a terrible job, I ended up buying something equivalent to two months of rent. It would be more cost-effective to quit the job and spend two months paying myself to look for a new one. What works for me as a survival strategy at truly awful jobs, is driving to work in a car with tinted windows. The car will have a steering wheel you can bang on, and it's relatively soundproof and quiet. In fact, being trapped in a torturous job is one of the best reasons I can think of to give up public transit.

The Los Angeles job was the gig I still consider the "most miserable; least quit-able" of my career. The three-month launch ended up lasting five months. Every day after the first week was depressing and soul crushing. Yes, there are plenty of positions worse than working for three men who are programming a station targeted to women. You could be canning salmon, or cleaning up one of those fun zones where three-year-olds have birthday parties. But in the quirky and emotionally dangerous world of broadcasting, working for three frightened guys in suits who think they know everything there is to know about women is pretty bad.

These three boss persons, of varying rank, had a sort of lions-in-the-Colosseum approach to managing me. They would call me into the biggest of their offices and hold a round-robin tournament complaining about my show. The most senior one, Zack, a florid blond who favored expensive suits and rococo ties, had a wife who hated me. The second,

Arlen, a rotund, affable fellow who built a career as a competent newsman, seemed perpetually at sea. It perplexed him to find his wife enjoyed my show; although, since she was a woman, that meant he must be doing something right. The one farthest down the ladder, Mick, had recently been a producer for another talk show. A well-groomed gay man with no discernable sense of humor or opinions of his own, Mick didn't really like or dislike anybody's show. He had two detectable concerns: keeping his domestic partner, who phoned several times a day, entertained, and knowing what the top boss was wearing, in order to come to work similarly dressed.

Each man was petrified of saying something nice, for fear the others would disagree and make him look bad. So they took turns finding things that were wrong with my program, and then agreed with each other that whatever it was, was terrible. There was just one problem with this approach: They almost never, so far as I could tell, actually *heard* my show, which aired in the middle of their office day, while they were working on their computers, talking to their various domestic partners on the phone, and waiting for the general manager to come out of her office; something she almost never did. Because of this, whatever my superiors said *I* had said on-air was almost always what *somebody else* had told them I had said. So my management team effectively consisted of three bosses and their three spouses, who considered it a matrimonial duty to critique the station daily. Anybody else they ran into, anyplace they went—from prospective client lunches to coffee runs—also provided input on my performance.

Take the vibrator show. I began one morning with a monologue about getting along without your husband or love interest while he/she is travelling. This was a topic close to home, because STP was not. He was still running a political campaign six states away. I didn't mention vibrators; only that there seemed to be a social absence while living in a city far from my husband. Callers helpfully spent the next twenty minutes suggesting strategies for amusing oneself, including use of various marital aids. Some women called in to recommend women-friendly websites or local stores.

"You can get them in all kinds of colors."

"Some of them are more powerful than what you may need."

"You'll wonder why you waited so long to get one."

"I have three!"

Nobody used any dirty words. Nobody mentioned any body parts. A ten-year-old might have assumed we were discussing kitchen mixers.

A summons from the bosses was waiting at my desk after my show. The meeting began two hours before airtime, with Mick, the fancy suit guy, speaking first.

"Turi, this is a station for women. Women don't want to hear about vibrators."

"They do if they don't own one," I replied, thinking of my listeners, and feeling sorry for the unequipped ones.

"Turi, I heard this from a woman. Talking about vibrators makes women uncomfortable," Zack, the uber-boss, continued.

Of course, I knew who didn't want to talk about vibrators: my boss's wife. And I could guess *why* he thought she didn't want to talk about vibrators: her husband had accidently heard my show on his way to lunch the day before. He'd gone home and asked her whether she had a vibrator, and she'd said, "I don't want to talk about it." So I waited in my chair for a moment, deciding what to say. For some reason, I didn't want to talk about vibrators just then, either. But when Arlen said to me, "Look Turi, this is a station for women, and we know what women want to hear. It isn't about vibrators. Trust me, I am hearing this from women," what choice did I have? I took a deep breath.

"From a lot of women…or from your wife?

That did it. Zack flushed beet red.

Sizeable Arlen stammered, "I don't think my wife would like it."

Sycophant Mick added, "Robert doesn't like it either."

I had just enough self-control to thank them for their insights and asked whether they had anything else. They didn't. By my own hand, the fuse to the detonation of my job was now slowly burning. It was like saying, "I quit," but in slow motion. I stood for a few minutes outside the office door, clutching a cassette tape of the offending show, like an airline life jacket that had failed to inflate. Then I slunk out into the parking lot, hid behind the tinted windows of my car, and pounded on my steering wheel for a while.

In my friend Howie's opinion, there are times when it really is necessary to blow up your job. My friends are much braver than I am. Howie once reached a point of such extreme frustration with his top 40 radio employer that he phoned me from his station's studio with an invitation to listen in on a speakerphone as he destroyed his job, live, on the air. I've loved him for it ever since.

Howie is a truly creative personality. He does cartoon voices, commercial voices, and some of the wickedest audio production and comedy ever, often using commercial radio as his fuel. But once upon a time, Howie had an evening DJ job at a legendary California radio station. The station hired a new general manager, who hired a new morning show team that sucked.

Howie, who would have been a far better choice as morning show host, was a good sport about it, until the mail arrived. There was a fan letter addressed to Howie's immediate boss, the program director, from Gus in Burlingame. Gus wrote that he made a point of "planning his evening so he could listen to Howie's show because the comedy was brilliant, and something the station needed more of," etc. Howie's boss was proud, so he copied the letter and distributed it to the entire staff, including his boss, the general manager. The GM appropriated the letter in full, recording it as an "editorial from management." Unfortunately, the GM decided to make one small editorial change. In the general manager's recording of the flattering letter, Howie's name was removed, and replaced with the names of the new morning show team. Howie heard it first during the station's midday show. By the time his evening shift started, Howie had a plan.

Shortly before the editorial cart was scheduled to play, Howie made an announcement.

"You've been listening to an editorial from management on our radio station all day. It includes a letter from one of you. If you're the person who wrote that letter, you're invited to call in." Howie verified the address and full name of the person on the phone to make sure it was really the letter writer, Gus from Burlingame. Then Howie put Gus on the air.

"So," Howie asked, "you're Gus from Burlingame, right?"

"Right," replied the slightly confused Gus.

"Gus, you wrote a letter to this radio station, right?"

"Yes," agreed Gus.

"And you said you liked the morning show team, because they're smart, and funny, and the station should have more shows like theirs?" prompted Howie, rattling the paper of the original letter in front of his microphone.

"Um, no. I didn't. Actually, I wrote the letter about you, Howie."

"So…it wasn't about the morning show?"

"No, ah, I think those guys really suck."

The following morning, Howie's direct supervisor was given a direct order to fire Howie, which he reluctantly executed, along with his signature on Howie's final paycheck.

If you work in a creative industry, you already know that you may sometimes have a harder time getting fired than you think. In radio, it often happens that program directors will forgive talent for showing up late, or drunk, because they are "creative personalities." A lot of really rotten behavior in the business gets written off as genius, providing you have great ratings.

If you ever do choose to blow up your job, Howie's approach is far better than mine. At least he had a good time doing it.

While You Were Out

Yet another "Talk Station for Women," programmed entirely by men, ended—first for me, then a few months later, for the entire airstaff. Almost simultaneously, Save the Planet's political campaign wrapped up with a victory. I flew to Chicago, gave my landlord notice, packed my things into a U-Haul, and wrangled them into Save the Planet's garage in St. Paul. We'd made the deal that we would list both our houses—mine in Oakland, his in the Twin Cities—and whoever's house sold first would relocate to the other person's home. This was a completely rigged arrangement. My California home, though it had received the kind of attention normally given to a contestant in the Miss America pageant to boost its "curb appeal," was languishing in one of the Bay Area's periodic real estate downturns. Save the Planet's house sold in a week.

I arranged to host some regular fill-in shifts in San Francisco. A smart, ambitious, Bay Area program director, Karl Blake, had just signed on yet another talk station for women (on FM, if you're keeping score). We rented another U-Haul. We strapped one of STP's two canoes and all his camping gear to the top of his rusty, ancient, Toyota. STP drove the rusty Toyota and canoe behind the U-Haul truck with our other car in tow. Please refer to the previous chapter on maneuvering U-Haul trucks. On this occasion, I did not run into my own car with my own truck, but I did get separated from STP's "chase car" just outside of Sacramento, where, despite a prolonged and well-signaled lane change, I managed to clip the front end of an ancient Buick sedan. The Buick's driver and passenger comprehended neither English nor turn signals. Nevertheless, they communicated that I had broken their headlight by passing me at seventy miles-per-hour, and then braking, hard, directly in front of me. That we all lived long enough for me to give them my insurance information is another of life's small miracles.

My Bay Area friends all showed up at our Oakland house to help us unpack. Haskell, the comptroller at my old radio station, K-Star, brought news, which he passed on as he was heading into my house while carrying a box full of my shoes.

"Hey, Turi, did I hear you say that you had a job lined up?"

"Yeah, but just part-time. I'm going to be working for K-Bomb. They're doing FM talk."

"So I guess you haven't heard that K-Bomb just got sold?"

"No."

"Yeah. Valley Vista Broadcasting bought them, and they're going classical music."

"Thanks for showing up, Haskell. For being the messenger, you get to unload the books."

The bad news on my return to the flowering spring of Oakland was that neither I nor Save the Planet would have a regular source of income. The good news was that for the next month, while staff and management at the soon-to-be-defunct talk station used their vacation days to travel for interviews and worked like demons to get off the sinking K-Bomb ship, there would be an abundance of shifts for me, the fill-in host, to cover. And, as it turned out, an excellent learning opportunity also awaited me.

Around the second week of my fill-in schedule, a major earthquake struck Iran. There was much discussion about whether we should send money to help with rescue and rebuilding efforts. Karl Blake solicited my opinion as I sat at the extra desk in the show prep area. It was my belief that we didn't have a big moral obligation to Iran, for reasons that anyone who lived through the US Embassy hostage situation might have found understandable. My boss waved the "Aid for Iran" headline in front of me like a red flag in front of a bull, opened the door to my studio, ushered me in, and waited. He knew me.

"I want to get this out of the way first thing. Because I know there are people who might assume something different, if I don't: If this earthquake had destroyed parts of Turkey, or Malaysia, or, heaven forbid, any number of other

Muslim countries, I would have been a major supporter of aid efforts. But I just can't get the 'Death to America, Death to Satan' chants out of my head. Tell you what. If Iran would like to officially rescind our status as the Great Satan, then the Great Satan, with its great concrete and its great bulldozers, might be more willing to send some help."

Maybe I'm a bad humanitarian, but I still feel that way. Of course, when you say things like, "I recognize those women out on the street begging for help. They're the same women who were ululating in the street in front of the US Embassy when the citizens of Iran took our citizens hostage," there will be fallout. The view that you might not feel kindly disposed to people who try to kill you is not the majority view in San Francisco. In San Francisco, the more people hate you, the more you consider it a challenge to win their hearts with love...and other stuff, like money. If you do not believe in turning the other cheek quite so quickly, you are bound to get calls and threats from some extreme people. And the more frightening, threatening calls don't come in during the show; they come in after it.

I arrived for my next day of fill-in to find the show's producer, who was used to producing a doctor's advice show, where the most controversial subjects were circumcision and whether or not to medicate children with

ADD. She was nearly apoplectic from fear. "We're getting bomb threats. We're getting phone calls. MUM is demanding a chance to respond to yesterday's show with an hour on the air." MUM, Muslims Unhappy with Media, was not my favorite organization. I had dealt with them before. They promoted themselves as an anti-discrimination group, but their agenda was actually much broader, and their idea of the parameters of "acceptable" speech was extremely narrow.

I tried to tell my producer that, since I wasn't planning to talk about the earthquake that day, and MUM hadn't called in during yesterday's show, we didn't owe them anything, but the poor producer made it clear that management wanted to give MUM some airtime. Since I was only a guest host on the station, I figured the polite thing to do was to accept the request. It if had been my full-time gig, I'd have fought it on principle. After all, there's always someone who didn't hear your show, but who, having heard *about it*, wants to respond. These responses usually make for very boring talk radio. I turned my attention to calming down my producer, who was waving a bunch of angry faxed letters at me. She looked as though she might cry. I took a packet of Kleenex out of my purse and was just about to offer her one, when the acting general manager's secretary materialized at my temporary desk and waved me into the general manager's office.

The office was, at that moment, a management no-man's-land. The real general manager had packed his files and left for a new job a couple of days before, anticipating the sale. Karl Blake was on an airplane, en route to his own job interview. The third person down the management food chain was the sales manager, Bonnie Slandar, a blonde-bobbed woman who, both times I'd seen her, had been wearing a navy-blue blazer with a yachting pin stuck in her lapel. Bonnie was hoping to stay with Valley Vista after the sale, as general manager of the classical music station. That position seemed, from the brief encounters I'd had with Bonnie, far more suited to her personality than being general manager of a talk radio station. To show how serious Bonnie was about claiming the GM title: with maybe two weeks left till the transfer of station ownership, she seized the initiative and moved herself into her former boss's corner office.

"Turi, I'm calling you in to my office to tell you, you are fired. You can go home now."

"Bonnie, I completely understand that you do not want to put me on the air, given the major PR storm that seems to be hitting the station right now. I understand that you'd like a smooth and quiet transition to the new station ownership. You might want to know that I was more than willing, at your request, to put a spokesperson from MUM on the show today. But if that's not what you want, I'm happy to head back home, no problem." I turned to leave, inwardly musing on the surreal sensation of having been "fired" from a job that I didn't actually have, since I was technically only a part-time fill-in talk host on a radio station whose remaining days could probably be counted on the fingers of two hands.

"Well, I'm telling the media that we're firing you for what you said on the air."

That made me turn back around. "What did I say on the air, specifically, that was so objectionable, and to whom?"

"You said you'd like to drop an atom bomb on Iran."

"Really? That's absolutely not the kind of thing I'd say. Did you listen to tape of the show?"

"No...but I've been getting calls from listeners non-stop. This group, 'Muslims Unhappy with Media,' has the papers calling, too. And they say you said it. Someone named Abdullah is threatening to firebomb the station. We just can't have it."

It was clear there was no point in arguing or explaining. I thanked her for her time and left Bonnie's new office. I dropped by the nervous producer's desk on my way out, to retrieve my packet of Kleenex and a copy of the tape of yesterday's show. She didn't have it. Had anybody in management actually *listened* to what I'd said? No. It appeared that management was relying on listener complaints; something any real talk radio program director or general manager knows is not, by itself, to be considered a reliable source. That's why we have tape.

I had a drizzle of hope that I'd be vindicated when a friend called to tell me that the station's afternoon host, Priscilla, was using tape of my show as the main substance of her program that day. "Aha!" I thought to myself. "Priscilla will back me up. She's a talk host. She knows better than to take angry, internet-generated phone calls from activist groups as gospel."

But Priscilla had another agenda. She spent her entire three-hour show blasting me on my inhumanity to mankind. She accused me of a lack of professional ethics. She called me a hatemonger and a bigot. Interestingly, Priscilla was not able to play any tape that sounded at all like I'd suggested bombing Iran. Most of Priscilla's show that day consisted of playing tape from my show the day before. I thought my show sounded pretty good. The tape of my show, re-aired with accompanying condemnations and harangues by Priscilla, was definitely the best work I'd ever heard her do.

Then the newspapers hit. "Talk show host fired. Says she wants to drop atom bomb on Iran," several columnists said.

Others wrote, "Management says Ryder has apologized for her show yesterday."

I would have gone away quietly, but I dislike it intensely when people take it on themselves to apologize for me. Fortunately, my husband, who as a campaign manager, is a veteran of many political crises, knew just what to do.

"You're going to do a media blitz, Turi. If there's one thing that other talk show hosts can't stand, and will talk about, it's someone who's been fired for doing what they pay you to do."

Thank goodness for Save the Planet. In a political crisis, he's the one you want. Within twenty-four hours, I discussed my "firing" on the number one San Francisco talk station, the number one Los Angeles station, and the number one talk shows in New York and Boston. Plus, I got to point out on all those shows the inherent anti-Muslim bias playing a part in my dismissal.

"It's interesting," I said. "If somebody named O'Donnell or Cohen calls or writes and threatens to blow up a radio station, nobody takes them seriously. But when a bunch of guys named Ibrahim or Nassar threaten to set the place on fire…everyone believes them. What does that tell you about our real attitudes toward Muslims?"

Two days after my controversial Iran broadcast, K-Bomb's actual program director, Karl Blake, called.

"Sorry about that," he said. "I owe you one. And we'll pay you for the week."

"I completely understand, Karl. There's just one thing I'd like. Can you get me a copy of the actual air check of my show? I still can't believe I ever said I'd like to drop an atom bomb on Iran. It's just not my style. But the papers say I said it, and the guy from MUM says I said it…so I'd like to know whether I said it. I'm starting to think I've gone crazy."

"Sure. I can get you that."

"Did you get that job?"

"We'll see."

A few days later, a cassette tape arrived in the mail. I listened to the entire show. About three quarters of the way through the half-hour I'd spent on Iran, I heard this exchange:

Caller: "Those Eye-ranians. I'd like to blow 'em all up. I'd like to just drop an atom bomb right on top of the place."

Me: "Seriously?"

Caller: "Yup. Just blow 'em off the face of the earth."

Me: "Well sir, *that* is why we don't let people keep those things in their garages."

I'm not sure whether knowing that a caller, and not the host, had made the remark they considered most offensive would have made any difference to MUM, but I felt better. The local reporters from both the city's major papers, who had been so quick to print my alleged statement, were absolutely not interested in correcting themselves. After all, since they'd put *alleged* in front of it, they seemed to feel they were under no obligation to make sure their "quote" was true. It was a timely reminder that the media is just a bunch of people going about their jobs. Some do their work with professionalism and care, and some don't. Even so, when you run in to the ones who don't give a rip, it's always a little disappointing.

The incident also prepared me for a growing trend in our industry. There are a lot of supposedly disinterested or impartial watchdog groups who have very specific agendas — and those agendas are not always what they put on their public position papers. MUM, in particular, has been behind the firings and suspensions of other talk show hosts they find objectionable. Usually, these hosts were hired to take on hot-button issues with drama and humor. But when MUM, or another pressure group, mounts a campaign, management frequently finds it easier to pull the plug on the host, rather than risk losing advertisers. It's increasingly rare to work for someone who will stand his or her ground under the pressure these kinds of groups can deliver. When you do work for a station owner, or a company that backs you up for doing the job you were hired to do, your gratitude is virtually boundless.

Del Stairs, the program director from KFFY, the LA talk station where I'd been a guest the day before, called me at home. Would I, he wanted to know, be interested in a regular weekend shift? I could commute. They'd pay my weekly airfare and expenses.

That is how I became, for the third time, a temporary resident of Los Angeles; and for the second time, a Bay Area to Burbank commuter.

.

Jesus Slept Here

If the universe ever played fair, and I'm not saying it does, then the LA job should have made up for some of the chaos and insanity of the past two years of my radio career. It did.

I was already a fan of the station's morning host, and I'd learned during my previous LA talk stint that he was a listener of mine. The highpoint of my experience with the Three Little Bosses Who Knew About Women was the day Wells, the number one air personality in LA, as well as a hugely successful businessman and attorney, called the program director's office looking for me. My boss's secretary thought it must be a prank, but the program director recognized Wells' voice, and put the call through. Wells' unmistakable gleeful cackle was the first shock; the second was that he actually wanted to talk about something I'd done on the air. His wife had suggested we get together for lunch.

At lunch, I was completely charmed with both Wells and his spouse, Jeri. They seemed to like me, too. When I came to LA to work for Dell Stairs, my manager at KFFY, Wells hosted mornings there. I commuted from Oakland to LA, every week, to work weekends. I also filled in for the evening host, my ex-boyfriend Paul, who had left Miami and was now on nights at KFFY.

When Del hired me, and I let Wells know, his first response was, "Do you have a place to stay? We have a guesthouse in our garden. Why don't you stay with us?" followed by, "Congratulations!" I hope Wells won't mind me mentioning his kindly side. He's known on the air as a tough cookie. I also hope he and Jeri have forgotten that I sort of ruined their new master bedroom.

About a year after I took up residence in their LA guesthouse, Jeri took me on a tour of their under-construction, custom-designed future home. The project was Jeri's baby, and it was nearly finished. Because Wells was by now hugely popular and often wildly controversial, they'd be moving to a gated community in the hills, where, unless you were a small dog that coyotes find tasty, it was much safer. A highlight of their new master bedroom was a just-installed, gorgeous, elaborately carved, centuries-old wooden headboard. Jeri had fallen for the piece on a "Travel with Your Listeners" trip to Europe.

After a stroll around their exquisite new home, Jeri and I began to make our way back to the kitchen, when her husband appeared at the bedroom door to call us for dinner.

"Wells!" I exclaimed. "The house is fantastic. I love every detail. The headboard is completely unique. And the carving of Jesus on it."

"Jesus? Jesus is over my bed? You're kidding." Wells boomed in a voice that could easily be identified by four out of five Angelinos, and heard two floors below in the gourmet kitchen. He ambled closer to the bed and, perhaps for the first time, took a *really* a good look at it. "Jesus!" he exclaimed, jumping back a few inches. "I had no idea he was there! Did you know Jesus was there, Jeri?"

Not only would Jesus be, in his carved aspect anyway, looking directly at the king size mattress of my friends' marital bed, but it bears mentioning that both Wells and Jeri are Jewish.

I realized immediately that I should not have said anything. Of course I should not have said anything. I guess I figured they had to have known Jesus was there, but liked the headboard for its artistic qualities. There were lots of other images on it—I seem to remember some lovely animals, and some fruit. Even though Wells makes a lot of fun of me for my very modest level of Jewish observance, and touts his absolute disregard for all things religious, I'm pretty sure I was not trying to make trouble. Pretty sure.

On the other hand, although I am paid to give my opinion, I should have known from past experiences that it's not usually a good idea for me to begin a sentence with, "You know what that looks like?" or "Has anybody told you that…"

Leslie, my LA savior, has been on the receiving end of my possession-spoiling observations more than once. The first time, I was helping her take some mildew stains out of a Norma Kamali designer seersucker print wrap dress; hand washing it over her kitchen sink. After about an hour of scrubbing and soaking, I casually remarked, "Leslie, did you ever consider simply stopping by a hospital supply room and replacing this dress with one of their robes? Maybe with some paper booties?" Although I got the expensive dress almost perfectly clean, Leslie has not been able to wear it since she began thinking of it as something that could easily be accessorized with an IV line. I messed up her $600 designer shiny black and silver vinyl raincoat, too, by pointing out that I had a box of contractor bags in my garage that looked about the same. In fact, I have a long and unpleasant history of re-casting my friends' clothes, cars, and even dates, in an unflattering light—a light, they tell me, that it is hard to turn off. If I were them, I might only hang around with me in the dark, and I would absolutely *never* let me near their closets.

I do not recall Jeri's response when I pointed out that Jesus was on her headboard. I *do* remember wanting to crawl back into the master bathroom and wash myself down the shower drain. I also don't know what Wells and Jeri ultimately did about the carved Christ over their pillows. I certainly never brought it up again. I'm guessing that they decided to do what many Jewish people do when it comes to Jesus: we don't worry too much about him.

Paul, meanwhile, had started dating another KFFY weekend host named Giselle, an alcoholic radio groupie. Giselle had landed a weekend program, as far as I could tell, by having an ex-husband in the business, and by assuming her maternal grandmother's Spanish last name (Spanish surnames were highly desirable in broadcasting at the time, particularly in Los Angeles). Giselle liked to do most of her show preparation at KFFY from the studio opposite the one where Paul was on the air. Her favorite show prep position was leaning over a counter, with her perky backside perched where Paul had an excellent view of it.

Giselle combined flaunting her tush with a romance-seeking strategy that almost no man can resist. I do not blame Paul one bit for falling for it. I have used it myself, more than once. You simply say to the gentleman in question, while looking at him with your most trusting and awed expression, "[Insert name of man here], you are the *most* amazing window washer (or race car driver or wild animal trainer or talk show host) I have *ever* seen. I would give *anything* to learn what you know. Would you teach me?"

This technique worked so well that Paul was soon engaged to marry Giselle. At Giselle's request, they made a huge event of it. Nuptials were held on the historic ocean liner, the RMS *Queen Mary*, now permanently moored in Long Beach.

Giselle was known to be jealous, and not a big fan of women in general. So I knew my days of simply hanging out with Paul were numbered; especially since, at his wedding, he made a joke about my returning the keys to his apartment.

While Paul requested I cover all his vacation days, Giselle tried every way she could to think of to get me fired. She was only successful in getting Paul to quit talking to me. This made it awkward to see him in the halls, but we managed. I didn't get my friend back till they divorced, a dozen years later.

We Don't Get Any Women

I once got angry enough to call a radio station. The host, Giles Brisk, was an ass who wasn't particularly fond of women, but being a misogynistic talk host and an ass wasn't especially unusual. To be a closeted, gay, libertarian talk host *and* a misogynistic ass was slightly more unusual. To be a closeted gay libertarian ass of a misogynistic talk show host in the city of San Francisco on its heritage talk station was however, something off the Richter scale entirely.

Giles Brisk prided himself on being cultured, a gentleman, and a fine dining expert. I don't know how much he knew or didn't know about fine dining, though he was definitely on the make for any dinner at any free expensive restaurant that would open a table and a wine list for him and his entourage of very non-closeted gay friends. They were known around town as Giles' boys. It was worth it to the restaurants to host a $3,000 meal, drinks included, for Giles and his companions, because they knew he'd be talking about their place on the air the next day. Giles' descriptions of the food he'd eaten, and the wine he'd drunk, made for stultifying radio, since he was never willing to describe the parties of young, hot, and wild gay men in a drunken state making passes at one another across the restaurant's banquette while flattering him. If he had been willing to talk, for instance, about the two *GQ* model twenty-somethings I'd heard (from Giles' former producer) had fed olive-oiled Spanish anchovies to one another by nibbling them simultaneously from either end, the show might have generated a larger, younger, hungrier audience.

The only women Giles welcomed on his show were chefs who had comped him cookbooks or meals; or in rare cases, worshipful sexagenarians who phoned in to talk about what a cultured, gentlemanly food expert Giles was, and to praise him for seldom taking sides in political discussions.

I could barely stand to listen to Giles for more than ten minutes at a time. Still, I considered it my professional duty, even though I worked for KFFY, the number one talk station in LA, to tune in and do my best to soldier through a quarter hour here and there whenever I was in the Bay Area. Which is how I heard Giles say, when a listener asked him why his station didn't have any women on the air, in serious and stentorian tones, that there were no women on talk radio because they didn't apply for talk radio jobs. "We can't hire good women to host talk shows, because they just don't apply. We just don't get any good women," he pronounced. "Women have never seemed interested in doing the hard work of hosting a talk radio show. Maybe they don't see the appeal of it," he continued, "or maybe they have families, and the hours are too demanding." Giles added that this had also been true for all of the other stations where he'd spent decades of his life, from Boston to Miami.

These were the early days of tiny cell phones, when minutes counted. I was darned if I was going to waste my precious seconds of talk time hanging on hold to get on the air, but Giles was still going on about women being their own worst enemies when I arrived home driving twenty miles over the speed limit. I nearly tore a side view mirror off my car as I whipped into the narrow driveway between my house and the one next door. I dashed up the back stairs and snatched my kitchen phone off the wall. I almost never remember numbers, but the digits to Giles' radio station phone line seemed, in that moment, to reside in my fingertips as I dialed.

"I'd like to talk to Giles about the lack of women in talk radio," I gasped into the phone, trying very hard to bring my breathing back to normal after my adrenaline-fueled sprint, "because I am one."

"Your name?" the phone screener asked.

"I'm sure Mr. Brisk will know my station, and probably my name, too, but I'd prefer to give them to him myself."

"Okay. May I tell him your station affiliation?"

"Sure. Tell him I'm a host on KFFY."

"Okay. Stand by, and turn your radio sound down," intoned the perfectly trained phone screener.

It took just a few moments to hear the telltale metallic hiss of a phone line going live on the air.

"Welcome to the Giles Brisk show. You're a woman in talk radio?" Giles asked, with more than a hint of skepticism in his voice.

"Yes, I am. In Los Angeles. And I can tell you why you don't have any women on your radio station."

"You can?" he responded, in the jovial manner I'd overheard department store Santas use with six-year-olds who climb on their laps and demand ponies.

"Yes, I can. You don't have women on your station because your mangers, and most managers of other talk stations, don't want them. They don't believe we can succeed without a man leading the show. So if we say we want to host our own shows, they don't hire us. Or if they do, they put us on in the middle of the night, or give us the lovers advice show, which they figure we can manage, because women, they think, are more emotional.

Sometimes they tell us to our faces that they won't hire us, but usually we hear about it from our friends who are men who work at these stations—stations that have openings, but not openings for women.

If you're a woman who can add, and you do the math, you'll see where women end up, if we can get on the air at all. Two shifts for us, maybe, compared to six for men.

So, Mr. Brisk, let me ask you a question: If you were a smart, funny, ambitious woman with original thought and great conversational skills, and you desperately wanted to be a talk radio host, but after years of trying, you realized you were going to get, at most, 20% of the opportunities that men get, especially white men, and by now you have an electric bill to pay, and college tuition for your kids, and a mortgage; would you keep on banging on the talk radio program manager's locked door, or would you take your smart, funny, talented self to some other line of entertainment, like TV, or movies, or comedy writing? *That* is where the women are going now. Because how stupid would you have to be to keep trying to get on the air in an industry that does not want you, no matter how good you are?

I'm lucky to work at one of the very few stations that hire women. We have a successful syndicated show run by a woman, plus four other part-time women who host regular shifts—six a week, not counting fill-in. The full-time woman, by the way, hosts a relationship show. I host two weekend shifts and fill-in, on average, three evening shifts a week—because I didn't want to host overnights. I did it for years, just like the men. I don't want to do it anymore, but I don't want to quit, so now I work part-time and swing.

And guess what? Our station is number one in Los Angeles; which, as I'm sure you know, is the number two radio market in the country."

"Well, you certainly are sure of yourself," responded a slightly less bombastic-sounding Giles Brisk.

"Yes. I certainly am."

"That's a very interesting approach. I'll have to give it some thought."

"Thanks Giles, and thank you for taking my call."

The line went dead. I turned on the radio that lived on my kitchen counter just in time to hear the past twenty seconds of delayed broadcast over San Francisco's heritage talk station. "You're very welcome," concluded a slightly bwildered Gentleman Giles.

I don't know whether Giles' views on women in talk radio changed one iota, but I felt orders of magnitude happier. As soon as my heartbeat returned to normal, I tromped back downstairs to the driveway to see whether I had scraped our neighbor's house with my side view mirror. I hadn't.

We Know Where You Live

I liked Dell, my boss at KFFY. He gave excellent feedback. If the listeners called with complaints, Dell insulated his staff from most of them. When groups like MUM threatened to picket, Dell would invite them to "Come on down. I'll have lunch catered." And he would. When one of the hosts created the on-air character of a megalomaniacal, witless, boob of a program director, and named it after him, Del got a kick out of it. And Del had the best strategy for dealing with stalkers and creeps.

Dell's method was never deployed on my behalf that I know of, but I'm told it worked very well. The station retained a well-connected former FBI agent who, in his second career, had morphed into a private investigator. He still looked like an FBI agent. When KFFY received mailed threats against staff that were not specific enough to meet the threshold then required for the police to arrest somebody, this private investigator would track down the workplace or home of the letter-writer, and show up there. Usually, all it took was for the author to see his missive dangling from the hand of a burly former FBI agent (an FBI agent who was making his way slowly across an office or shop floor) to be personally returned to sender. When it comes to creepy, violent, racist, or threatening letters, knowledge that you are no longer writing them anonymously tends to have an inhibiting effect.

Stream of consciousness radio was both my strong suit, and my weak spot. I was so notorious for veering off from one topic in an entirely new direction that my producer and I came up with a signal to steer me back towards whatever I'd promised the audience I'd be talking about. She'd hold up a plastic picnic fork on her side of the soundproof glass. Sometimes I was so far down the road to wherever my new idea had launched me that she had to wave that fork around.

I think that's how I ended up warning all parents never to let their kids join a youth group. It was an unplanned departure from something else.

"Youth groups are set up to lull you into the belief that your kids are safe from all harm. They are doing meaningful community service, or helping them grow spiritually, or teaching them some important life skill. Yes. But not the way you think. If, by community service, you mean increasing the population by adding to its birth rate; by helping them grow spiritually, you mean giving them a chance to make out behind the synagogue altar; or by life skills, you mean learning how to kiss or undo a brassiere with one hand, then by all means—sign your kid up for your favorite youth group. That's pretty much where I learned all that stuff—because we were out of class, and together with a bunch of other kids our age with raging hormones, often for overnight or late-night activities, with either minimal supervision, or overseen by youth group leaders who were not much older than we were.

I distinctly remember 'lock-ins' where we were supposed to be spending the night on some worthwhile project, like making food baskets for poor families, and we'd have to wait twenty minutes for whichever couple was lip-locked in the pantry to finish whatever they were doing so we could bake whatever we were allegedly baking to put into the baskets. I think it was supposed to be challah bread. When the couple came out, they were covered with flour from the giant paper sack they were lying on, and one of them had a bruise that stayed on her thigh for a week from rolling onto a can of poppy seed filling."

As sometimes happens in these cases, my audience has more experience than I do. Turns out my youth group escapades were fairly tame, and the real revelation, at least to me, was what other kids were up to at their youth groups and parochial schools.

"Monica from Encino, you're on KFFY"

"Hi Turi. I just want to say you're totally right. The sluttiest girls I ever knew were in my class at Catholic school."

"Really? Catholic school? I thought those nuns kept pretty good order. And didn't you have to wear modest uniforms?"

"Well, they had no control over what we did before and after school. So we used to bring pins, and pin our skirts up as high as we could. Then at home, we'd remove threads from the plaid material, so our skirts would be see-through."

"Who thought that up?"

"I have no idea, but we all did it. Some of us pulled so much fabric out of our skirts that we might as well have been wearing plastic baggies. And we all stuffed our bras. It was an all-girls school, but there was a boys' school across the street, so we'd get together after class and, um, *study*."

"Wow. I'm impressed. Thanks for the heads up. I don't have kids yet, but I'm putting parochial school on my list of things I'm gonna need to watch out for."

"No problem. Glad to help."

"Brad from Culver City…"

"Yeah, Turi. You're right on about the youth group thing. I was a Boy Scout. We spent most of our time lying about sex and—can I say jerk off?" My board operator hit the delay button, which removed twenty seconds of Brad from Culver City.

"No, Brad, you can't. So let me help you with your language here. You say you spent most of your time at Boy Scout Camp lying about sex and pleasuring yourselves?"

"Yeah. And we stole the scout leader's stash."

"No!"

"Yeah. What are they gonna do? Report us? They were high all the time anyway."

"Brad, you are wrecking my fantasy of Boy Scouts. I always thought of you guys as frontiersmen trained to live in the wilderness for days with nothing more than a pocket knife."

"A pocket knife and few joints, yeah. We could do that."

"Thanks, Brad. Tiffany from Seal Beach. It says on my screen that you got pregnant while you were in the Masons? How does that happen? I didn't even think girls could *be* Masons."

"We couldn't. We were 'Rainbow Girls. I'm not the one who got pregnant, but two other Rainbow Girls did."

"What do you do in Rainbow Girls?"

"It wasn't what we were supposed to be doing, that's for sure. We were supposed to be memorizing this stuff about faith and each color stood for something—love and faith and service—I can't even remember. Our dads were all Masons, so this was what they had the girls do, and then there was this boys group called the DeMolay, which was also supposed to be about service…."

"Don't say it."

"I won't say it."

"*Two* of you?"

"Yeah."

"What did you tell your parents?"

"One of the girls was older, and I think she had the baby and her parents raised it, and I think the other girl went to Mexico and had an abortion."

"And I thought making out on the altar was a big deal. That guy—the guy I made out with on the altar—he's a rabbi now."

"Well, maybe you inspired him."

"I never thought of it that way. You've just made me feel a whole lot better about my youth group experience, Tiffany."

"Cool."

"Would you let your kid join a youth group?"

"You know, I'd forgotten all about that part, till you brought it up today. And I'm married, and I have two kids, but they're little. I'm not sure."

"You've got time to think about it."

"Yeah. I will."

"Brandi from Tarzana, you're on KFFY."

"I was a Mariner. That's a kind of waterborne Girl Scout. I'm a lesbian, and that's where I had my first experience—it was on a boat. Most of the girls were really into boys. They used to joke that they wanted a badge on their sash for…ok, let me say it this way. Um, they spent a lot of time *talking about their techniques*, which I thought was pretty gross…but I guess if you're into it…"

"Yeah. If you're into it, technique is important."

"For us too, for other stuff."

"I suppose it would have to be."

"So I just wanted you to know, if your kid is gay, youth group can be great."

"Thanks for calling."

I spent a full hour taking calls from people who spent their youth group years up to every kind of mischief, from shoplifting to running their own youth group event bars (courtesy of their parents' liquor cabinets) to simply lying about being at youth group altogether.

When it was over, I gained a new perspective on the creativity and treachery of fifteen-year-olds, and my producer had long since put down her plastic fork.

I loved my shifts at KFFY. In the second year, however, word came that if I were not willing to do an overnight shift, the only full-time shift that might become available, the station wouldn't be able to continue the commuting arrangement. There were a lot of reasons I couldn't go back to doing overnights. One was that Save the Planet and I were thinking of becoming parents. But if I were ever going have a kid, time was running out.

Feeling the Ice Cube

Married for over a year, unemployed, and rapidly approaching forty, it seemed like a good time to have a baby. It also sounded much better, when people asked why I was no longer on KFFY, to say, "I'm taking time off to have a baby," instead of saying, "Because I couldn't bear the idea of being back on overnights, and I'm tired of moving." After giving the baby line to several people several times, I started to believe I might actually be ready to have a baby. In my secret heart, I knew that would never be true. But Save the Planet, I was convinced, would make up for my nearly complete lack of maternal instinct and my silent, or possibly non-existent, biological clock. I figured that by this time, old as I was, there was also a reasonably good chance that I wouldn't be able to get pregnant anyway, and then I could say I'd tried to have a baby, but hadn't been successful, and I'd get sympathy and never have to live whatever kind of masochistic life I was convinced was involved in having an actual, non-verbal, diaper-wearing baby. I was so anxious and conflicted at the idea of motherhood that I completely neglected to be anxious about pregnancy itself. This turned out to be my biggest miscalculation.

When you miss playing a commercial on the radio, you give the client what is called a "make-good" commercial to compensate. As soon as I'd retrieved my few household goods from Wells and Jeri's guesthouse, I started planning a trip to Spain and Morocco. I considered it my "make-good" honeymoon—compensation for the disaster that had been Glacier National Park. As often happens on honeymoons, I came home from Spain with a few lovely souvenirs, and a pregnancy.

Books have been written about the things you don't get told about being pregnant. All of them are true. To escalate the misery of the uncomfortably pregnant middle-age woman, America's obstetricians, midwives, and doulas frequently recommend a social/educational experience called the "birthing group." My doctor required all his patients to enroll in a birthing class, so I picked one that met near me, where I would learn, presumably, what the American hospital birthing experience of the fully insured would be like.

I recently checked around to see if modern birthing groups are still set up along the same lines as the one I attended. They seem to be. One website stressed that the groups are about having babies "from a place of positivity instead of fear." Another encourages women to "take back childbirth." By my fifth month of pregnancy, I would have been only too happy to delegate the task to somebody else.

Even before we began our first session, the birthing group building gave me a sample of the escalating discomfort of pregnancy. It met in an airless, unclean room at the top of three dusty flights of puce-carpeted stairs. The neighborhood required street parking several blocks away. It was summer. Save the Planet and I struggled into the small, hot space a predictable—for us—twenty minutes late. There were eight other couples, each containing one late-third-trimester pregnant woman. The group was already dispersed on pillows and low cushions around the walls.

"Welcome! Take a seat, please." The leader, a no-nonsense looking woman wearing snugly fitting, size fourteen jeans, short brown hair, a purple T-shirt, and no makeup, beckoned us to join the circle of couples. There were absolutely no chairs, so I tried to find a position on the floor from which it looked fairly certain that I'd be able to get up. There seemed to be handgrip opportunities in the corner. I settled myself on a slightly grimy fuchsia velour pillow. "I'm Sage, your doula coach for the class. We've just been working on our first experiential birthing assignment. Would you care to take an ice cube?"

I knew what an ice cube was, but most of the rest of what Sage said left me feeling that perhaps English wasn't my first language after all.

"You have missed our first assignment. Would you like to grip a large ice cube in your bare hand until it melts, and draw a crayon picture of your emotions about how that feels?"

I did not want to hold an ice cube in my bare hand. I was already holding a seven-month fetus in my bare uterus. The ice cube experiment had produced some interesting art already. One partner drew a large anvil in orange, suspended over his head, like something from a Wile E. Coyote and Roadrunner cartoon. Another made a series of asterisks and exclamation points like a swearing comic book character. One husband colored his piece of paper entirely black, obscuring, with time-consuming diligence, any sign of the white paper underneath. (Shortly after relocating his wife and, by then, two children to Washington DC, the Black Crayon of Doom father deserted his family for one of his employees. I have no idea whether the crayon incident was foreshadowing, but his picture did make me glad that I was sitting next to somebody else.)

I surreptitiously dropped my ice cube on the floor, and waited for our next assignment. We were all supposed to go around in a circle, answering, for the other members of the group, the question, "What do you want to get from the class?" Some hopeful answers included:

"I want to involve my husband in more of the birthing process."

"Can you tell me whether it's too soon for my daughter to benefit from the classical music and stories we are playing and reading for her every night?"

"Is there a spa in the Bay Area where I can have a water birth?"

I went last, because we'd been late, but I was ready with my question. "I would like to know what drugs will be available, and when I can get them."

I could feel the oxygen leaving the room, the way you feel your mouth collapse when you try to suck up a too-thick milkshake. You might have thought I'd just opened up a bottle of scotch at a meeting of Alcoholics Anonymous. Everyone looked at Doula Sage.

"We'll cover that," she said.

I actually cared less about chemical intervention at that moment than I did about the panic in my heart that had set in over my lack of "bonding" with the not-yet-born-baby. Never one of the legions of women who melt at the sight of an infant, I assumed that the actual pregnancy would enhance my insufficient maternal sympathies. But by my third month, when nothing seemed to have changed, I checked to see whether there was a word for what I had. I found the word for fear of pregnancy and childbirth (tokophobia) but there wasn't one for the fear of regarding your newborn with indifference. I went around the house singing "Nothing" from *A Chorus Line* for a half hour straight. STP eventually took notice.

"Are you worried that you will feel nothing?"

"That's very perceptive of you," I responded, with the suppressed snarl that had marked every month of my pregnancy since conception.

"Don't be worried." He would say, in his most soothing voice.

"Why not? Because you have enough paternal impulse to safely shepherd an entire baseball team of babies from birth to puberty? Why shouldn't I be worried? What if, while you're grinding up special organic baby food for our son, I take our child out in his stroller, and accidently leave him at the park, returning with a sense of calm and well-being?" I responded. "Why wouldn't I be worried? Other mothers-to-be are massaging their bellies and singing at the grocery store, and I'm sleeping forty-five minutes at a stretch, hurling *sotto voce* epithets at our unborn child, and can't fit into my shoes. If the doctor hands me a puppy and says, 'here's your baby,' I'm not so sure I'd be all that disappointed. I like puppies, and you don't have to send them to college. I like children when they are old enough to argue with—say—about eight."

"Turi, you're a pretty good actress. Just fake it till our kid turns eight."

Strangely, I found this advice helpful. I was going to fake liking my kid till he turned eight. I could do it. Then I almost got divorced over a $20 parking space.

Your Zone of Cheapness
Part 2

My husband is a generous person. He volunteers at food kitchens. He helps near-strangers load their possessions into rented moving trucks, and all his pets are adopted. I managed to avoid dealing with Save The Planet's parking Zone of Cheapness by working from home, keeping odd hours, and driving my own car. There's no snow in the Bay Area, so I had no problem walking an extra few blocks every now and then to indulge him in his quest for free parking.

The parking Zone of Cheapness didn't have much of an impact on me—I even made jokes about it—until I went into labor with our firstborn. Sometime between the epidural and the pant-and-push, my husband left the room. I was slightly relieved, because he had taken the advice of Doula Sage:

"Labor can go on for hours, longer than a day. You should pack some healthy things to eat." Save the Planet had packed a Tupperware container of very garlicky homemade hummus. If you do not already know this, learn it now: *Do not breathe into the face of a laboring woman when you have eaten half a tub of anything with a lot of garlic in it.*

Save the Planet breathed into my face twice before I banished him to the other end of the bed. I noticed he was missing when the smell of the garlic died down. I looked around between contractions—no spouse. He came back, though. And I banished him to the end of the bed again, where his breath would be less obnoxious. When he disappeared a second time, about two hours later, I finally figured out what was going on: My husband, the father of our about-to-be-delivered child, had left the "coaching position," abandoned the entire labor and delivery suite of the hospital—to feed a parking meter.

My friends couldn't understand how a man who could cheerfully review and pay hospital bills totaling in the thousands would balk at a $20 garage fee, but I knew I had run smack into his Zone of Cheapness.

I watched, in a happy, epidural-enhanced haze, through a mirror as my firstborn emerged. The doctor and Save the Planet handed me an approximately five-pound boy. I was a little dismayed at his size. He looked pretty scrawny. I was sure it was my fault. Even after several weeks of medically necessary bed rest, I'd been chemically induced to have the baby a few weeks early. Later, when I mentioned to my Grandma Rose my regret at not being able to carry the child until he could reach a larger size, she comforted me with this practical suggestion: "Who needs to give birth to a ten-pound baby? Let him gain it outside."

The baby was spirited away seconds after being presented to his mother so that he could be warmed up under

what looked like those lights they use in fast food places to
make sure your fries are served hot. This gave my doctor a
moment to consult with me on our post-partum plan of
action.

"You're going to want to take him home tomorrow,"
advised my doctor.

"Really? Are you one of those doctors who pitches
women out of the hospital before they're ready?" I asked,
rather unfairly.

"Oh, you can stay longer if you want to," my obstetrician
nodded sagely, "I just don't think you'll want to."

That's how I discovered the technique by which hospitals
help keep their discharge rates high: in cases where you do
not have a private room, they figure out what you like to
watch on TV, and how loudly you like to watch it. Then, they
put the ear-splitting *Wheel of Fortune* watchers in with the
Masterpiece Theater watchers. After twenty-four hours of
hearing the big wheel spin, or polite British wit—whichever
you abhor—you will call up your relatives and demand they
bust you out at two in the morning.

But on the very first morning, when the *Wheel of Fortune*
watcher in the bed next to me had been evacuated by her
extended family, I had a few minutes alone with the child my
listeners came to know as the Big Cutie. I was watching him
in his blue, pink, and white flannel swaddle blanket, in that
clear plastic drawer on wheels in which they store newborns.
A nurse bustled in, took his temperature, and advised me that
he needed another round under the French fry warmer.

"Do you think," I asked, "that I could just hold him, and warm him up myself?"

"Sure," replied the nurse, and brought the little pile of wrapped flannel to my bed. I un-swaddled him carefully, and stashed him under my hospital gown, next to my skin.

Have you ever wandered through a strange house, turning on lights as you move from room to room? Putting the baby next to my body gave me the sensation that I'd just flicked on the light and stepped into a room in my heart that I hadn't even known was there. After a few minutes, I was pretty sure I wasn't going to trade the Big Cutie for a puppy.

Nursing a grudge came second to nursing the baby, so I forgave Save the Planet for his parking meter vanishing act. But I didn't forget. Two years later, for our second son, I prepared a strategy: I made Save the Planet swear on a stack of cotton diapers that he would not use a parking meter. I presented him with a $20 bill as though it were a sacred token, and told him he absolutely positively *must* put the car in the hospital's garage. Under no circumstances, I warned him, would he be leaving the labor and delivery room to feed a parking meter. He agreed.

Since childbirth was induced again, we planned the logistics like a military campaign. STP was going to send our oldest to preschool; then, when called, he would pick him up and drop him off with a friend. STP would transfer both kid and car seat from one Berkeley Volvo to another at the Whole Foods parking lot just around the corner from the hospital. Then he'd drive to the hospital, park, and join me in labor and delivery.

Labor began, as expected, mid-morning. My friend called my cell phone to say that the child handoff had been accomplished smoothly, and Save the Planet was en route.

Then…nothing. No husband. No call. By my calculations, he'd been four blocks away for about twenty-five minutes. Delivery was moving right along, so in between contractions, I placed an anxious call. "Where are you?"

I would not have been more amazed by what I heard at the other end of the phone if my husband had suddenly decided to try out for *American Idol*. Panting. *PANTING?* He was panting. I was supposed to be the one panting. "I'm having this baby right now. Where the fuck are you?"

"I'll be there in a minute [*pant pant*]. I'm not far away. Don't worry. I won't be leaving to feed a meter."

Therapists say most couples divorce not over cheating, sloppy housekeeping, or compulsive sports-watching, but over money. I could have done an Alec Baldwin-versus-the-paparazzi temper tantrum through the floor and called a lawyer over the fact that it was only by luck that my spouse, who had cruised the neighborhood until he found the only free parking blocks within half a mile of the hospital, arrived in time for the birth of our child. But…everybody has a Zone of Cheapness.

The Changing Table

I lied. I had told Save the Planet that he could work to his heart's content in whatever underpaying but worthy occupation he preferred, because I, the capitalist tool, would be creating wealth for our family. *Ha.* The minute I took the Big Cutie home, I was unwilling to do anything that required me to be away from him for more than a few hours at a time. (Which is not to say that we were one of those mother-child couples who seem to be attached at the abdomen. On my first foray from the house without a diaper bag, I felt as close as I believe a human being can feel to actually flying.) What I experienced was something between inertia and sloth. The baby was like a sort of quicksand into which my hours and days could be poured. Gaining any traction on moving off the living room floor and back to work seemed uninteresting, and therefore unlikely.

On the other hand, I was abstractly worried about the possibility that I might never work in radio again. At the point where I had amassed a significant store of frozen breast milk, I was ready to go, at least for a few hours a week, somewhere—anywhere—where I was not known as "Mommy." Fortunately, there was a big heritage talk station just across the Bay Bridge. It looked like I might be able to get my hands on a few night shifts, or possibly even weekend work. I packed up my breast pump and headed in for training. The shifts did not go well. Maybe I was out of my element, since the station followed a more traditional host-interviews-guest format. Maybe I just wasn't sounding so great. I had only covered a few shifts when I found I was in trouble with management. "Why did I interview a not-particularly famous guest over the phone, instead of asking him to come into the studio?" the program director's right-hand woman wanted to know. Also "Why did you choose to talk about your union's strike against commercial producers? Wasn't that a little self-serving?"

Actually, they didn't ask me about these things. I found out when I called for the third time to find out what had become of the week of holiday shifts they'd asked me to host. That's when they told me. If they had actually asked me, I could have answered them:

I like people to be on the phone, because if they turn out to be boring guests, it is easier to get rid of them. I don't think your audience cares whether an interesting guest is across the table from you, or in another country, providing the sound quality is good. Conversely, if you have the most famous actor or politician or celebrity sitting virtually in your lap, if he or she can't string a sentence together, it just takes you longer to say "goodbye" and move him out the door.

The union strike came up as part of a conversation with a local guy who had recently found a small amount of fame, if not fortune, by becoming the spokesperson for a neighborhood pizza chain as the character "Big Wally." I asked Big Wally whether the performers strike was going to put an end to his pizza-pitching career. Technically, it couldn't have been self-serving, because I wasn't doing any voice over work at the time.

I was disappointed. Then I was invited to a bizarre exit interview where Jay, the program director, whom I'd never met before, informed me that he'd never wanted to hire me in the first place. The whole thing left me confused, and further convinced that I'd dumped my career in the diaper pail.

I also felt a little bad for the program director's assistant, who seemed to have gotten caught between Jay and her desire to put some diversity into what was, at that point, a strictly old-boys network. I was called in one more time at the last minute to cover for the restaurant reviewer's Sunday food show...and that was it—almost.

The city's former mayor, a major political power broker statewide, had always dreamed of hosting a talk show. The program manager hated the ex-mayor's guts, but the GM owed the ex-mayor a favor. Consequently, the city's former leader was going to get a three-hour, one-time radio talk show. There were just two problems: The ex-mayor was legally blind. He was also extremely vain. Although his suits and shoes were the stuff of newspaper columns, the ex-mayor was losing his ability to put on his own diamond cufflinks.

But nobody was supposed to know that the ex-mayor couldn't see well enough to read commercial copy, or the programming log, or the names of callers displayed on the studio's computer screen. So a person with "genuine radio experience" (me) would stand by in the on-air studio and function as a text-and-screen reader for the ex-mayor. My descent was complete. I'd gone from talk show host at a major market talk station to human seeing eye dog in less time than it took for one baby to start crawling.

It was back to the stroller and changing table. I blended my own baby food. We adopted a German Shepherd. I did every maternal thing I could think of, except those "mommy and me" music classes. Those were more than I could tolerate. In fact, any "mommy and me" classes made me want to be disruptive in a way I hadn't been since fifth grade. I blame Berkeley, where I found many mothers intolerably self-righteous. A random stranger at the fruit and vegetable market gave a friend of mine a hard time about the bottle in her baby's mouth. Kelly, who had a physical anomaly that had left her unable to make breast milk, fled the store in tears.

"What do I say?" she beseeched me on the phone. "I just don't know what to say to these women. They come up to me all day long, telling me what I'm doing to Seth's IQ by giving him a bottle. I'm afraid to leave the house."

"Tell them…" I thought for a second. "Tell them you'd like to be nursing, but your chemotherapy makes your breast milk toxic."

I didn't really mind not working for the next year; but at the two-year mark, life grew difficult. My Grandma Rose died just before our second baby was born. Rose spent most of her last few years holding court from her recliner chair in her courtyard-facing New York City apartment. Rose really knew how to get a two-year-old to remember her. Her genius with product placement and promotion employed a philosophy I've used ever since: "Give them as much candy as they want."

Whenever our firstborn would visit, Rose would offer him candy. Then more candy. Then still more candy. "Grandma," I'd protest, "that's a lot of candy."

"Let him have as much as he wants," she'd respond. "He'll remember."

He did. If you ask Big Cutie what he remembers about his great-grandma, he will say, "She got stuck in her power-lift recliner chair when it went all the way up, and she let me have as much candy as I wanted."

(Rose's advice on abundance also proved useful when I was back at work. Listeners will remember you if you give them not only something they really want, but also as much of it as they want. If they like your show, make a podcast for them, and show up at their community events and charity functions, too. Be generous.)

Grandma Rose, on the other hand, often did not remember her visitors, from the young women volunteering at the Jewish senior service agency who came to study with her (my Grandmother loved to learn. Mostly, though, she loved to find "matches" from her congregation for the twenty-two-year-old religious college student volunteers) to her daughter and son, who phoned daily. So we installed a whiteboard next to her recliner chair, where her caregiver wrote the news of the day, along with which of her children and grandchildren had telephoned. When I arrived at her home, a couple of days before Thanksgiving, for Rose's funeral, the whiteboard was inscribed, in big blue letters: "Turi's baby due March 3."

Part III

My Name is Not Mommy

The new baby, born over a month early, was not healthy. Our insurance, through my union, was coming to an end. Save the Planet had consulting work, but it didn't come with insurance. Like so many other American families, we had to start paying for our coverage, and it was going to be expensive. I figured if I could get even a part-time union radio job, I could amass enough hours to qualify for the healthcare plan. That's how I became Lila Wright, traffic reporter for Million Mile Traffic.

I would be lying if I said the baby's health was the only reason I took the traffic reporter job. The compromise I made between childless, career-obsessed, move-anywhere-for-a-lucrative-contract performer, and stay-at-home-mom was this: No matter how many hours I spent lying on the floor channeling the inner thoughts of terry cloth stuffed animals in a wacky voice, I needed somewhere I could go where my name was not "Mommy." The all-night news and traffic gig filled that need. I didn't feel quite like the cool career woman I had once been, since it is difficult to impersonate a cool anything when you have a large blue plastic case containing a breast milk pump slung over your shoulder where your boho purse used to be. At least at my new job, people looked at me without wondering whether perhaps I might be hiding a spoonful of mashed sweet potato behind my back.

Lila Wright got a lot of the karma I had coming to me for not having understood, over the years, what demands are placed on a radio station's traffic reporters. These reporters usually do not work for an individual radio station. Instead, they work for a traffic service, likely across town in some other building. I had no idea what these people did when they were not providing, with various levels of competence, traffic reports for whatever station I was on. I didn't know they wrote reports and often newscasts, under several different names, for four or five stations. I didn't know that they reported for those stations at a set time every hour, not to mention calling up the sheriff's department or the local police or fire departments for details on traffic incidents, often coordinating with the airborne reporters as well. So when I was a DJ or a talk host, if I were late to my traffic report, and my reporter wasn't there when I "tossed" to her, I thought it must be her fault. She must not be paying attention. Lila Wright taught Turi Ryder the truth about traffic.

I was now providing overnight weekend news, plus traffic, to the market-leading station that had given me those few talk shows a year and a half before. Eventually, somebody there was bound to find out who I really was. And, when word inevitably made its way to Jay, he did a gloating turn around his newsroom.

"How far the mighty have fallen," Jay crowed. "One day, you're hosting talk radio on the number one station, and the next, you're doing midnight news and traffic from The Million Mile Traffic Center."

Jay's midday show producer, Whit, was also a weekend news and traffic reporter at Million Mile. By marvelous coincidence, the audience for Jay's snarky monologue included Whit, who was sitting in the newsroom at that exact moment.

"Jay, did you know that Turi just had a baby with health problems, and that she's taken the traffic job so she can keep her insurance and take care of him?"

I was not there, but several witnesses reported that Jay first visibly paled, then turned rose-pink, and finally, retreated in silence to his Bay-view office. The debt I owe to Whit, now a successful news anchor in Sacramento, is one I will be happy to repay anytime.

As Lila Wright, I snuck out two or three nights a week, more during holiday seasons, with my breast pump, my cooler, and my files of "kicker" stories—the "just for fun" stories you hear at the end of many newscasts. A few months into the gig, I learned some bad news: The Million Mile Traffic Center's contract did not include union health benefits. I'd become a traffic reader for a modest paycheck, period. But I stayed for a couple of years. We needed the money.

Sometimes I supplied the morning news for stations a hundred miles from our studios. I was the traffic lady on a country station in Santa Rosa where the female member of the wakeup team treated me like a bad waitress. I was the appreciative audience for the midday host's bad puns at Jay's number-one station. And I was the bête noir of Jay's overnight weekend host, Dr. Bob Rattleberg. Dr. Bob was known, in station promotional materials and to his listeners, as the "Smartest Man on Radio." Bob was an archconservative, a cop groupie, and a research scientist. The rumor was that he worked from home so as to avoid getting a DUI after his shift. On a certain evening, Bob took exception to a story I'd excerpted from a major newspaper, with attribution, on pension spiking among the state's sheriffs. Pension spiking, for those who do not have, or spike, their pensions, works this way: You want to retire. Your pension will be calculated by a formula based on your salary at retirement, and the years you've worked at your job. It will, or it is supposed to be, less than the salary you made when you were on the job. However, if you have a sympathetic boss, or political clout, or management wants you out of the place, you may engage in pension spiking. You get a whopping big raise. You work at that salary for a year. Then you retire with pay similar, if not identical to, your salary in the year before you spiked. When public employees game the system like that, it costs the taxpayers plenty. So the investigative piece about the state's sheriffs spiking their pensions was pretty big news, which is why I put it at the top of my newscast, and got about halfway through it when Dr. Rattleberg interrupted.

"See, there you go, picking on law enforcement. That's just the kind of radical liberal crap I expect from some minimum wage traffic reporter."

"Excuse me, Bob?

"You heard me. You have some kind of radical liberal agenda, like all these so-called news media. You're nothing but a bunch of punks."

"I didn't make that story up, Bob. It's from *The Sacramento Blaze*. I attributed it to them."

"Don't give me that crap. You know you're putting these lies out there because you're nothing but a liberal punk."

I have learned a few things from being a talk show host. One of them is this:

The audience does not like you to abuse your power. The audience likes to believe you will treat them fairly. And they imagine your subordinates and support staff are more like them than the host is like them. So treating your subordinates unfairly, or unkindly, does not go over well with the listeners. To fix Bob's wagon, I became sweet—very, very sweet.

"Well, Bob," I said in my most sincere and innocent voice, "that's why, after my five-minute news cast, you have a three-hour talk show: to undo all the damage you feel I'm doing. I'm sure you can correct whatever misinformation I've given out in this small item in the next talk show hour that you're about to do." Then I gave my traffic report, and turned my microphone off.

Dr. Rattleberg, at the end of my traffic and weather report, turned his microphone volume up about as high as I'd ever heard it, and demanded I come back on the air with him.

"Lila Wright," he taunted, "you're nothing but a liberal coward. You're nothing but a minimum-wage hack. An idiot. A stupid member of the stupid anti-police majority of spineless morons who beg the cops to show up when a stray dog relieves itself on your lawn, but doesn't think our men in law enforcement deserve a dime for risking their lives for punks like you. That's why you won't talk to me."

I maintained radio silence.

"You think you're so clever. Investigative news article, my ass. You wouldn't know a piece of journalism if you fell over it. Answer me!"

Having spent years on Bob's side of the talk microphone, I was content to keep quiet. I knew, just as surely as if I'd had a crystal ball, what was about to happen: Bob's phone lines were about to light up like an airport runway, and not with people sympathetic to his cause. Bob demanded I come back on the air with him. He called me a coward a few more times. He escalated his tirade of insults to the point where I was confident that every call he'd take for the next hour would be about how bad his audience felt for Lila Wright, that harmless newswoman.

As I've mentioned, when it comes to a controversial show, the calls to management the next day are always worse than the ones that come in during your shift. Jay, Bob's boss, arrived at his office Monday morning to find an inbox full of messages. The switchboard rang like a fire alarm. How could the great Dr. Bob Rattleberg have been so mean to that sweet little newsgirl? Jay is a pro. He actually pulled the snooper tape of the incident and listened to Bob's meltdown. Then he called my boss and asked that his apologies be conveyed to "Lila." I can't recall whether Bob himself apologized. I didn't care. Every now and then, it's good to be the cupcake.

But the occasional duel with a drunken weekend talk show host wasn't completely satisfying, professionally speaking. I still had a need, perhaps a pathetic one, to gather stories and material for the show I hoped I'd once again have. Or maybe by this time, show prep was simply as much a part of the rhythm of my life as cooking dinner. In any case, I realized I was still living my life as if it were twenty-four hours a day of show prep. That's why I couldn't resist returning the dead guppy.

Belly Up, or Return of the Dead Guppy

The guppy cost $1.25. Returning it was an exercise in self-indulgence. I had a feeling the effort would give me a story, and material for a talk show—always a good excuse.

The guppy lived for less than forty-eight hours in its new home, the aquarium in my children's room. It didn't look happy from the moment we let it out of its little plastic bag, swimming listlessly in a lazy circle, which became an oval, which soon became a sideways float. It was not the first time a fish from this particular store had not lived long. Gouramies had gone to their makers, platies had plotzed, and tetras had terminated in the course of my life as a fish-keeper. But for the most part, we had a tepid tank with a one-gallon per fish compliment of only mildly algae-laced, de-chlorinated city water. The fish seemed content. Three of them; a neon tetra whose red, silver, and blue-green colors could frequently be seen swimming around a three inch high plastic baseball-player birthday cake ornament, pressed into service as aquarium décor, so that it looked as though the batter were swinging at somebody's hallucination of an iridescent football; a cherry barb that was starting to look a little more grapefruit than cherry; and an angel fish, which had survived by acting in a manner completely inconsistent with its name, and was known by the Big Cutie as, "the mean one;" were all older than my youngest offspring.

But something about the store's gaudy warrantee intrigued me: "We guarantee all our pets for seven days," they bragged. The idea of bringing in a dead pet was irresistible. Was the store accustomed to taking back dead guinea pigs, lizards, and parakeets? What did they do with them? The dead guppy gave me a perfect opportunity to find out.

I put it in a baggie and took it to the store. To be honest, I didn't run off to the store directly. I went to the store by way of my post office box, the grocery market, and Costco. My car is black. It gets pretty hot. By the time the dead guppy, in its baggie, entered the air conditioning of the pet store, it looked much worse than it had when I'd netted it out of the fish tank that morning. I had my receipt with me. When it was my turn at the front of the line, I removed the dead guppy from its temporary morgue, my purse, and placed it gently on the counter. "He's dead," I announced. The woman behind the counter looked a little puzzled. I pressed on. "We just bought him two days ago. Your store says it guarantees its pets for seven days. So I'd like to return him."

I've sometimes wondered whether the return policy for clothing stores means they simply refold or re-fluff items and place them back on the racks and shelves. My lack of faith in other people's hygiene means I wash nearly everything before putting it on. To the pet store's credit, I'd never once seen a dead fish returned to a tank, though there had been many occasions when I'd noticed deceased inhabitants floating right beside their healthier brethren under the "Special! Three Family Tank Fish for $5!" sign. The woman continued to stare at me. Then she called her manager over the loudspeaker system. "Fish return at the register."

Eventually, the manager appeared, and glared at the baggie with its sad cargo. If you've ever wondered whether name-brand Ziploc bags really work better than the generic ones, they do. For safety's sake, though, I also put an extra layer of plastic between my fish-casket and the air-breathing world. The gentleman in the shirt with manager tag asked me to step out of line. I repeated my request.

"I'd like to return this fish. Here's my receipt." I paused. "He didn't even live twenty-four hours."

"Did you bring in any water?" asked the manager.

"Well," I said, eying the bag doubtfully, "there's water in the bag, but I don't think it's going to help the fish any."

"We need to test the water before you can return the fish."

"Why?"

"To make sure there's nothing wrong with your water."

"My other fish like the water just fine. Why would there be something wrong with the water if the other eighteen fish are swimming around, and the new fish keels over? Have they changed the models on the fish, so that the new ones are no longer compatible with the old ones, like phone chargers?"

"No, it's just store policy. You need to bring a sample of water for us to test, so that we can help you if there's something wrong with the water in your tank."

"Your sign doesn't say, 'Our pets are guaranteed, provided you can prove you didn't kill them.' It just says they're guaranteed."

By now, the fluorescently lit, cat-litter scented space around us was starting to accumulate an audience. It would have been hard to say who was more surprised: the assorted dog treat and lizard-bowl buyers looking at a manager holding the fuzzy remains of my double-bagged guppy and demanding tank water; the manager himself, who wasn't sure why his customer didn't seem to be able to follow simple directions; or me, an oddly determined woman who had begun her day with a mission to see whether the store would really take back my dead fish, and who was now discovering a labyrinth of increasingly stringent return regulations designed to prevent customers from walking out with an unjustified $1.25. For a few more seconds, the manager stared into the fish bag, as if checking to see whether the fish was truly dead, despite the fact that its fins were now attached to its body at a most unnatural-looking angle. Then he yielded.

"Okay. This time, I'll do it, as a courtesy. Next time, you'll need to bring in a sample of the water."

"Next time I'll try to pick out a healthier fish," I said. "Do you need my credit card?"

"No. You can have cash."

I heard the register open behind me.

Radio can make you drive a dead fish around in a hot car to see whether you can get back $1.25 and have something to talk about when you get to work. I still didn't want to go to law school.

Secret Agent

The joke about radio used to be that it was one of the few kinds of work you couldn't do in your garage. However, with the increased availability of a specialized phone line, called an ISDN, that gave high-quality audio in real time, and one rather expensive piece of equipment that made the ISDN line work, many radio personalities started broadcasting from their spare bedrooms and broom closets. Michael and Tom, my two friends from high school (the same ones who made my original audition tape), got together at my house and helped rig up a home studio in my attic. Tom sent me a shopping list, and thanks to eBay, Craigslist, and Guitar Universe, I was able to assemble everything I needed. Michael, by now the chief engineer of a major-market television station, and Tom, an IT executive, crawled around my "studio" with wires and staple guns, and made it possible for me to work—just as they had twenty-five years before.

It was tremendously liberating to be able to host talk shows in any time zone, live, as if at the end of a very, very, long microphone cord. As soon as the studio was up and running, K-Bomb's former program director, Karl Blake, offered me a regular part-time gig for KIIO, the talk station he was now managing in the Pacific Northwest. I also picked up occasional shifts on stations in DC, Chicago, and suburban Los Angeles. Even with the KIIO shifts, I was still only working part-time. So I formed a tiny ad company. Shebops Productions is to conventional ad agencies, as a neighborhood Popsicle cart is to Baskin Robbins.

My first client, Stan Bellevue, didn't exactly hire me. He hired Save the Planet—a political consultant with a winning track record and a lot of credibility—and Save the Planet hired me—a one-woman advertising agency who was still wearing her maternity clothing eight months post-childbirth. It was nepotism, to be sure, but nepotism that we both figured would get Stan Bellevue elected as a moderate judge in a rural, conservative Northern California county.

First, we needed the candidate to approve our concepts. We sold him on the idea that if he was going to stand out from the pack, his ads would have to be creative, memorable, and depict him as a reasonable jurist who was neither a spineless marshmallow allowing rapists and child murderers to wander back into the community, nor a fire-and-brimstone, one-way ticket to jail for anyone caught with a joint in his glove compartment. While I hadn't come into advertising by the conventional methods, as someone who read and wrote copy for my show for years, I was pretty sure I could produce something more interesting than the pompous, flag-waving piffle that most campaigns used. After all, I had different sources of inspiration.

Some people think playing with educational toddler toys is what you do to help your kid acquire skills that will get her into the university of her choice. Others love the fun aspect of watching their child solve problems and develop. I like kids' toys when I can use them for my own purposes—as props for political ads.

Our candidate wanted to use his judgeship and the courts to divert convicted non-violent criminals into mental health, drug treatment, and restorative justice programs. The concept of not sending people to jail for non-violent drug crimes was particularly popular in parts of the county where the main cash crop was high-quality marijuana. We needed to make the point that the judge believed prison wasn't necessarily the best approach to California's pot-growing industry. We didn't want him to look soft on crime.

I'd stuck my bare foot into the baby's shape-sorting, yellow plastic bucket as it lay on the floor of the nursery about seventy-three times. I'd retrieved its red, blue, and green plastic pieces from under the couch and behind the dog's water bowl. The toy, it seemed to me, ought to be good for something besides causing me to limp to the medicine cabinet for a Band-Aid once a week.

For my first ad, we labeled the yellow and blue plastic cylindrical shape sorter's three holes, Treatment, Prison, and Reparation, and showed plastic shapes labeled, rather innocently, as Drug User, Mugger, and Vandal being dropped into the places the Judge thought they belonged. With a children's music soundtrack, and my earnest narration, it worked pretty well.

On paper, I looked nothing like the owner and creative mind behind an ad agency, and in person, looked even less so. We decided it would be best not to tell the candidate, when we arrived to shoot the second ad, that the wife of his new campaign manager, who for some reason, came along on the commercial shoot with a baby, a stroller, and a diaper bag, was Shebops Productions.

These were to be man-on-the-street interview pieces. We'd build a montage of whoever the voters thought did (or did not) belong in jail. STP is a soft-spoken person by nature, and doesn't usually approach people on the street asking their opinions on the possible fates of house burglars and child abusers. But we figured it wouldn't be all that hard to make him into my Remington Steele—the hunky male, faux-front for a TV detective agency run by a woman. I pointed out the likely interviewees, and then STP would zero in on them, with a locally procured camera operator trailing. He'd ask what kind of criminals they thought should go to jail, they'd answer, and we'd have the footage we needed. The candidate, who was going to come and watch, need never know that the woman nursing an eight-month-old on the town square park bench was actually his ad agency—his *entire* ad agency.

We managed to maintain the fiction that STP was simply a devoted father, who checked in with his baby-toting wife a lot, for about twenty minutes. The interviews, however, were not going so well. By the end of the first half hour, we'd both figured out that not just anybody can buttonhole passersby for Man-on-the-Street footage. You have to have a little interview experience, and a willingness to get in people's personal space. That's me. That's not Save the Planet. People were waving him off like a guy with a bad pickup line. The only things people said to him couldn't be put on the air at all, and were also accompanied by gestures that are not considered polite. I was going to have to leave my post by the stroller and unmask myself in front of our candidate. The Judge, who was probably already on to us, got a full confession. Fortunately, he didn't care. In fact, he said it confirmed the suspicions he'd harbored ever since he'd seen the toy sorter spot.

The baby was invited to attend his first political event: Judge Bellevue's victory party. Everyone was very proud. The ads had done their job. I now had something to post under the "ad agency" page on my website, although I still refused to have a new publicity picture taken. I had launched an ad agency, but I was still wearing my maternity clothes.

Who Would I Tell?

Jealous. I was jealous and furious and frustrated. Before it was over, I'd also be devious.

Devon McNally, a woman who'd had great success as an outrageous music radio host in San Francisco and Los Angeles, but no talk experience, had landed the job I coveted. A new network of FM talk stations—this time targeted to men—was launching. Its goal was to replicate the success of one radio genius and legend who just retired from terrestrial radio for a show on a satellite subscription service. On satellite radio, he'd be able to do all the things he hadn't been allowed to do on conventional airwaves, where different standards of language and content applied. The gaping hole left by his departure was so vast, his old radio home was going to try to build a whole new format, in most major markets, just to keep as many of his listeners as it could. And the San Francisco station I lived practically next door to wasn't even willing to meet with me about a job.

I called Paul, who was by now the darling of the TV and movie crowd in Los Angeles, due to his brilliant talent for creating an entire cast of callers (all of whom were played, in real time, by him) and told him that Devon had gotten *my* perfect gig.

"Devon?" Paul choked back a combination laugh-snort of disgust. "Devon is a raging alcoholic. I give her three months before she blows herself up."

It didn't take that long. I actually enjoyed a few hours of Devon's shows. Then one day, she simply vanished from the airwaves. Her co-workers told me that Devon had been stashing bottles around the studio and drinking steadily throughout her shift almost since she'd started. She showed up for work one day completely loaded. She made a sloppy mess of her show, verbally assaulted her boyfriend, whom she'd hired as a producer, and eventually passed out in the studio. Live. On the air. The audio went around the internet, complete with the usual nasty comments and snide remarks. Drunken, pathetic, and yet talented Devon became entertainment fodder for a major morning show out of New York.

Never let it be said that I don't owe a debt to the alcoholics of this business. Technically, Live FM couldn't replace Devon, who was on medical leave. So I was invited to host the midday shift as a temporary fill-in, while management decided their next move. The company eventually succeeded in getting Devon into rehab, but her addiction was so extreme that she reportedly relapsed (there's yet more audio of the New York hosts, and what sounds like a not-very-healthy Devon, to give some weight to this version of events) and died within two years.

Meanwhile, I held the fort on middays on Live FM, and hoped the general manager, Chris, who was programming the station, would keep me permanently. Chris was having a great deal of difficulty making up his mind about whom to hire. He was known among former co-workers for being indecisive about everything from what his station should sound like, to whether he would sail his boat or fly to Cancun on any given weekend. Some at Chris' prior radio stations were known to dodge lunch offers from Chris, because he took so long to decide on a sandwich. It became clear to me after a few months that Chris was going to replace me with a male team, as soon as he could find one he liked. Hoping against hope I'd be on the air long enough to generate a ratings blip in the right direction, I made it my goal to prolong my temporary stay at Live FM. To do it, I resorted to sabotage.

Whenever I tell my husband or a friend or one of the kids a professional secret, I demand that they tell nobody else. My husband and my kids and my friends never ask, "Who would I tell?" because they have heard this story:

"Do you know a talk host from Raleigh named Dillon?" my friend Raven asked as we perched over her stove, tasting the lunch Raven was preparing. Raven was a good hostess. Whenever somebody showed up at Raven's house of worship, and was new in town, he or she could count on a lunch invitation.

"No. How do you know Dillon?"

"He was at services last week. I invited him for lunch. He's here shopping for a house with his wife. I think he's going to be working at your radio station."

"Really? I didn't know," I said to Raven. Which was the truth. But now I did. And in the interest of keeping my paycheck coming in, I knew I'd have to act. Dillon must not be hired.

Monday morning, right after my fill-in shift, I dropped by Chris' office—the same Chris who'd taken three months to locate Dillon and fly him into town so he could house hunt. Because I had always been told my gig on middays was temporary, and because I'd smiled and said I was fine with that, though I'd like to stay on if I could, I had no problem sticking my head through Chris's doorway, and into Dillon's career prospects on Live FM.

"Hey Chris. I hear you're talking to Dillon from Raleigh about taking over Devon's show, since she's not coming back."

"Yeah. I think he'll do well. Do you know him? What do you think of him?"

I channeled the guy who did in Stan the Scam at Drivin' 99 all those years ago. It helped that I was trying to confuse a person who had so much difficulty making up his mind that he never ordered any toppings on his pizza.

"Well…I could recommend a few other people you might want to listen to."

That was all it took. Sowing the seeds of indecision into Chris' brain bought me another month of work on Live FM. I never told Raven what her act of kindness had ultimately done. She might hate me for it. But when anyone in this business says, "Where's the harm if I tell my best friend's brother? He's a carpenter. Who could he tell?" I tell them the story, and that Raven is a librarian.

Gone

The real joy of Live FM, for me, was listening to its afternoon show host, Jack Reno. Reno once talked for ten minutes about his purchase of the world's most luxurious socks, and how these socks, costing more than five times what he normally paid—nearly as much as the shoes he wore with them—had been such a revelation of comfort, as near to ecstasy as he could experience with his clothes on, etc.—that now he could never go back to wearing ordinary socks. He described the feeling of the $40 socks in such loving and heavenly detail, that I briefly wished for an excuse to buy some. But there's only so much conversation to be had about socks, before you start hitting the buttons on your radio, looking for a little music while you drive Bay Bridge rush hour traffic. So Jack made the hour about "regular things you can never go back to, once you've had the luxury version." It was brilliant, although it did make me embarrassingly aware of the fact that I no longer tolerate grocery store sandwich bread or buy generic shampoo. That's one of the best things about radio: you listen to an hour of a really great show, and you see the world differently.

Still, something was a bit off about the afternoon show. I knew Jack had a fascination with strippers and hookers and took every opportunity to verbally eviscerate his ex-wives on the air. That's not all that unusual for a guy who'd come successfully through years of hosting morning shows on rock radio. But Reno seemed to have a special hatred for one of the station's other hosts—a famous comedian and Las Vegas performer, who, though he'd been a guest on talk shows for years, was trying talk radio as a host for the very first time. Jack, and most listeners, to judge from the comedian's sparse ratings, didn't think it was going very well. Jack believed you ought to pay your dues.

It's a common complaint among talk hosts. Most of us work for years to get good at what we do; and then, because we make it look easy, management assumes that there's nothing to it, and hires some comic or actor to be a talk show host. Most of the time, the show bombs. We, who work for years to do radio well, are more than a little resentful at the plum jobs going to people who want to try our career as a hobby or a lark. So the rest of Live FM's airstaff and producers were not entirely upset at the escalating series of verbal swipes Jack was taking at the big name, talk-host-come-lately.

Then one day, Jack Reno launched a diatribe against the other host, reviling him as a talentless, egomaniacal boob, and culminating with a joke offer of payment for his assassination. It was, beyond a doubt, going too far. Jack refused to apologize. The victim of the threat made it known to the network that it could expect a well-funded lawsuit, and Jack, ultimately, was fired. His agent backed away from him for unexplained reasons. He launched his own syndicated show. Somehow, it didn't gain traction. Jack faded out of mainstream radio, with only legal briefs from his countersuit against the station in the distant pages of a Google search to mark his passing.

Several years later, somebody sent me a video he'd found on YouTube of Jack's testimony as a born-again Christian. The strippers and the hookers and the death wishes for the ex-wives were evidently part of a meth and coke addiction. That's one revelation I was definitely not expecting. Which itself is a surprise, considering my history and fascination with addicts. You'd think the fact that I liked Jack's show and humor as much as I did would have set off some sort of advance addict danger warning—but it almost never does.

Leaving Las Vegas looked like déjà vu to me. I actually cannot count all the talented people I've heard, and with whom I've worked, who have spent huge chunks of their lives fighting substance abuse and addiction. Some of them have gotten their acts together and been sober and clean for years; some for a while; and some never did.

Laura Geary, the woman who worked for Zeke Sada at Crazy103 in LA, was a regular holiday hostess and generous patron of young broadcasters. If you were scheduled to work on Thanksgiving, Laura would invite you to stop by her home after your shift and serve Thanksgiving dinner all over again, just for you. When I met her, she was proudly clean and sober. Years after she retired from the station, I looked her up. She'd moved to Oregon to farm. When I called her, a decade since I'd last seen her, to thank her for her kindness to me, she didn't sound good. She died a few months after our conversation. I only learned recently that she'd ultimately hired a famous sexual harassment attorney and sued Zeke. I hope she won.

How much can you blame on a rock and roll industry where creative people's wild behavior was tolerated, even encouraged, in the name of entertainment? How much is the fact that people who need to be seen, heard, and want permission to behave outrageously, are welcome in broadcasting and entertainment? It's a subject that's back in the news again. This time, the excesses and transgressions are sexual. People's lives are damaged. It's not yet clear how great the ultimate toll will be. Creative people can be just as normal as everyone else; and yet, entertainment attracts those who seem to be, by their very nature, extraordinary.

There's a wonderful man named Art Vuolo who's spent his career collecting archival tape and video footage of on-air personalities. Someone's posted a compilation of it on YouTube; it's called "The Greatest Rock and Roll DJs." I knew a lot of them, and a lot of them are dead.

While Supplies Last

Radio people look for show prep with the constant intensity of those guys on the beach waving metal detectors over the sand. A good show topic is more valuable to us than an antique coin or an old wedding band. You know you have radio in your blood when you volunteer to MC the local Men's Club's "Belt Sander Races" and you leave the event thinking, "I have one of the most skull-splitting headaches I have ever endured, but at least I got some material out of it." The quest for material never leaves you. Never.

When you live in San Francisco, you avoid Fisherman's Wharf as though the wax museum were ground zero of an Ebola outbreak; but when your houseguest from Minneapolis finally talks you into a boat trip to Alcatraz, or a cable car ride, you think, "Well, at least I might get some material." I lived in Chicago for years, and never took one of those cruises down the Chicago River, until a visitor invited me to join him. "Oh," I said to my friend, about five minutes into the trip, "*now* I understand why people do this!" It can also be that way with "calendar-based" show prep—you avoid the "Going Out in the Woods to Chop Down a Christmas Tree" story, or the "Getting Married in an Unusual Place Valentine's Day" story; and then, one day, you realize you've never gone out in the woods to chop down a tree, and you've never joined anybody for their wedding in a hot air balloon, and you think, "Maybe I should check it out."

That is one reason I decided to cover Black Friday, the much-promoted first shopping day after Thanksgiving. The second reason was because KIIO scheduled me to work the weekend after Thanksgiving, one of the slowest news times of the year, and I was going to need some material. The third reason was that I wanted to buy Save the Planet a giant cheap television.

There are calendar-based events you know will be covered by all the news media, even though they're not necessarily news. The news, or rather, a five- or thirty-minute show that's called "the news," is a gaping maw that must be filled. Certain seasonal stories that predictably generate some colorful video footage on days when news is almost always slow will help to fill it. There's the drunken St. Patrick's Day Parade story, with a reporter wearing a shiny green leprechaun hat. The reporter often participates in the "story" by cheerfully getting doused with green beer as he or she is surrounded by rowdy, not-necessarily-Irish, parade-goers. There's the local Pet Adoption Day, where the reporter gets a kitten stuck to his or her chest. There used to be Tax Filing Day, where the reporter stood outside the post office; which, before internet filing made this whole exercise unnecessary, stayed open till midnight, and talked to people's outstretched left arms as they drove by the mail box and stuffed in their tax return envelopes.

Talk show hosts have it much easier than news reporters when it comes to calendar stories. We don't usually have to attend ethnic parades, unless our stations have a float. We don't have to stand outside in the dark or the rain on opening day of the baseball season, or get hit by wrapped boxes of puzzles as people toss them into barrels at the Toys for Tots Christmas drive. We just ask our listeners to tell us, or tweet to us, or post on their Instagram pages what it was like, or keep our news reporters in the studio to chat with us for a few extra minutes after their broadcasts. I've always felt a little guilty about this

On Black Friday, TV stations turn out to interview frostbitten fans of impossibly cheap loss leaders, as shoppers queue up for extra special discount deals. To ratchet up the manufactured drama, quantities, the ads remind you, are limited.

I avoided this mob scene for years. So on my first Black Friday, I couldn't have been more stunned if I'd turned on Monday Night Football and discovered the entire Seattle Seahawks lineup playing in high heels and feather boas. Although a great deal of Black Friday advertising was targeted at women, the five-block long line snaking around the heavy industrial area near my local appliance and electronic superstore was almost exclusively male. Its starting point, outside the store's giant glass front doors, was so heavily guarded, it looked as though the store had experienced Black Fridays in the past where people decided that, while cheap was good, free would be better. This day, the store's parking lot was turned into a festival campsite. A crowd of hundreds had been feasting on ramen noodles and nesting on piles of "Seven Hour Special" newspaper inserts. The line at 4:30 a.m. twisted its way past five sleeping homeless people, three foul-smelling dumpsters, and snaked along next to the elevated 101 Freeway.

"Why," I asked myself, "are there so few women here? Don't women watch TV? What about the great deals on washers and dryers? Do women not wash?" For the life of me, I couldn't figure it out. I surveyed my neighbors in line and found the answer: the newest gaming devices were on sale for roughly a quarter of their usual retail prices.

So there I stood, freezing in the chilly San Francisco, post-Thanksgiving morning air, memories of my recently consumed turkey and stuffing growing fainter with every passing semi-truck.

Doors were not scheduled to open for another hour and a half, and the city was still layered in fog and darkness. The Black Friday shopping line had yet to inch forward. The greatest source of illumination came from the freeway across the alley and above us. Our secondary light source was from people's tablets, phones, and portable video games. You could hear, against the noise of passing traffic, an occasional low conversation, as boys called their friends or texted them information on how closely positioned they were to the store's entrance. A couple of parents carried kids who should have been in bed hours ago.

There were also a few, but not many, line crashers. These were dealt with in a variety of ways. Sometimes, a small group of bundled-up shoppers would surround the people who had attempted to sneak into a preferred spot, and loudly shame them until they slunk away. Others were reported to the store's employees, who were passing out tickets entitling waiting customers to purchase one of the coveted loss-leader items. In the event that the store employee took no action, the shaming shifted to these employees—twenty-somethings wearing their employer's bright blue polo shirts under open jackets.

"How can you let that happen? She cut the line. You can't give her any tickets!" The store employees tried to stay above the fray. When conflict broke out over a high-value item, they'd cool things off by offering more pedestrian options. "Vacuum cleaners? Anybody here for a vacuum cleaner?" they'd cry out. You could raise your hand and get a ticket. Almost nobody was there for a vacuum cleaner. "Computer? Camera? Sound system?"

The woman standing behind me raised her hand for a ticket. I learned that she was planning to use her new computer to stream video chats with an amply proportioned burlesque performer she'd recently met at a sober living conference in Panama. My fellow customer hoped to see, in exquisite hi-def detail, what she had been promised in a photograph: the curvy lady of her dreams, wearing a white feather boa, and nothing else. She proudly shared with me an image of a rather hefty burlesque performer of indeterminate gender. I was glad the parking lot was still pretty dark. "She looks intriguing," I said. "Tell me more about her."

You can pass an hour in line hearing perhaps a little more than you'd like about somebody's visit to a transgender burlesque house, a triple strand of pearls, and a jar of Chinese pepper sauce.

Standing practically underneath five lanes of freeway at 5:00 a.m. on Black Friday morning also teaches you things you may not learn about your neighbors any other way. Our city's panhandlers, people who might register in your consciousness only when you hand them a buck or your bagged-lunch leftovers, turned out to have amazing hidden skills. One of the waking homeless, still prone and swaddled in his sleeping gear, under a verge of scrub near the store parking lot, managed to pour his beverage directly from a small beaker into an even smaller flask without spilling a drop. This, a near miracle in itself, was accomplished while the pourer remained in a horizontal position under piles of cardboard and blankets. Only his hand and the receptacle were visible. I wondered briefly whether there was any way this fellow could make commercial use of a talent like that. It was like watching an alcoholic Cirque du Soleil. For a while, I forgot about the cold.

I thought about how excited Save the Planet would be with his big holiday surprise hi-tech TV. I just knew he'd love it. I wasn't so sure about liking hi-def TV myself. In fact, it worried me a little, especially the idea of commercials in high-definition. Did I really want to experience ads as though they were happening in my living room? Sure, beer fans might welcome a bikini-clad volleyball team pouring them a cold one, but the flip side would be life-like animated bathroom sponges spinning on moldy tile, or oil change experts who looked like they might actually smear 10W-40 on my carpet.

At 6:00 a.m., the doors opened. The crowd, brandishing ticket numbers, began to move forward. I reminded myself that life would still go on, even if I did not score one of the super-giant-high-tech-latest-model TV sets at a price roughly equal to that of a good restaurant dinner. It didn't look like I was going to be one of the first five hundred people through the door, or even come close.

When I finally passed through the store's holiday-decorated, massive glass portal, it felt strangely normal inside. Nobody was pushing. Nobody was shouting. Not until I got to the TV department, where there was a drama playing out that resembled the deck-clearing scene from *Titanic.* It was chaos. Of course all the cheap TVs were gone.

I wasn't able to get everything I learned about Black Friday into my show that weekend, but we did spend an hour discussing the "while supplies last" approach. The listener consensus was that the phrases "while supplies last" and "limited to stock on hand" really mean "limited to the supply that we have in our vast warehouse sixty miles outside of

town, or any other place we care to stash them." It was thanks
to Grandma Rose, and her "you don't ask, you don't get"
school of consumer training that I knew to check if the limited
supply offer was really all that limited, providing I was
willing to pay for my TV then and there.

A few days later, I wrestled the giant box containing our
new, enormous TV onto one of the kids' old baby strollers
and maneuvered it into our neighbor Oscar's garage. I hoped
that by stashing it three doors down from our house, I would
be able to conceal the TV until Save the Planet's upcoming
birthday. That turned out to be a complete waste of energy,
since Oscar invited my husband into the garage the very next
day to look at some cabinets he was building. When STP
remarked on the presence of a boxed flat-screen TV on what
looked like our kids' old stroller, Oscar confessed. STP made
his best attempt to appear surprised when the new set rolled
into our home three days later.

It's been over ten years since my one and only Black
Friday sale purchase, and that TV is still going strong. Which
is a good thing, because my aversion to lining up to shop at
4:00 a.m. with a stomach full of turkey has lasted far longer
than the TV's extended warrantee.

The Exceptions

It was time to give up Lila Wright and Million Mile Traffic. I was certainly grateful for the gig, but I also considered assembling radio newscasts made from re-written stories culled from newspapers' websites to be participating in the murder of genuine newsgathering. It didn't matter that I credited my sources. There were fewer and fewer newspapers paying real money for professional staffs of hard-working, beat-covering reporters. What I was doing was providing radio stations with a newscast that *sounded* like it came from an actual news staff, except that it didn't.

The second reason was a suggestion from my LA friend Leslie, who was getting tired of hearing me whine about a chronic problem in talk radio: giving standup comedians their own talk shows. In general, though there are exceptions, standup comics make lousy talk show hosts. Why is this? They're funny. They're smart. They're good talkers. Why shouldn't they be brilliant radio hosts?

For one thing, standup comics tend to need a live audience. A radio studio doesn't typically have more than one or two people in it. And since those ancillary people are often being paid to support the host, you get a feedback loop where the support staff laughs uproariously at everything the comic says, whether or not it's funny.

Here's another problem with hiring standup comics to create entertaining radio for three-to-four hours in a studio every day: comics are used to preparing and honing an hour or two of killer material which they will then use, in similar if not exact form, over a long tour. The idea that you have to generate new material every day for a radio show strikes panic in their hearts. The solution to the need for something fresh to talk about is obvious to anybody who has ever been on a date, or sat with friends in a coffee shop: ask a lot of questions, and listen to the answers. Your job is to be curious. When you need something to talk about on the air, you ask your newsperson, your callers, a guest, or your listeners, to give you their opinion, or experience, or a story, or information. But the opinions of comedy club patrons go by another name: heckling. And while some comedians have built careers out of dealing with hecklers, most of them regard vocal audience members as something between a challenge and a curse. For perfectly understandable reasons, comedians, though often astute observers of life, tend to be extremely bad listeners.

Also, for someone who is used to the late-night comedy club or theater circuit, getting up at 3:00 a.m. for a morning drive shift is not much fun. So when managers hire standup comedians who imagine they would like to do radio, or managers persuade a comedian to do radio, it often ends fast, and badly.

At that moment, the radio industry was on a comedian-hiring binge. Managers were falling all over themselves to get the hottest nightclub acts on the air as full-time radio hosts, while overlooking truly talented radio pros who had taken years to polish their skills. It was tough to watch. I'd been complaining about it to Leslie, who by now had built a successful career as a broadcast consultant. She was losing patience with my constant moaning about how hiring a standup comic to host a radio show was like hiring a mime to conduct a symphony orchestra.

"Why not try something short form? Build your brand that way. Sometimes a little Turi Ryder goes a long way." That was how she put it. My friend and I have a deal. We are honest with each other, even when the truth is not flattering. So I had to consider whether this "little bit goes a long way" might have something to do with my mean streak.

It is true that sometimes on the air, I was known to be a little unkind. Like the time I put the woman who married a jailed child pornographer on the air, and kept after her—pliant, guilt-ridden, and aching to think of herself as a victim—until she admitted that she couldn't honestly say she'd had no idea what her husband was up to.

"Really? You saw kiddie porn on your husband's computer, and it never once crossed your mind that he might have an actual interest in real children? Or filming real children?" I asked her.

"No."

"So you figured this was, what, like travelogue night at the library? 'Now showing a Film from Bora Bora, a place I have no real plans to visit?' And you never suspected your husband might actually be going to Bora Bora, even though Bora Bora, in this case, is not half a planet away, but as close as the nearby Little League team?"

"No."

"No, you didn't think of it, or 'no, I really *did* know, I just didn't want to deal with the fact that I was financially and socially dependent on a demented child abuser?'"

"I didn't think he was really doing anything with it."

"Except, of course, that even if he wasn't, he was creating a market for it."

"I guess so."

"You mean you have no idea that people make money distributing this stuff to creeps like your husband?"

"I never thought of it that way."

"Please tell me you and this man do not have children."

"We have a son."

"And you left your son with his dad, the kiddie-porn watcher?"

"He would never hurt our son."

"But other people's kids are okay?"

You see what I mean? I am not always very nice when I'm working. I can also get a bit carried away with what seem to me to be logical solutions to problems—solutions I feel other people are missing. For instance, for years some of Chicago's poorer and more dangerous neighborhoods had an extreme lack of access to medical trauma centers. Community and youth leaders had my support and sympathy when they organized to pressure a local teaching hospital to add a trauma facility. But I had a different reaction on a day a story crossed my desk about several gang members who had organized to march and picket the hospital. I suggested that these very same gang members might consider using some of their drug-sale-generated millions to open a trauma center themselves. They could redistribute some of the money they made off their privileged wealthy suburban customers, and create medical education scholarships in their own communities. That way, I said, kids who do not want to deal narcotics and shoot innocent by-standing schoolchildren for a living could instead find work as fully trained medical professionals. They'd be employed in gangster-donated hospitals, built with money provided by the same people who would one day create the most business for these young doctors, nurses, and technicians.

Leslie thought it might be a good idea for me to brand, or market, myself with short humor features. I could control them, and they could be funny, but not mean.

That's how "Turi Ryder's Exception to the Rule" short features started. One of my very first ones was about how people will tell you their salaries and whether they've ever cheated on their partners before they will tell you what they've spent on their pet's teeth. I based this on what I'd just spent on my dog's teeth.

Because I am lucky enough to have friends who are program directors, one of them in Sacramento started airing the three Exceptions every week. I didn't charge him, and he got cool free content for his news-talk station. So far, things were going well. The features were topical, seasonal, and occasionally political, but never partisan. I made fun of stupidity on a non-denominational basis. We started describing the minutes as "Erma Bombeck with a razor blade." The Exceptions spanned topics ranging from outdoor living room furniture, to the time I fumigated my house for chicken mites, thinking they were lice.

I met my guardian Exception to the Rule angel, Hal Silver, at a radio industry conference. Hal agreed to distribute the minutes on his network for free for about a year. Then he found, in his news budget, a small amount he could pay me. "Because," said Hal, "it's the kind of thing we should do."

I loved creating the "Exception to the Rule" features. They were well received, and soon in regular use as news "kickers" from Seattle to Washington, DC. As tends to happen, the people who knew me and my work eventually left their stations and moved to other sorts of jobs in the business. I needed to make new contacts and find new program and news directors to interest in the features. I didn't figure that out right away. It also didn't occur to me that selling the minutes on behalf of the stations should be my job. I thought the radio network people, like magic leprechauns, should do it for me, or were doing it for me, or perhaps I never thought about it at all. I locked myself into my studio every Monday night and created three of the features. If they were good, I considered it a job well done.

File the experience under "cheaper than an MBA." At the end of about seven years, Hal let me know that there weren't many stations currently using the minutes, so they were going to stop taking them. I felt terrible for Hal that I had not done a better job of marketing the features. I still hope to make it up to him one day, though he's been wonderful throughout the process, and claims to not have a single hard feeling about backing my ultimately unsuccessful venture.

I shouldn't say the Exceptions were *entirely* unsuccessful. I still have a small collection of emails from listeners who loved the Exceptions. A DC-area woman wrote to tell me they were the reason she'd been able to drive her kids' carpool without losing her sanity altogether. Those kinds of emails can make you feel like you really do something useful for a living. A Delaware man emailed to eviscerate me about what he thought was a political jab at the president. He eventually sent his compliments on the minutes, and the fact that I personally responded to his complaint to the station's program director. There are a couple of talk show hosts who used the features as "starter yeast" for topics on their shows, and I was proud to appear on a few of their programs as a guest.

Most importantly, because of my commitment to Hal to produce these features every week, on time, I started to think of myself not only as a talker, but also as a writer.

The Minivan of Surrender

The woman who wrote to me that the Exceptions minutes kept her from losing her cool when a squirt-pack of yogurt hit her in the back of the neck while she was driving the kindergarten carpool was not only my listener. She was my kindred spirit. She would have understood that the thing I was missing most after our second child was born—the single thing that was the difference, to me, between being a single woman and a married mom, was the auto body shop.

I could mourn over my wardrobe of tight fitting jeans and slinky black velvet vintage skirts, but the auto body shop was my favorite luxury. It pained me to let it go. I loved the auto body shop the way some women love spas. I felt soothed by the smell of car paint and polish. I liked to wander around and see the collectable cars being restored over periods of months, or even years, for the shop's regulars. When I picked up my car from the body shop, I experienced the feeling of calm and wellbeing many people say they get after a deep tissue massage.

I still own my last "single girl" car, a now-vintage, thirty-something-year-old Toyota Supra. My eldest, who drives, doesn't have a hope in heaven of getting the keys.

I learned that the Supra was not supposed to be a single girl car at a suburban car dealership back when it was new. The salesmen, four of them wearing suits without ties, were sitting around on top of a bunch of unsold cars when I entered the showroom. I wore my usual work attire of blue jeans, a flannel shirt, and boots. The salesmen ignored me the way you ignore someone who is trying to catch your eye in order to hand you religious literature. I approached the group.

"I'd like to test drive one of these," I called out, pointing to a white Supra on the sales floor.

One of them turned to gaze at me over his shoulder for a moment.

"We don't take those out for test drives on Wednesdays."

"But I'd like to try it out."

This time he turned from the group to face me. "Why not take a look at the Miata? Most girls prefer the Miata. It's a cute car." Astonished, I pivoted on my booted heel and left.

Two days later, I parked my new black Supra, bought from a different dealer three miles away, in front of the showroom. This time, when I entered the salesmen noticed me.

"Hi," I smiled at the salesman closest to me. "Remember me?" I pointed to the car outside. "Look what I bought!" They were still watching me when I left.

I still have, and love, that car. But it doesn't look quite as fresh as it did the first thirteen years that I owned it. During my single girl years, if anything—from a shopping cart to a moving piano—put a dent in it, it went straight to the auto body shop and emerged like new. I treated the charges like a doctor bill: one of the basic costs of good health, not to be second-guessed.

Then, for three years, I watched my not-as-careful spouse put a series of scrapes in it, most of which got repaired, though not as quickly. Instead, I would wait till the car had amassed about six months' worth of dings, then I'd bring it to the shop and have them all taken care of at once—like waiting till you have three chins to get a full face lift. Most of the year, the car looked like new.

Then, in my seventh month of pregnancy, I discovered that even with the steering wheel tilted all the way up, I could only get out of the car by parking it next to something I could use as a hoist. "No problem," I thought, "as soon as I have this baby, I'll be able to get in and out again." The fact that the baby would actually be coming along in the car with me had not yet registered. I gave little thought to how I'd install the car seat, or load the stroller; neither of which were designed for the tiny rear of the sporty single girl car. The day I accidently slonked my nearly newborn infant on the head with the hatch as I tried to fold down one of the back seats to make room for the "Snap'n'go" wheels, I realized as I hyperventilated, examining the still-sleeping child for any signs of damage, that it was time for a more accommodating vehicle.

The official pace car of motherhood is the minivan. My cousin recommended a minivan. I did not want a minivan.

"You'll love it. You'll never go back to a regular car again," he said.

"I'm not one of those people," I protested. "First the minivan, then the handmade craft-decorated boxes. The only way to make sure I never ornament my or anybody else's clothing with puffy paint is to resist the minivan."

We bought a used Volvo station wagon instead. The Volvo wagon is to driving in the Bay Area, as a set of golf clubs is to living in the Hamptons. You have to have it. I used to get a kick out of San Francisco and Berkeley residents putting bumper stickers for Democratic candidates on the back ends of their Volvos. It seemed redundant. The Volvo was a stereotype. I had become a stereotype. I was a genuine, homemade-baby-food grinding, cloth diaper washing, Bay Area mommy.

But the price of repairs to the safe, comfortable, leather-interior, airbag-featuring, Swedish station wagon made me nuts. There was this one part, the rear turn signal cover—a red plastic piece on the corner of the rear passenger side panel—that I broke so often, I thought of contacting a Chinese factory to do a manufacturing run of knockoffs just for me. After the fourth replacement, I bought a roll of red duct tape, and stuck it over the damaged lens. I was avoiding the auto body shop. I had, unaware, come to view the high-ceilinged, industrial shop space not as a spa for a metal portion of my body, but as a giant industrial fan blowing my cash—cash I would soon need for preschool and music lessons and summer camps—out its air vents.

I now believe there is a moment in a woman's life when she realizes she is destined to drive a minivan, the same way I believe there's a point in a young girl's life when she has to come to terms with the fact that she will need to wear a brassiere. The minivan isn't really something to which a single woman aspires. It's the thing you wind up with. And then you look wistfully back on your single youth, and think, "Why didn't I hang on to my sporty car?"

It's true that hanging on to the car of your single years is a lot more difficult than keeping your size six jeans in a box at the bottom of your closet. But some people make life harder than it needs to be. Those people don't think, "I will drive this minivan, and I will come to terms with it eventually. The money from the sporty car would pay for speech therapy for my three-year-old's lisp, so it needs to be sold." Instead, they put the sporty car in the garage, and leave the minivan, like an unloved dog, at the curb. Then they wander into the garage occasionally, and stare at the sporty car, and wonder how long it will be until they can drive that car again, even if by now, the kids' bikes have run into it a few times, and your spouse put a noticeable dent in it with his elbow when he was carrying the carton holding the fragile holiday china with specific instructions *not* to let it get broken, and he tripped and was just about to drop the entire box, but instead caught himself on the car at the last minute, leaving the passenger door with an impression of his entire forearm.

The minivan moment is different for every woman. It might be the point where you are trying to strap two kids into two car seats in the back of a sedan, and your diaper bag falls out and opens and two Tupperware containers of Cheerios and apple slices go rolling down the street. Then, when you try to get yourself out of the car in a hurry to catch them, along with the sippy cup you just noticed has dropped into the gutter next to the teething ring, you catch your foot on the seatbelt anchor and bang your head really hard on the edge of the door. It might also be when your nearly twenty-year-old Volvo station wagon, which seemed like a good compromise between something fun and something practical, breaks down for the third time in a month and the AAA driver says, "Hey, didn't I just tow this car last week?" followed by the experience, one week later, of standing on the shoulder of the 580 Freeway, traffic passing close enough to unbutton your blouse, while you call the school office to see whether somebody can come out and rescue a carpool of first graders. That's when I was done. It was minivan time.

Minivans do not command a lot of respect. Nobody has done any scientific work on this yet, but I would venture to bet that if you took a fairly attractive woman and had her drive by a police officer at fifteen miles per hour over the speed limit in a minivan, and that same woman drove by that same officer at the same speed in a Porsche convertible, she'd get pulled over both times, but she'd only get a ticket behind the wheel of the vehicle with two booster seats in the back, and Ziploc baggies of pretzel snacks on the passenger side.

My self-loathing over my minivan grew exponentially when our own government tried talking people into getting rid of them for a while with their "Cash for Clunkers" program. I took it personally. Where was the "Cash for Schleppers" program, where the government gives you money if your vehicle is used to drag around your entire family, kids' soccer teams, and the food pantry collection barrel?

Minivans may be low on the glamour scale. But without the minivan, how will America's next generation see the Grand Canyon, Mount Rushmore, or the Museum of Pez Memorabilia? Minivans make a different statement than a smug hybrid. They say, "I am serene enough to lock myself into a small metal box with several people I already know very well, and spend fifteen hours stepping on granola bar wrappers and crayons. I care nothing for material goods, other than air conditioning, sun block, and my first grader's special blanket."

When listeners write or call to tell me they enjoy my show or my short features while they are driving the carpool, it makes me happier than I'd be if it turned out Martha

Stewart's Three Cheese Macaroni had fewer calories than a bowl of fresh strawberries.

My old Toyota Supra is parked in the garage. And even if we are on the verge of the energy revolution, and will soon be driving mini-pods that run on food leftovers with solar panels on their roofs—when the kids are done with college, I plan to have it re-painted.

Nothing Right Now

If **I practiced** astrology, I'm pretty sure my chart would read, "Things are going well for you. Beware." My regular KIIO gig had expanded to include a lot of fill-in work. I'd asked for a raise, and received it. Then, without warning or rumor, KIIO was sold to a different broadcasting company—one that didn't understand why they should pay someone who lived two states away to be on the air at their station. It was also true that the new program manager of KIIO had had to relocate his wife and family from a city he described as being "perfect for them." And he'd left a house that his wife also described as being "perfect for them." By golly, if he had to move three states away, why should I get to stay put? I knew I was in trouble when I called to let him know that I'd be flying up to meet him, and he didn't seem to have any idea who I was. A few months later, they gave my shift to a local guy, who worked for half of what I'd been earning. He lasted just a little less time than the new program manager who went back to his perfect house in his perfect city eleven months after he arrived at KIIO.

What I had going for me was Hal, my patron saint at the national news network, and the Exception minutes. It wasn't much, but it kept me writing, and gave me something to talk about at broadcasting conventions. The Exception to the Rule features made me feel that for a few hours every week my job description was not "former broadcaster," or worse.

A broadcaster of whom I think highly once introduced a group of radio pros to each other by going around in a circle: "This is Gena Gallatin. She's with K-Luv. Lisa Lifton reports for W-Hip. Sheila Soll is middays on K-Breeze. And…oh, Turi, I guess you're nothing right now." The Exceptions provided an excuse for me to keep returning dead guppies and collecting material. They gave me a reason to pay attention. The minutes created a place for that content to go. I wrote notes on giant yellow legal pads that I kept in my huge, disorganized diaper bag, and later my purse. I used any story that seemed interesting, from NASA crashing a research vehicle into the moon, to the positive aspects of hoarding. It also turns out that I find deadlines useful.

As an extra gift from the universe, MacFlanagan Keys, an experienced and successful programmer, decided it was time to launch his brainchild: a weekend, live, nationally syndicated talk program. The idea was to create eight hours of original programming on Saturdays and Sundays to spruce up the insufferably boring paid long-form content that lives during the weekends on most commercial talk stations. There'd be twenty-minute "US Weekend" segments, followed by ten-minute breaks. Inside these lived the Garden Show, or the Fix Up Your Home Show, or the Invest in Real Estate and Become a Mogul Show, in small installments. The idea was to keep the hosts of these gardening-repair-investment shows, who were paid advertisers (though not usually talented broadcasters), from boring a station's weekend audiences to the point of stupor. I chose Dasha as my producer. Dasha could find an entertaining guest on any subject, even grisly ones like airline crashes and international kidnappings.

From my home studio, I now spent Sunday mornings talking to everyone. You might hear a guy who matched potential dates by analyzing the contents of their refrigerators; an expert in flying Americans out of combat zones; or any of a generous assortment of actors and rock stars—though not usually A-list actors, and more typically, *former* rock stars.

US Weekend was, in fact, a wonderful idea. There were a few hurdles, of course. By now, a few companies had collected huge numbers of stations. To get a single one of those stations to sign on for US Weekend was nearly impossible. They tended to do things in groups. The stations owned by smaller broadcast groups (I hear they loved me in Mississippi) often delayed the show to suit their own programming needs, which made it impossible to execute the show's original concept: live, quality, call-in talk radio on the weekends.

We worked hard—as hard as we would have if we'd been assembling shows for Los Angeles and Boston. We sent each show live down the special ISDN line, and hoped—along with the other four hosts and MacFlanagan Keys, that we could gain listeners in enough smaller markets to make the big market groups take notice. It was a race against the clock. Everyone—hosts, producers, engineers—was being paid out of MacFlanagan's pocket. Kind, creative, and visionary though he might be, MacFlanagan and his co-investors couldn't run the show at a loss indefinitely.

Meanwhile, although the kids were now both in private elementary and middle schools, the City of Oakland was providing a great deal of additional education at no cost. I already crossed one threshold of possibly irresponsible parenting when one night at bedtime, after the kids were tucked in and Save the Planet was out of town, we were startled by a loud, familiar noise. Instead of rolling from their beds and dropping to the floor, as we had taught both boys to do, they argued with me for a few seconds that the sound was not a garbage can being pushed to the curb ("Mom, it's not even trash pickup night"), but gunfire. Then, to my chagrin, the kids ran to the window and excitedly pointed out the domestic argument unfolding directly across the street.

A young woman behind the wheel of an older Nissan sedan had pulled up and was driving, slowly, down the left-hand side of the road. She was rolling at walking speed, halfway on the sidewalk, while shouting out the window at an armed youth hiking purposefully, a few feet away and parallel to her. He presumably had just gotten out of her car, tired of either her personality or her company.

"What, are you gonna just shoot me now? Is that it? You gonna shoot me?" taunted the woman, as she cruised gently down the block, half-on, half-off the curb. The young man's response was to fire his weapon for a second time, in the general direction of the vehicle. Whether he missed because he was simply trying to make a statement that he would prefer to be alone, or due to a lack of proper target practice, was beside the point, since the bullets had plenty of other places they could do damage; including the barred-but-open windows of my neighbor's house, located catty-corner across the street.

In Through the Out Door

It was time to come home to Chicago. We had a list of reasons why. These included the fact that our firstborn would soon be ready for high school. Public high school, in Oakland, California, is like one of those "Would you rather" party games, as in, "would you rather spend your old age collecting recyclable cans from the roadside in order to buy canned kidney beans for dinner so that you can send your child to a safe, private high school now; or save money now and spend your retirement savings on therapy for your traumatized-by-Oakland-public-high-school-student later?"

Another reason I was considering a move to Chicago was that my father had been diagnosed about three years before with Alzheimer's disease. He'd been telling us for a couple of years that he was pretty sure he was becoming mentally incapacitated. Since he'd never been able to remember names, faces, or much of anything about people he'd met dozens of times, including my former best friend Kristal, who was in and out of our house from high school till years after I graduated college, we didn't pay much attention. It wasn't until one visit with the grandkids, when he turned west instead of east to walk the two blocks home from his neighborhood ice cream shop, that I had an inkling that something might actually be wrong. When he and my mother made an official announcement during a holiday visit, he told us, with his usual scientific directness, how things would progress.

"I'm going to start taking some medicine. It will work for about two years. Then, it will stop working, and I will deteriorate. It will be much harder for you than for me. I won't be in any pain at all."

In general, my father proved correct. Except for the idea that it would only be hard on us. He didn't—how could he—anticipate some of the intermediate phases of the illness. For example, there was trouble when we worked together to shut down his lab and donate the expensive equipment to a variety of educational institutions. Dad and I would go over the items and assess their usefulness and value for tax deduction purposes. (He'd become obsessed with tax deductions. These fixations, which came and went, I later learned were part of the progress of the disease.) We'd agree on where each item would be donated. Then, as the items were shipped to or collected by their designated recipients, my dad would grow enraged at not having been consulted about getting rid of them. It was clear that my mother was going to need some help.

I'd always said I wanted to move back to Chicago. It felt more like home to me than any other city. I knew the signs of winter: storm fencing along the city's entire twenty-eight miles of Lake Michigan waterfront; and of spring: bursting gutters and flooded potholes. I loved its theater, music, and the way people talked to one another over the course of shopping or doing business around town. I'd tried to come back a few times, but mostly it felt as though I'd exited through the closing-time gate at the zoo: those giant iron cheese graters that only spit you in one direction. How I would manage to get back to Chicago was something I hadn't seriously considered.

Save the Planet, who loved his job for years, lost his boss to the charms of a government appointment. The person who took over for him wasn't content to manage my spouse from the other side of the continent, as his former superior had. She wanted him to relocate to Washington DC. Instead, he landed a position with a different political organization. By sheer luck, it was in Chicago. It was decided that STP would go to Chicago immediately, and live temporarily with my parents. If I ever doubt my good fortune being married to STP, I remind myself that he has many skills I lack—like the ability to live for a year with my mother, a woman who could not understand why a working person wouldn't want to take a day of medical leave in order to drive her to her podiatrist.

We expected that STP would commute for a year while the children finished fifth and eighth grades, and then we'd follow. I could continue to create the Exceptions, and host US Weekend from Chicago, thanks to my home studio and my ISDN line.

Sometime around November, about two months into STP's commuting schedule, I read that the big name talk station in Chicago, WING, was looking to hire a local. And, the trades reported, they thought it would be a good idea to put some women on the air.

When I called their program director, I pointed out that I was both an experienced talk show host and a Chicagoan. I also sound very female. We set up our first radio date: a week of holiday fill-in. They liked me. I loved it that they liked me. But…could I work from my home studio for a few months until the school year ended? We'd be moving, expenses paid by STP's new employer, and I was, after all, a "local." Yes. My boss would let me finish the school year from my remote location, and I'd be in the station's studios by July. I was so happy, I believe I actually used the cliché, "dream come true" to some of my friends. But this is radio. I should have known better.

Taste This

The station that hired me was the one I'd made fun of, privately, for years. Other hosts and jocks with whom I'd worked had poked fun at WING much more publicly. They were the old-line talk station; the one many of our parents had listened to when we were kids. WING was everything a soul music loving, concert attending, FM rock alternative station playing Chicago youth detested. They helped people find lost dogs. They gave away panty hose as a "thank you" present—which to women of my generation, is like giving a coffee mug doused in lead-based paint as a hostess gift. Those shows were the reason I avoided talk radio until all the personality had been completely sucked out of music radio. And there always seemed to be somebody on the air offering tips on cooking. Teenagers at the beginning of the microwave era were not turning up our dashboard radios to learn new ways of making cheese balls and green goddess dressing.

If you had predicted, when I started out in rock radio, that I would spend five minutes on the air talking about food, I would have hit you with a package of ramen noodles. Food, as it appeared on radio when I started thinking about radio for a living, meant reading aloud the school district's lunch menu. But a Chicago radio host I admire more than he will ever know once forced me to pull over to the side of the road and take deep breaths until I stopped crying with laughter when he explained the things he would rather do than eat liver, and why. And I found that the school lunch menu can be its own form of poetry ("…fish fingers, and a pudding cup.)

Food turned out to be one of those things that came up a lot on my new WING show. There was the time a Chicago-based national manufacturer of bourbon decided they would save their customers the trouble of watering down their spirits by diluting their bourbon ahead of time. The company let it be known, via a news release, that thenceforth, the bourbon in their trademarked bottles would also contain water. "After all," reasoned the company's PR person, "that's what most people who open a bottle of our bourbon really drink—bourbon and water. So our customers will like it if we water down their bourbon for them." I mentioned on the air the day the press release hit the internet that this logic struck me as defective in a few significant ways. The most obvious, of course, was that it's kind of nuts to pay for water inside your bourbon bottle that you can add for free from your kitchen tap.

On the other hand, I mused, to give the bourbon company the benefit of the doubt, lots of people drink only bottled water. So perhaps the company planned to add a special variety of water— maybe some fancily named imported water—assuming their customers would appreciate a less bourbon-y bourbon, providing it was mixed with water that cost money. But the logic that I found most curious in the "pre-watered-down-bourbon" marketing campaign was the idea that they, the bourbon distillers, actually knew what you, the bourbon buyer, were going to do with their bourbon. I had to ask my WING listeners.

"So what if most people want their bourbon with water? What if you're not most people? What if you, for example, make steak, or salmon, with a bourbon, mustard, and maple syrup marinade? Do you want your bourbon maker to include a piece of raw meat with every bottle? Do you really think focus groups and customer research entitles a company to treat *all* their customers like the *majority* of their customers? I suppose it might be good for competition. Some other company can start making bourbon with fish or meat with the slogan: 'Bourbon of the Sea' or 'Just Add Mashed Potatoes.' And another can advertise that theirs is 'Turbot Free.' That could be where this ends up."

It didn't escape my attention where this monologue had led me: discussing recipes on WING. I had just transitioned into a twisted version of my parents' radio station, without the panty hose.

Playing Ball

People say terrible things about kids, but kids often come through in the most astonishing ways. From January to June, Monday through Thursday, my children, known to listeners as the Big and Small Cuties, made sure our house moved like a fast-picked bluegrass number.

My air shift, 10 p.m.—1:00 a.m. Chicago time, meant I had to be in my Oakland studio by seven. So after whatever post-school activities—baseball, soccer, music lessons—the kids had, we'd walk the dog, zoom home, eat dinner, and then I'd hustle downstairs to work, while the cuties began homework and music practice. I'd scoot upstairs again, just before airtime, around 7:45 p.m., to make sure everyone was okay, and give Small Cutie a goodnight kiss. They put themselves to bed, and I checked on them when my shift finished at eleven. Never once did a child in a snit or a squabble burst into the on-air studio. Nobody had a nightmare. Nobody got a stomachache requiring my immediate attention. I got amazingly lucky.

I did once manage to lock myself into my studio. The door between my studio, which was in a walkout basement, and the rest of the basement, which communicated with the house, had a push-button lock. For some reason, I still don't know why, I came down to go on the air after a bathroom break, and locked it. I could walk out of my studio, onto my front lawn. I could perambulate all around my house, where my children slept. But unless I wanted to break a window, I could not get back into the main body of the house. It took about half an hour for the locksmith to arrive. From then on, I kept a full set of keys to the house in my studio desk drawer. I still have them here, although the Oakland house is three thousand miles away from where we now live. You only want to make some mistakes once.

Two or three mornings a week, with no makeup, and wearing the outfit most closely resembling pajamas that I could find, I watched my kids eat oat cereal and milk; observed them as they hoisted themselves and their backpacks into the mommy van; opened the hatch for the large barking German Shepherd and sped off to pick up the kindergartener and second grader from two other families who comprised our carpool. I hauled everyone up to the hills, dropped them off at school, hiked with the dog, and drove back down the hill to begin my workday of preparing the show. The days I didn't drive, the kids woke themselves and watched for the carpool parent. They even fed the pets and set the alarm when they left. I remain in awe of how organized they were.

Meanwhile, I begged Save the Planet to change his commute schedule from every other weekend to weekly. Although he had negotiated clearance to work from the road two days a week, STP's supervisor was not as happy with the reality as she'd been with the idea of her remote worker. It is one thing to accept something in principle, and another to walk by an empty desk every Friday afternoon and Monday morning.

Still, the meter was running on leaving the Bay Area. We put our home on the market, and it sold in days. I got bids on movers. We chose a house in Chicago and navigated the maze of entry into the city's sought-after public high schools.

I only had one seriously bad mommy moment. I think it may have been my worst yet: I warned my eighth grader, the Big Cutie, that if we had to move to the suburbs because he had fucked around on his tests or homework so that he couldn't get into one of the city's selective public schools, I would never forgive him. The braces came off the younger kid. We gave away a heckuva lot of toys and clothes. And then…everything fell apart.

Just as we were closing on our Chicago house, Save the Planet's boss told him his job would end. As a severance package, she kept him employed till our mortgage was approved, and agreed to honor their commitment to pay for the move.

Days later, the broadcast industry trades reported that a new GM, Frank DelSilvio, a market veteran, with charm, salesmanship, smarts, and a reported plan to change the programming of our venerable talk station, had been given the keys to the historic WING Tower offices and studios. The media columnists speculated that his idea was to build on the sports teams we already carried with an all-sports talk format.

The patient, even-tempered program director who had hired me was let go before he had a chance to reap the rewards of any of his programming decisions. I immediately regretted having spent money on a new computer. My days, I knew, were numbered.

Before the week was out, I got this voicemail:

"This is Josephine. I'm Mr. DelSilvio's secretary. Would you give him a call this afternoon?"

You'd think after all these years, calls like this would get easier. They don't. With shaking hands, I dialed Mr. DelSilvio.

"Mr. DelSilvio? It's Turi Ryder."

"Call me Frank."

"I'll try. And I know that when the new boss calls, it's polite to just listen. But if it's ok with you, could I have a minute first, to say something?"

"Sure."

"Mr. DelSilvio, You get major Human Being points for making this call. I know you are going to be making changes to the station, and I'm guessing you want to let me know it's unlikely I'll be kept on. And I'm thinking you're telling me now, because you know I'm moving to Chicago, and you don't want me to move for a job that's not going to be there when my truck pulls up. Some people wouldn't care. So thank you. I appreciate that you'd like to save me from moving for a vanishing job. But I want you to know that I'm from Chicago, and my parents are there, and one of the main reasons I wanted this job was that I'm moving home to be closer to them. So if it helps you to keep me on till you hire my replacement, I'm happy to do it. And I understand perfectly that you'll want to do something different with my shift, probably sooner than later."

There was a longer than usual moment of silence.

"Thank you," said an audibly shocked Frank DelSilvio. "I really appreciate that. I think this may be a first. By the way, do you have a mover? I've got a great mover. I can give you his name and number. And, if there's anything else you need while you're in transition, just let me know."

The last thing disassembled in my Oakland house was my studio. I hosted my final night on WING, the Chicago station I had never met in person, on the night the movers left with all but a few of our essential worldly goods. I balanced my studio gear on cartons, and sat on a folding chair as I thanked management, and my listeners, for six months of talk radio that was so much fun, it felt like flying. When my shift was over, I looked around my just-emptied home and remembered a similar scene, decades ago: the dish-packs, the empty house, and my big Bay Area rock and roll radio job that disappeared the day I closed on my first mortgage. If I were creating a tarot deck to tell my fortune, the death card would show, in place of a skeleton, a large, unpacked, moving box.

Free Advice

City dwellers get a lot of opportunities to cross paths with the homeless. Columnists for big city newspapers also have opinions about the homeless problem. But a "homeless problem" can be written about from a safe, clean distance. An actual homeless person may be, as our newsman on The Big Rock discovered at 5:00 a.m. one morning, using your cute little MGB convertible's passenger door as a toilet seat. That's where things get complicated.

In the interval while I was still working for WING from my remote studio in Oakland, before I lost my job and we moved back to Chicago, there was a lot of long-distance house hunting going on. At last, we found our future neighborhood. In my high school years, it had been a forty-nine square-block den of vice. It took me a while to believe Save the Planet when he swore the neighborhood had changed. The main business district of Uptown still has, though only two of them are currently in use, three of the best, and most beautiful, vintage concert venues in Chicago. Uptown, in addition to being a good spot to hear successful acts before they start packing stadiums, was also the only place I ever did any running.

I don't run for planes, classes, or busses. I do run for an escaped toddler who is about to get onto the luggage conveyor belt at the Omaha airport; and sometimes if I'm late for the theater and I fear the ushers will hold me in the lobby till intermission.

But in high school, I ran every time we parked in Uptown. We found a spot and we ran. We dodged the broken glass and needles, hoping to make it to the safe zone under the marquee before we were mugged or kidnapped and forced to be teen prostitutes. Prostitutes of all sizes and descriptions were then as abundant in Uptown as concertgoers, and certainly more common than anyone sober.

Just as Save the Planet and I settled on buying a place in a quarter-mile stretch of the recovering portion of the war zone that had once been Uptown, one of Chicago's major newspaper columnists got into a spat with Uptown's alderman. I thought the alderman was being judged a little harshly on his effort to ban a soup truck from serving meals to a homeless encampment located under scenic Lake Shore Drive, an eight-lane boulevard in the easternmost section of Uptown. So I invited the columnist to be a guest on my show.

"The alderman thinks this soup truck is a disincentive to the homeless finding homes," the columnist told my listeners.

"Well, I don't think he's entirely wrong. If you're putting out a whole buffet every day, who'd wanna go anywhere else?" I replied.

"It's not a buffet. It's a cup of soup." The columnist didn't see any problem with the homeless people staying where they were, since there wasn't any place else being offered to them. Of course, the soup itself wasn't the problem. It was all the other stuff that comes after digesting the soup that was the problem, which the alderman had been hearing about, presumably in disgusting and graphic detail, from his constituents.

I was of two opinions about the alderman and his war on soup—or war on the homeless, depending on your perspective.

"On the one hand, you want to be kind to the homeless, and help them find shelter. On the other hand, as someone who leaves radio stations at extremely odd hours, I'm not too fond of having to run a homeless gauntlet, leaping, like something from a military training exercise, around sleeping bags, needles, and garbage," I told the columnist.

"Well," he responded, "there are going to be poor people in this economic system, and they're going to float to the bottom of the opportunity ladder, and then we can either exterminate them, or find some way to take care of them."

Neither of us was in favor of the first option. We had different ideas about how to accomplish the second one, and about whether banning a soup truck was equal to an attack on the underprivileged of our city. Since the homeless problem wasn't going away, we agreed to talk more about it at some future time.

Even though I told the columnist, who did not live in Chicago, residing instead in the suburb that boasts architect Frank Lloyd Wright's mansions, that his opinion of the appropriateness of the homeless encampment's location might change if he actually needed to step gingerly around its inhabitants on his way to work each day, I still wanted to believe I was a deeply compassionate person. But I know myself better now.

As you know, the Chicago job vanished before we arrived, without my having set so much as a toe in the station's famous pheasant-under-glass street-front studio. That was actually the only thing about being fired that cheered me up. I feared being the pheasant-under-glass so completely, it had given me nightmares.

There was the fantasy that some maniac would elect to drive a semi right off the street and onto my lap.

Or, perhaps, I would forget that passers-by could see everything I did, and I would accidentally pick my nose or remove my undergarment from an inconvenient sticking place in front of someone with a smartphone.

I feared—and it was possible—that a publicity-seeking, violent nutcase would show up with an assault rifle (management's assurances that the glass was "bulletproof" comforted me not one bit—I don't believe in bulletproof glass, any more than I believe you can tell by looking at him whether someone has a good marriage).

Weeks after my return, there was still the flickering, fading hope that, should the station not make its move to sports, which was the rumored trajectory, I might be invited to fill in on occasion. I made an effort to get to know the new program director, who politely joined me in the WING building's coffee shop for a cup of tea; and thenceforth, equally politely, avoided me.

An assistant program director, who'd helped bring me on for my prior six months of evenings, took it as an honor pledge to give me the chance to work in the station's studios for a shift or two. So before the station committed to its next evening talent, I was invited to fill in for a week, from the pheasant-under-glass studio. I was honored. I was petrified.

Show prep the first night was easy. I had a problem the listeners could help me solve: I had just discovered a homeless person living under our front porch.

Since the house we bought wasn't ready, we rented a place in a perfectly pleasant, working-class neighborhood of Chicago. On the main street, half a block south, you could find a variety of businesses, from a Mexican-style ice cream parlor, to a boutique selling hijabs to the area's large Muslim community. Directly next door to the hijab haberdashery was an establishment dedicated to the eradication of all modesty: the city's largest adult theater, whose name my youngest misread as the "Admirable Theater." Patrons of the theater, many of them inebriated, would leave its tolerant confines and seek the comfort of young women who offered their services up and down the avenue, and some would collapse in the doorways of the neighborhood businesses until morning. But all of this, we believed, was a safe half-block from our front door.

We didn't notice the signs of occupancy immediately, but our German Shepherd did. First thing out the door one morning, she zoomed under the porch. We figured there must be an opossum sleeping there, and called her off.

After two or three days of this, I peered behind landscaped evergreen bushes, and saw what had made Sasha so excited: a sleeping bag, a nest of plastic bags containing various items of clothing, cigarette butts, and a small pile of empty half-pint bottles, which had once contained a brand of alcohol that would be equally useful as skin toner. Fortunately, there wasn't an actual person there.

Save the Planet and I did reconnaissance for a week, peeking under the porch each morning, to see if the human nest was a one-time, sleep-it-off event, or something more permanent. In a few days, the pile of bottles had grown, as had the collection of cigarette butts. The sleeping bag was now located on a cushion of several flattened cardboard boxes. I couldn't figure out what was going on with the bags of clothes. They looked the same. But there were also small heaps of something that might or might not have been human excrement.

Since we didn't own the place, if anything were to be done other than respectfully clearing out the man's possessions, including the wadded up sleeping bag—an item so rank I dared not touch it—we would have to ask our landlord for help. Plus, once emptied, the space would need some sort of drunk-resistant fencing.

I had the altruistic idea that I should don gloves, crawl under the porch, carry out, launder, and return the man's bedding to him, neatly, anonymously, but with a gentle note explaining that he would have to find somewhere else to bed down. I was convinced that this was what a good human being would do, especially the kind of good human beings we see in movies. I wanted to be that kind of human being.

On the other hand, I was scared to touch the stuff, lest every communicable disease, including several for which I was almost certain I had been vaccinated, overtake me. Plus, I dislike crawling around in the dirt for any reason. So on my first trembling night in the pheasant-under-glass studio, on my first actual night inside the station, on the same shift for which I had originally planned to move back home to Chicago, I laid out the entire scenario, and asked for advice from many of the listeners who had been with me for my brief tenure at WING: What should I do about the homeless drunk sleeping under my front porch? These people knew me. They'd heard me talk to the columnist, and rant to my newswoman. They knew I wanted to do the right thing. I felt they'd support me.

"Don't touch the stuff."

"Are you crazy? Don't go near it."

"You can try getting it out for him with a garden rake..."

"Maybe you could burn it for him."

"You could leave him a note, and give him twenty-four hours to move it—but don't handle it yourself."

"Tell the guys who come to put up the fence to do it."

"He could be dangerous. Call the cops."

"Turi, I think you should move. This is not a good neighborhood."

Not one person told me I had a humanitarian obligation to remove the vile bedding, bring it into my house ("Are you kidding? Don't even take it to a laundromat. Would you want to use that laundromat?") and wash it.

What excellent, what brilliant listeners! They all made me feel super-duper and marvelous for even *thinking* about washing the homeless man's stuff. I got so much more ego satisfaction out of just *talking* about doing something nice for a stranger than I would have reaped for actually *doing* it, that I didn't feel even a twinge when I called the property management company to report a "problem under my porch," and requested that the crew "be sure to remove any stuff they found under there before they sealed it off." Talking about virtue can also be its own reward.

Why Not Write Something?

You can ask the universe to grant just one wish—you can keep asking for years—and never get your heart's desire. But sometimes you get lucky.

And sometimes your good fortune doesn't look exactly as you thought it would.

For many of the mommy years, I lusted after a full-time radio job like it was the perfect piece of pecan pie. Mostly, there was a whole lot of fill-in work that added up to *almost* a full-time gig. Only one of these opportunities was in the city where Save the Planet and I were raising our kids.

Having moved around a lot as a child—I attended eight schools before I was fourteen—I was absolutely determined that the boys would be raised in a community that would get to know them. So the home studio was my way of making a living and staying put. This had its pros and cons.

Working from a remote location, no matter how often I flew in to visit and soak up the local scene, made me feel incomplete. I missed the pleasure, the occasional horror, of meeting people who listened to the show as I went about my daily routines.

But as radio metamorphized into a home for political ranting, name-calling, and soapbox preaching, it lost a lot of its sparkle for me. I was always a fan of the quirky caller, the entertaining host, and the chance to hear the back-stories of artists, world events, and people who'd done unusual or world-changing things. There was less and less of that on commercial radio, and more of it on public and community supported radio. I didn't know a soul in public radio. I believed it must be like another planet, with an incompatible atmosphere.

Meanwhile, a lot of creative air talent had been so beaten down by managers who wanted only one type of host, or only one brand of politics, or even only one topic all day long, that we got queasy at the thought of what would happen to our souls if we took the kinds of work that were out there. Add to that the very real disadvantage of being a woman in the business, and you pretty much figured out that radio was going to be a part time thing, if you could do it at all.

In case you think opportunities have gotten all that much better for women in radio over the last five years, I submit the following recent events: A general manager told my producer, "What we want is a woman who knows about sports that guys want to fuck," and a very pleasant fellow who, when he realized he was going to have to put a woman on his station, hired a husband-and-wife team, so that he could also have a man on the air at the same time. It's just as bad, and probably worse, if you're any other minority.

If you still don't believe me, and you want to get really depressed, visit a get-together of morning show hosts (there's at least one convention just for them, every year) and see who's in charge. Watch the women. They're still expected to defer to the men, laugh at their jokes, and look pretty. The guys will all tell you "I couldn't do the show without Betty Sue," and Betty Sue will tell you she's totally respected, and as big a part of the show as all the guys are—exactly as she would have done twenty-five years ago—except that twenty-five years ago, Betty Sue might have been a trained journalist. I'm not sure whether reporting skills makes playing the part of playground monitor or locker room referee, under the guise of delivering the news, better or worse. I'm embarrassed to admit that I've been worried about speaking out about this system. Will it sound like I have a case of sour grapes, or, heaven forbid, that I'm angry? Should I know more about sports? Do I still have anything to say if the men who are listening aren't actually thinking about screwing me while I'm talking? Just writing this makes me nervous. If I were prone to drama, which I am, I could think of this book as my radio suicide note. No man in this business hires a woman who makes trouble. With this book, I am officially making trouble.

So I asked the universe for a part-time gig, a job that would use some of my broadcasting skills, and require a bit of creativity, but that wouldn't demand of me all the hours of work and energy that a daily talk show requires. My syndicated show and my short network features were still going concerns, but I didn't think they would last much longer. And what I wanted, I decided, was a chance to do creative work, for an audience. That audience could be live, or it could be curled up on a couch. I wanted to finish this book and create a live performance piece. I wanted what I've always craved: attention.

My phone rang. A worldwide business broadcast network needed someone to write and produce their promos—those are the commercials a radio station or network makes for itself, usually using pieces of the shows that are on the air—the same kinds of announcements that my friend Patrick had made for me, in Minnesota, years before. In fact, it was Patrick who'd recommended me. He was the station's voice.

The job was exactly what I'd asked of the universe. It was like the final naptime location for Goldilocks: not too big, not too small, but just right. They needed someone half-time. I could put in my hours in the middle of the night. I could string them together like beads on a necklace with anything I wanted to do in between, and take time off to travel or perform. I was grateful, but completely untrained. I had hardly done any production. For my own shows and projects, I'd always put my creative thoughts on paper or tape or phone message, and left the nuts and bolts of cutting and pasting the whole thing together for somebody else to do. I'd resisted learning sound-editing software. That was the production director's job—not mine. I never let on, when I said yes to the gig, that for the first few months, it took me twenty hours to assemble four hours' worth of work. My wrist—the main appendage used for sound editing in the computer age, felt like a rotten orange—swollen and squishy—but that was the least of it. I had to stuff my ego into a small, small space, and concentrate on showing off the network's clever, informed, and expert hosts.

But the book progressed, so I was happy.

Then Patrick started to make uncharacteristic errors. Normally, Patrick is the very best in the industry at voiceover work. He can read something three times, and each time it means something completely different. He can speed something up without it sounding any faster. He has a sense of humor, which he can convey seemingly effortlessly, for any script that requires it. Patrick has some kind of ESP for understanding how the voice in my head hears any given script. Nobody in the business is as gifted and adept as he is. Except that he had long ago split from the talented Broadway director. After a series of relationships that made me wonder whether the odds of Patrick choosing an appropriate, healthy partner were any greater than me suddenly winning an Olympic gold medal for ice dancing, Patrick fell in love and married the man of most people's nightmares: a violent drug addict. Scarred and beaten, Patrick and the nightmare divorced. His ex let him keep the drug habit. Here's the most awful part: no matter that Patrick was a meth addict, and frequently made no sense before and after his sessions—his work was still brilliant. You just couldn't count on him to show up and do it. Our boss noticed it first. "Do you think there's anything wrong with Patrick?" He asked me one day. "I've noticed he's behaving a little strangely. He's out sick all the time. Could he be using drugs?"

"That's not Patrick. I'm positive he'd never use drugs. He hardly drinks. His dad was an alcoholic, so he avoids the stuff like poison."

Apparently, Patrick had developed a taste for poison. We watched his life disintegrate like a slow-motion scene. I called everyone I could think of: his ex, his personal assistant, his sister, and the union's health insurance office. Everyone who knew (which was almost everyone but me) had been trying to get him to rehab for over a year. Once, he'd been willing to go as far as the door of the intake office of a prominent hospital, then turned back.

Our boss made a decision. Patrick, who in my head, I still see as that perfect, innocent, barely grown man whose audio love-poem to my show had found me in the middle of a blizzard; Patrick who made his way to the top of the Hollywood Hills, figuratively and literally, was destroying his own life, and might not survive. Some angry lover or dealer hacked his Facebook page, and put the sordid details of his substance use out into the wired universe for all to see. Patrick compounded the damage by posting inane, drug-addled videos. He was dying on Facebook. I could do nothing. But I could use the gift Patrick had gotten for me — the job I said I wanted so I could finish the book — to finish the book.

Epilogue

"What gives someone** the right to expect an industry to stay the same?" That's what the guy at the fancy New York City party said to my friend Leslie, who had just mentioned to him that I was finishing a book. The book was part middle-age mommy diary, but it was also about falling in love with radio, and then—just like for the people who made cars or bath towels or watches for a living in America years ago—what happened when the radio industry changed.

Leslie called to relay the "What gives someone the right" question.

"Well," I agreed, as I wandered the kitchen in my bathrobe, waiting for the microwave to finish heating/exploding my morning oatmeal, "that is a very good observation. Nobody has a right to expect an industry to freeze solid. But that's not the point. The point is that next to family, radio was the love of a lot of people's lives. In some ways, this business gave a lot of radio nomads a second family. And I'm sad because, even though it was never perfect, now it's *extremely* not perfect. It's getting trashed by people who never loved it at all. And even though I'd like to take the attitude of Mr. What-gives-someone-the right, it's still like watching the guy you baked cookies and made mix-tapes for break up with you for a girl you *know* is going to throw his blue jeans out of her apartment window in exactly two months. You can see it coming, but you can't stop it. Was that guy at the party drunk?"

"Yes. Very. In fact, he came on to me with his wife standing twenty feet away."

"What does he do?"

"Something in publishing."

"You don't suppose his problem with my radio story has anything to do with the fact that the publishing industry is allegedly a more dangerously leaking boat than radio, do you?"

"It might."

"Well. I hope it does. Even though he's technically correct: Nobody has a right to expect his business not to change. Not doctors. Not bankers. Not even tree trimmers."

"What about the tree trimmers? What's changed for them?" Leslie asked, revealing her background in journalism.

"I have no idea. I just threw them in because I didn't want to sound classist."

"Oh. I wonder whether tree trimmers' businesses have changed…"

"Before I give you my list of how many ways I could guess a tree trimmer's business has changed, starting with the availability of cheap, yet possibly unreliable, chain saws imported from China, and working my way through hideously nitpicky internet reviews of tree trimming services on Angie's List, where women with obvious anger issues complain that the tree trimming service left dust on their patios, could we get back to radio, and my book, please?"

"Sure."

"So do you think anyone will want to read about what it's like to spend your childhood underneath a dining table listening to old Shelly Berman and Severn Darden routines, take a job in a completely unstable yet creative industry, and then find out, after thinking she'd given up marriage and kids to move to seven different cities, to be on twelve different stations, that absolutely everything she thought she wanted in radio and life is different?"

"Well," said my friend, "it isn't exactly a new story."

"Yeah. I know. But it's just like that thing I think when people ask me why anybody should listen to my show. That thing that you're not supposed to say, but every single talk host secretly believes. That when we go to the bank where we've had an account since we left college, to clear out our old boyfriend's guilt gifts from our safe deposit boxes, it's always *our* safe deposit boxes that go missing, and not other people's. And it's not because we didn't send in some form…it's because we'll tell it better."

"Finish the book," Leslie said, "and you'll find out."

Acknowledgements

Many thanks to my radio community, family, and friends, including these kind souls:

Valerie Geller told me to write this book. She's almost always right. Linda Matlow said, "Let's go over to that book festival. You never know…"

Bountiful support, wiring, and pizza provided by my two favorite engineers: Tom Demos, who I miss every day, and Michael Englehaupt, who shows up in any emergency.

Roz Varon willingly keeps me company on the air, even when she should be sleeping.

Dave Tipton reminds me that the music matters.

I would never have made it to a Top 40 survey without Bill Richwine. Chuck Britton taught me how to tell a story. Larry Lujack, whose memory I treasure, encouraged me to "Leave the pauses in." John Landecker is as fine a radio spouse as anyone could want.

Steve Dahl—you got me a lot more work than you'll ever know.

Jim Smith remembered me from 3000 miles away and Jack Silver saved my life two ways, one time.

Howard Hoffman makes me laugh, and loves radio too.

Virginia Morris for being almost inhumanly patient and kind.

Cassandra Fish can do anything, and she shows me how.

Phil Hendrie adds character to my world.

Bill and Marjorie Handel gave me a place in their home, and a fig tree to look at.

David G. Hall, a champion airchecker.

Bobby Cole plastered personalities all over his radio station.

Ken Beck found a purpose for my home studio. Margo Whitcomb was first to read and to help. Dave Delk offered a place where my name wasn't "Mommy." Alan Eisenson took a chance.

John Mainelli taught me that the audience likes to peek behind the curtain.

Harvey Nagler will always be my hero for providing me a place to write, and for being honest. Kipper McGee for letting me help with his vision. Jan Cattron for lending me hers.

Thanks to my OHDS, Netivot, Beth Israel, and NTEHEM communities, who inspired and supported me when I wanted to be a mom and a grownup, but never insisted that I be too much of either.

Steve Lanzone, Anthony Mancini, and Fran Sharp, allow me room to be creative every day.

Leslie Kirk Campbell, Tanya Shaffer, and Jean Schiffman rescued me from any number of truly horrible ideas. Thanks to Dana Dworin for her vision, and to Richelle Lieberman for her *joie de vivre*.

Barbara Blake is beloved for her courage, and her couch. Matrona Malik knows how to make waves. Sam Downey Smith is the ultimate caller — plus, she's from Texas.

Robin Gluck reminds me of why I love books. Art Vuolo really IS radio's best friend.

Thanks, in no particular order, to Karen Blackwood, Ken Cocker, Mark Lyons, Daryle Albert, Rachel Slavick, Rich Johnson, Bill McMahon, Mark Howell, Bill White, Mitchell Miller, Jim Farley, Ursula Reutin, Herb Anderson, Phyllis Malitz, Randol White, Judith Gidden, Lorene Hopkins, CRW, Bo, Vicki Keyak, Stephanie DiPalma, Michael Martin, Doreet Stein, Jessica Nutick Zitter, Gary Cohen, Ben Patrick Johnson, Debra Grobman, Karen and Steve Bovarnick, David Levine and Joanna Weinberg, Marci Persky, and Ruth Anne Hohfeld — for her innumerable kindnesses, and pie.

I will always be abundantly grateful to Jerry Brennan and Leanna Gruhn, the Tortoise team who pulled me over the finish line, and made this book real.

About the Author

Turi Ryder is a music and talk radio host whose voice is known to listeners in Chicago, San Francisco, Seattle, Los Angeles, Minneapolis, and Portland, Oregon. Her not-quite-empty nest features a broadcasting studio and, variously, one spouse, two children, a rescued German Shepherd, and numerous marauding chickens.

About Tortoise Books

Slow and steady wins in the end, even in publishing. Tortoise Books is dedicated to finding and promoting quality authors who haven't yet found a niche in the marketplace—writers producing memorable and engaging works that will stand the test of time.

Learn more at www.tortoisebooks.com, find us on Facebook, or follow us on Twitter @TortoiseBooks.

Made in the USA
Columbia, SC
15 September 2019